SOLDIER'S HEART

An Inspirational Memoir and Inquiry of War

By

LEE BURKINS

To Tom,

Lee Burkins

10/24/03

ISBN: 1-4033-9481-4 (e-book)
ISBN: 1-4033-9482-2 (Paperback)

Library of Congress Control Number: 2002095737

This book is printed on acid free paper.

Printed in the United States of America
Bloomington, IN

1stBooks - rev. 01/24/03

Dedication

This book is dedicated to my wife Bonnie for the love and support she soulfully shares with me.
It is dedicated to the many Doctors who work to bring peace to combat veterans.
It is also dedicated to the men and women of the armed services.

Acknowledgments

My heartfelt acknowledgment to the encouragement and manuscript editing done by Larry Foster, Tom Jerome and Michael Askew.

Go To: www.onetao.com for historical photographs

soldier's heart: *Pathological. See* cardiac neurosis, [1895-1900]

cardiac neurosis: *Pathological*, an anxiety reaction characterized by quick fatigue, shortness of breath, rapid heartbeat, dizziness and other cardiac symptoms, but not caused by disease of the heart. Also called effort syndrome, irritable heart, neurocirculatory asthenia, ***soldier's heart.***

Table of Contents

Forward From Here

Years ago, a very fine doctor, compliments of the Veterans Administration, enjoined me to write about 'the war'. When he said it, I immediately experienced fear. Because I felt fear I knew I must do as the Doc suggested. When I did write, trying to get at the words to break beyond the conflict and frustration inside me, I broke my hand. Phantoms from the past disguised as unknown memories propelled my penned hand to violence.

I was sitting on the floor and writing about the war when I began to feel ill. My stomach knotted. My eyes burned. My breathing labored and a knife-sharp pain stabbed into my throat. I stretched out on my back on the floor and began taking strained deep breaths. The pain in my throat increased and I felt like I was going to explode. In my mind I hadn't a clue as to what was happening other than losing control with my existence. Something gave way…

Like a bullet out of a barrel, a bolt of overwhelming rage exploded throughout every fiber of my being causing my body to violently thrash and flop like a fish out of water. Without conscious will, I twisted and spun from my back over to my belly and my fist, propelled by some psychic wrath, flew in an accelerated downward arc to meet the oak floor. I felt the bones crack. A prolonged, vehement scream escaped from my guts. The pain in my throat left with the scream and in that moment I began to cry. My hand throbbed but my soul's anguish diminished. Despite the tears, the trauma and the pain, there was an unmistakable emancipation. My attempt to write about the war, as unclear and difficult as it was, helped make it so.

But every time I attempt to write about what I feel needs discovering I find myself in an obstacle course. It's not writer's block. I have a plethora of anecdotes literally littering my thoughts. But the words I seek fail to reveal my desired and needed self expression. What I experience is fear. Fear of liberating the unknown. As a warrior though, I learned that if I had fear, the best way to be rid of it was to put myself right in the middle of it. So I write.

I've filled two cubic feet of yellow sheet paper with words. Piles of words strewn beyond juxtaposition and conflicting segments with no obvious connection in the literal sense. Writing filled with hesitant expression, unclear rambling and frightening demons. I've written and rewritten of battles but war is still lost to me in understanding. I need to express something besides the obvious battlefields. Horror and trauma are too familiar to us all. War is hell. Actual combat is a motherfucker. What I want to know is, what does a man do when he seeks to end war within himself?

When I was nineteen I was ready for everything life had to offer. It was my first opportunity to test the world with what I knew. I knew little and I didn't know the world. I knew my high school stressed the necessity of college and career but at the same time it religiously ignored discussing our country's war in Vietnam. They taught us to get jobs, I wanted to learn what life was all about. In my noble innocence, I believed there had to be a definitive answer. Once I knew what life was all about, I figured I could really do something great! I was joyful to be nineteen.

History made me curious. I somehow felt it held the answer to life's meaning. History classes impressed upon me that the world was pre-occupied with the struggle between war and peace. Conflict was the most recorded reactive aspect of the human condition. I observed from history people would do anything for something they believed in or felt forced to react to.

When I graduated from high school I didn't know what to believe in. I had a shiny new Chevy, a passionate girl friend and a job I had held for four years in a hunting supply and gun store. I knew there was a war going on in Asia and because I hadn't the finances for college I knew I would be drafted. I toyed with the idea of this being my big chance. War. History was in the making. History made in the present which would become my future. War. The essence of humanity's struggle to live. Live for what I wondered? I had enough sense to know I was only nineteen and had no sense of the world outside of high school. I did believe though, that if I became an active part of history and went off to the front lines of war and lived, perhaps I would learn something. Not just in the isolated incident of war but in the nature of all men. As a nineteen-year-old boy, I wanted to become a man. I wanted to ask my own questions and find my own answers. I would discover what life was all about by throwing myself into the finest experiences war could allow me. I knew I would learn something of great value to the world and myself or be killed in the process. The thought of it excited me.

So the writing continues and the past becomes my present looking for a future in it all.

Guardian of the Mountain

When I was a Green Beret, one of my duties was to recruit, equip, train and lead Indo-Burmese tribal men in guerrilla war against the Communists in South Vietnam, Cambodia and Laos.

These indigenous mountain people, because of the remoteness of their environment, had a cultural history that was unaffected by any of the world's great traditions, religions or teachings. Their origins are not well documented but it is believed they migrated from the early races of India and Southern China to establish themselves throughout the highlands and mountains of the Indo-China peninsula.

Within the country of South Vietnam there were approximately thirty-three different tribes distinguished by linguistic factors. These tribes did not exist as separate groups living in distinct settings. The tribes themselves consisted of many different size villages of varying populations spread over large definite areas.

Their population, at one time estimated to be just under a million, composed only a small percentage of South Vietnam's total population but they were the primary inhabitants of about fifty percent of South Vietnam's land area. They lived in the more remote highlands and mountainous areas with rain forests and dense jungles dominating their environment. Because the Communists were forcing them into service, stealing their crops and using their land for insurgency operations, these sturdy little people, being quite friendly and trustworthy, volunteered to fight along side the men of the U.S. Army Special Forces.

I was twenty years old, a sergeant with little combat experience, standing quietly before a group of eight combat hardened tribal warriors, the men I was supposed to lead, who were presently laughing so hard some of them were rolling on the ground holding their sides while tears rolled down their brown skin cheeks. My first day on the job and already they have broken into total laughing hysteria several times as I attempted to train them in map reading. It seemed to me that when my name was spoken by my interpreter the laughter begins. I had no idea what was going on between them.

I wanted to say "what's so damn funny?" but I patiently and quietly sat on the green sand bags of one of the camp's perimeter bunkers and waited for the laughing to subside. Having read my government manual on the tribes and their culture and customs I realized I am the foreigner, the intruder, the guest and I must not lay my immediate judgments, needs and authority on these men whom in the near future my life would certainly depend on…

****

After several minutes of this comical scene, my interpreter Gai, trying to contain his laughter, stands close to me and places his hand on my forearm.

"Oh, sergeant, sergeant. Not to worry." His smile reveals his filed down front teeth, a social custom of some tribes. He speaks softly, "You see sergeant, it is your name that makes us so joyful. Forgive us please and I will tell you a story." He turns and yells at the other tribal men to be quiet.

"You must realize that this earth is inhabited by many mischievous and evil spirits. Good spirits too but these are of no consequence. The evil spirits are constantly making plans to invade and disrupt our lives. They bring misfortune, disease and death. It is important to protect ourselves. When children are born they are most vulnerable. To protect them from these evil spirits we give our babies such names as 'dog', 'idiot', 'buffalo dung' or the names of the sex organs."

Gai turns to the other men and says something to them. This elicits more giggles. They jostle and poke at one another like kids on a playground hiding a secret. Gai continues.

"Excuse me again Sergeant Burr-kai." This time I think I hear what sounds like my name. It brings a riot of uncontrollable laughter from all the warriors, Gai included. Again I wait, amused myself and curious as to why my "name" makes the men laugh riotously.

When the French Army previously occupied Vietnam they too worked with these highland tribal people and bestowed upon them a name that was to signify any one or all of the many existing tribes. The French named them 'Montagnard' (mohn'-tahn-yar), literally meaning 'guardian of the mountain.' These 'Montagnards' now worked with the Green Berets and we affectionately refer to them as 'The Yards'.

The laughter is subsiding and Gai and the rest of the Yards again bring their attention back to me.

"Oh Sergeant Burr-kai. Forgive us again but you see the name is important. No self respecting evil spirit would ever inhabit someone with the name like 'buffalo dung'. But your name, Burkins is very close to a Montagnard word, 'Burr-kai'. Not every child is named after something awful or gross. Some children, because they are born into a wealthy or important family get names that are powerful. Like 'elephant' or 'tiger'. Evil spirits are afraid of those so powerfully named. Your name 'Burr-kai' is powerful. It means 'Lizard'. So we will call you 'Burr-kai' because it has power and protects you from bad spirits". More giggles and stifled laughter infect the Yards.

I am in no position to refuse so I accept the 'honor' they have histerically seen fit to award me. If my birth name of Burkins were pronounced with a long "i" it does sound something like 'Burr-kai'. Besides, if the name contains power that is something I want while in this war. Although deeper down I think all the laughter reveals a lizard as something comically gross. Either way, I trust the evil spirits will leave me alone.

Now that the secret of the laughter has been resolved, Gai interprets my point by point teaching of map reading to the other

Yards. The eight men that comprise my team are from different tribes. Their names are Hyak, Diu, Boon, Deng, Yubi, Pei, Than and Gai. The war has displaced them many miles from their original villages and has forced them all to no longer be unaffected by foreign influences. Within the last few years they have moved from slash and burn farming, crossbows and spears to canned food, automatic weapons and grenades.

Gai, the interpreter, is physically typical of the Yards. He is just under five foot tall, light brown skin and stocky. He has cropped his straight black hair short. He wears a tattered, green canvas jungle hat that is shaped like a derby. In keeping with the times he no longer wears a loin cloth but U.S. government jungle fatigues tailored smartly to fit his smaller physique. He speaks many of the different tribal languages, French, Vietnamese and English. He speaks proudly of the fact that one Montagnard (in the entire nation) went to America and learned to pilot an airplane. He is my communicative link to the others. Presently, I only know a few general phrases of tribal language; the Yards know even less English. In spite of that fact, each Yard watches and listens intently to my lesson of map reading. The pace is slow and deliberate with Gai dutifully translating.

The map reading is important. If I am ever killed on an operation the Yards must know how to locate their position. In addition to the map skills, I teach them how to talk on the radio, in English, so they can call for help and give their location to the pilots who will try and locate them for rescue. For the remainder of the day we practice over and over, again and again. Each man takes his turn deciphering the grid points of a location I point to on the map then uses the radio to simulate calling for help. Most of the men do well and express their pride in their success. At first a couple of them have difficulty with the lesson, but they are coaxed and encouraged by the others until every man is confident the others can depend on his ability. We are becoming a team. Led by a lizard.

Of the eight Yards, Hyak is the most fierce, both in manner and looks. He is thirty years of age. His pearl black eyes exude a rock piercing seriousness although his dark face occasionally breaks into large smile revealing a mouth full of gold teeth. Gai told me when Hyak was a teenager he was taken from his village by the communists and forced to fight for the North Vietnamese regular army. He became a squad leader and had many battles against the French and South Vietnamese. After several years of fighting he managed to escape. He is the Yard team leader. None of the others would dare question his commands. I observe how, by his presence only, he demands accomplishment in the Yards' task of reading the map and using the radio. Hyak's eyes meet mine. He gives his head a slight nod in my direction. By the end of the day both he and I are satisfied with each man's ability.

"Gai, tell the men we are finished for now. Have them head over to their mess hall and eat chow. In two hours I will come to your team room to inspect everyone's gear. And tell them they did an outstanding job today."

"Yes, Sergeant Burr-kai." Gai smartly snaps to attention. This is unnecessary but I believe it is more an act to entertain me and show his approval of our first interaction as a team. He takes a serious look at the watch on his wrist then he crisply does an about face and translates my words to the others.

As Gai and the Yards walk from the camp's bunkered perimeter in toward the larger buildings near the center of our heavily fortified compound, some of them hold hands and sling their arms about each other's shoulders. I can hear them softly sing-songing "burr-kai, burr-kai, burr-kai" and giggle among themselves. I am quietly amazed at how despite growing up with decades of war they can still keep laughter in their heart.

The securely established compound we occupy is one of three top-secret bases under the authority of a group called MAC-V-SOG. (Military Assistance Command-Vietnam-Special Operations Group). The camp is called F.O.B. II (forward observation base #2) Command and Control Central (CCC). The camp's perimeter is a roughly laid-out ellipse of green sand-bagged bunkers. Each sand bag is made of woven forest green cloth fibers and is about eighteen inches long, ten inches wide and four inches thick when filled with earth. Each bunker is dug down into the ground about four feet, and measures approximately twelve feet wide by fifteen feet long. An additional two feet of height is built above ground. The exposed sides are four interlaced sandbags thick. Bunker roofs are made of heavy timbers then covered with corrugated tin sheeting with another four or five layers of sand bags on top. In the rear of each bunker is an opening about eighteen inches wide and five foot high for entering and exiting. A snaking labyrinth of trenches and shallow tunnels connects every bunker in the perimeter. Inside the bunker there is about five feet of head clearance. The light is dim. The floor is dirt. The smell damp. The inner side walls of the bunker are sand bagged. The more the better. There is a long, narrow, horizontal firing slit in the wall of the bunker that faces the outer perimeter defenses. Looking out through the firing slit you see the rows of wire entanglements and the ragged jungle treelinc bcyond.

On the inner ledge of the firing slit lay a half dozen hand held firing mechanisms that connect to claymore mines, thirty-gallon metal drums of foo-gas and other creative pyrotechnics. All these explosive devices are positioned and contained within a forty-foot wide perimeter. The entire area of this perimeter has tangle wire that is strung six inches above the ground to prevent someone from crawling up to a bunkers' position. Then there are several additional perimeters of four foot high barbed wire triangulated fences that are six foot wide at the base. Intermingled and atop all this barbed-wiring, snake rows upon rows of spiraled rolls of razor sharp concertina wire stacked six foot high.

Strategically placed along the defensive perimeter are eight larger bunkers known as command bunkers. These command positions are a second story built above the normal bunker emplacement. They resemble a look-out tower structured out of sand bags. Although they have a fortified roof, the surrounding walls are only about four foot high leaving an open area of about two feet on all sides for viewing. These bunkers have .50 and .30 caliber machine gun emplacements.

Inside the defensive ellipse of bunkers are a few dozen buildings. Most are built long, low and squat, out of concrete block, two by fours and tin, screen and sandbags. They house the Recon company office, the Montagnard Army Headquarters, the Vietnamese Special Forces Headquarters, Tactical Operations Center, Yard team houses, Recon team houses, Supply (S-4), Medical dispensary, store houses, mess halls, a motor pool, a helicopter pad, a mortar pit and a bar. It is jokingly said that once a perimeter is secured by Special Forces, the first fortified position built is the bar.

Within all this defensive construction there is one anomaly. The elliptical defensive perimeter of the camp is dissected by a dirt road designated Highway 14. This makes the compound a deadly bottleneck to any major attempt to attack the city of Kontum from the South. Both sides of the road within the camp's perimeter are lined with bunkers, sand-bagged walls and explosives creating a deadly gauntlet for anyone trying to infiltrate through this area.

The F.O.B. is located one mile south of and on a rise of land above Kontum. Looking toward the city, an open plain of tilled fields and farm houses border Highway 14 as it gently slopes down and away from the compound through the fields to a long, narrow red wooden bridge that spans the broad Kontum river. From the F.O.B. you see the dirt road cross the wooden bridge, wind through the city and snake its way up into the heavily-forested, mountainous peaks to the north. Looking to the south side of the compound you see the road run straight-away from you and traverse slowly downward across a three hundred foot-wide denuded brown plain that abruptly ends at a forty foot high wall of jungle foliage. Here the road cuts a narrow swath into the forest and continues to wind south past small villages, farm land and jungle forest for fifty miles until it reaches the large military base on the edge of Pleiku city.

Highway 14 is about twenty feet wide. On one side of the road is the Montagnard Army Company compound. On the other side of the road is Recon Company compound where I reside. The 'Yard' Army compound is home to a few dozen Americans and 250 Yards who make up two Infantry companies. They are affectionately know as the 'Green Hornet Battalion' because of attitude and certain medicinal empowerment. Their job is to basically set themselves in the middle of enemy operations and do as much destruction as possible without being destroyed.

The Recon Company compound houses around fifty Green Berets, a few dozen Vietnamese Special Forces personnel and approximately one hundred and fifty Yards. There are a dozen recon teams each with an average of ten Yards and two to three Americans per team. These teams travel deep into enemy territory to carry out reconnaissance, prisoner snatches, rescue missions and ambushes. Teams usually deploy with a total of eight men or less. On most missions the teams have to play a deadly cat and mouse game with an enemy of much greater number. Sometimes after a team deploys they are never heard from again.

It is nearing sunset as I walk toward the Yard's team room. Day patrols are returning and night ambush teams are preparing to leave the compound. Bunkers are silently being manned by men carrying their weapons. They also carry a blanket to ward off the chill of the Central Highland nights and dampness of the bunker. The heavy barricades of steel and wood and wire are pushed and wheeled by several men into position fortifying the openings created in the camp's perimeter by the bisection of Highway 14.

Out of habit I have mentally made a note of the number of steps I have taken from my quarters to the door of the Yard's team room. I grab the metal black loop handle and pull the galvanized-tin covered door so it swings open past me. I step into a windowless cinder block room lit by several independently hanging bare bulbs. The light seems olive drab. The floor is gray concrete. Aligned on each wall are double stacked army bunk beds. A total of ten. At the head of each bunk hang personal weapons and tactical gear. Metal wall lockers stand vertical between the bunks. Brown wooden foot lockers are scattered around a small dark green folding table. Sitting on the foot lockers, dressed either in shorts and boots, loin cloth or fatigues are the Yards. The air in the room is filled with the acrid smoke of a tobacco favored by the Yards. Some of the Yards are busy checking their gear, others play cards while they smoke and snack on C-rations. Gai-Yak, sitting on his bunk, quickly stands at my entrance. The other men look at me then seemingly unconcerned look away until Hyak sharply barks an order at them. They quickly turn from what they are doing and center their attention on me.

"Gai, tomorrow we will practice immediate action drills and in two days we will be going to Dak-to for two weeks." I wait for him to translate this to the other men. "I am going to inspect the gear of each man and I want you to help me do this. I'll start with you. Have the men go about their business until it is their turn to have their gear checked."

Gai tells the men to prepare their gear then tells me he is ready for the inspection. Hyak comes over to me. His eyes tell me he is prepared to assist me. I nod affirmatively.

Gai grabs his weapon and tactical gear hanging from the head of his bunk and lays them on the card table. I pick up the black steel CAR-15 (.223 carbine), make sure the safety is on and detach the fully loaded clip from it. Weapons are kept locked and loaded for use in an instant if needed. I draw back the t-handle of the weapon's bolt ejecting a live bright brass round to the floor. Gai retrieves it. The weapon is clean. Gai tells me it has functioned without fail for him. I reload the weapon and hand it to him. He hangs it back at the head of his bunk. Hyak's steely eyes are meticulously inspecting Gai's web gear.

Besides the soldier's personal weapon there is his tactical "web gear". For our unit this consists of a webbed pistol belt that is threaded into a two-inch wide nylon harness. This harness is like a pair of suspenders that drape over a man's shoulders. The pistol belt weaves through loops sewn into the harness. Two at the belly and two at the lower back. On the harness where it connects to the front of the belt there are steel D-rings, one on each side of the belt's buckle. Where the two straps of the harness connect in the back to the web belt, the harness continues in length with two longer straps, about eighteen inches in length, that have a steel snap link at each end. The purpose of this is to let the back straps dangle down so they can be grabbed from the front from between the legs and snapped to the D-rings on the front of the webbed pistol belt. When the straps are pulled tight this encases the body completely within the harness. Where the harness crosses the top of the shoulders there are two more small steel D-rings. Once a man is in the harness he can 'attach' himself to long ropes dropped from a helicopter to be lifted out of the jungle if necessary. Most times the mountainous jungle areas of operation won't permit a helicopter to land to retrieve a team. Ropes, a hundred feet in length with snap links connected at their ends, are dropped from the helicopter through small openings in the jungle canopy down to the team members so the harnesses can be attached to them. As many as four men at a time can be hooked to the ropes and lifted up through the jungle canopy. This is a standard method of extraction in our areas of operations.

Hyak and I systematically inspect each man's gear while Gai translates. I get the silent 'look' of 'I know what I'm doing' from some of the men as I go through their personal equipment. I must subtly assert my authority and show them I also know what I am doing. Preparedness is essential when going into battle. If you don't have a piece of gear with you, you can't use it. As I look over the Yards' gear, Gai tells me a little bit of personal history of the men.

Boon and Deng want to be inspected together. They are the older men of the group, somewhere in their late thirties. Both are short and thin and originate from the same tribe. They prefer to wear loin cloths and canvas jungle boots when they are not on duty.

"These men have only each other." Gai says. "All their family and their entire village were killed by the Viet Cong. Since then they have been inseparable. Like brothers." I look into Boon's passive eyes and can almost feel the painful emotions of his many traumas. Deng, on the other hand, responds to Gai's conversation by expressing his outright hate for those who murdered his family and destroyed his previous way of life. For a short flash Deng's speech spews until a lone wet tear of rage slides from his eye down his brown cheek leaving him silent. "Deng is a good man", says Gai.

Yubi is next. He wears his web gear, a pair of army issue green boxer shorts and rubber sandals made from discarded tires. His straight black hair falls to his shoulders. He holds his arms out from his sides and turns his little physique around in a diminutive manner as if he is modeling the latest fashions. The other Yards begin laughing and Yubi beams being the center of attention.

"Yubi the pretty boy," announces Gai. "He is so pretty even the Vietnamese girls want to have his baby."

Attached to the 'web gear' are several brown canvas ammo and canteen pouches. Only two of the canteen pouches actually have a canteen in them. The rest hold "baseball" hand grenades. Generally each Yard carries six hand grenades. I carry ten plus two white phosphorous grenades. Each man carries five hundred rounds of .223 carbine ammo. Each man carries both a smoke and tear gas grenade. Other items attached to the web gear may include a knife, compass, side arm (.45 or .38), bandages for wounds, morphine, amphetamines, strobe light, gas mask, a coil of ten feet of rope, personal self destruct devices (in case you decide not to allow yourself to be captured) and any talisman or good luck piece you feel necessary.

Diu and Pei are the next Yards to have their gear checked. Diu is the tallest of the men, standing nearly six foot. Gai said all members of Diu's tribe were tall. Diu, like the others, had lost friends and family in the war. He stood and observed quietly while his gear was being checked. Pei whose hair, skin and eyes are the color of chocolate also was silent while we looked over his gear. Gai's only comment was, "Pei has drunk the blood of his enemies." My government manual spoke of a tribe that at one time had practiced cannibalism.

In addition to the personal weapon and web gear is the rucksack (backpack). In here you carry canned and dried food rations, ground cloth and poncho liner for sleeping, foot powder and several pairs of dry socks, and a claymore mine on top of it all. In my rucksack is the addition of one, twenty-five pound radio, because of its weight, affectionately called a "Prick-25". A lot of gear, but all necessary for combat survival.

The last man Hyak and I inspect is Bunh. Bunh is squat and broad and has a smile that openly expresses affection. Buhn's weapon is a single shot 40 millimeter grenade launcher. It looks like a small sawed-off shot gun. It can throw a high explosive round nearly three hundred meters accurately. It's kill radius is about one meter. Other rounds it can fire are flares, tear gas and there is a round called a 'flushette' that holds dozens of what look like miniature steel missiles replete with fins. These are used for close combat and cover several square feet of area when fired.

All in all the inspection goes well. There are some weapons that could be cleaner and a few items on some men's web gear that could be made more secure and quieter. I tell this to Gai and he in turn translates for Hyak who makes sure these changes are quickly attended to. When the changes are made and the inspection is complete, I tell Gai to tell the men they have done a good job, and that we will depart at zero-seven-hundred hours tomorrow to go and practice battle drills. After Gai does so, I start to leave the Yard's team room when Gai makes a request.

"Oh Sergeant Burr-kai. Before you leave we would like to talk with you. Come. Sit here with us." He speaks to the others. They gather around Gai's bunk and leave a space on the bed for me to sit.

When I sit down, Gai puts his arm around my shoulders then says, "We need to know something…"

I nod in acceptance and wait for him to begin. A thick air of anticipation closes around me.

"As you know, Burr-kai, your president of America has promised the Montagnard people a country of their own when the war is over."

I have heard of this promise and affirmatively nod. Gai continues.

"But do you see, Burr-kai, the war is not what it seems."

I'm a little confused by this statement but sit quietly allowing Gai to go on.

"These lowland people, the Vietnamese are mean to us. They do not allow our children to go to the schools. They do not allow us to sell our crops openly in the markets. They call us "moi", savages. There are no laws to protect us from sometimes violent abuse from them."

As he speaks the other Yards seem to weave an invisible unity of mind and spirit between them. At the moment I am feeling much the foreigner.

"So tell us Burr-kai," Gai's voice suddenly becomes demanding. "Tell us Burr-kai. After we kill ALL the communists, will you help us kill ALL the Vietnamese. WILL YOU?" The room is dead silent. The atmosphere like a storm ready to be born. "WILL YOU?".

Without pause I immediately answer. "I will. I promise I will." I say it as I look at each of the faces of my men. "I will!"

Gai says something short and direct to the Yards. They all nod in what looks like serious agreement.

“Good”, exclaims Gai. “We can talk more later. Now we are done.”

I nod in silent agreement. I feel my heart swimming into my head as I push the door open and walk out of the Yard’s team room and into the dark night full of insect chirps and shrills emanating from the surrounding jungle.

As I walk to my hootch I wonder to myself, *‘What the hell is going on here?’* I feel the first piece of my innocence fall from grace…

On The Couch

It was not until World War I that specific clinical syndromes came to be associated with combat duty. In prior wars, it was assumed that such casualties were merely manifestations of poor discipline and cowardice. The syndrome that we know today as Post Traumatic Stress Disorder was first recorded during protracted artillery barrages in 'The Great War' and was labeled 'shell shock'. The experience of World War I showed that over 97,000 men were admitted to hospitals with neuropsychiatric disorders resulting in considerable cost to the government through the payment of Veteran Administration benefits. During the early years of World War II psychiatric casualties increased some three hundred percent over those of World War I. (Goodwin, <u>Continuing Readjustment Problems Among Vietnam Veterans</u>, Disabled American Veterans, Cincinnati, Ohio; 1980)

****

Doctor Brooks is the psychiatrist who owns the hands into which my care has been most recently placed by the Veterans Administration. Until now, I had spent the past year, an hour a week, 'talking at' a social worker who was out of his league when it came to counseling me and other combat veterans who chose to live isolated in the jungles on the Big Island of Hawaii. While serving in the Hawaiian Army National Guard I had what higher-ups called 'events' that paved my way into counseling. These events could be described as having difficulty in differentiating 'training' situations from a reality imposed by war psychoses. Training became too real for me.

In local psychological circles, we veterans were called 'Trip wire vets'. One small physical, mental or emotional nudge and BOOM!.. I too was a walking bomb. Why I didn't know. I just knew I had to defuse myself. Hopefully Doctor Brooks was with the bomb squad.

I prefer to call Doctor Brooks, 'Brooks' and he is okay with that. He is comfortable in his small office, decorated in shades of browns and the worn backings of old texts that sit on the shelves of many bookcases. Prominently positioned on a shelf, was a tastefully-carved, small wooden sign, artfully painted with the words *"Thank You for Not Asking Me Not to Smoke."*

Brooks likes to smoke a rare, liquor soaked, dark Turkish tobacco cigarette. His ritual for the beginning of our sessions was to sit his large body comfortably into his custom made recliner chair, draw a cigarette from its pack, light it with a butane flame, and thoughtfully suck in just two draws from the thin, dark tobacco roll. He'd do it without any sense of stress or tension. It was as if he absorbed the moment to calibrate and center on the present.

The doc is twenty years my elder and a veteran of the Korean War. He looks like a cross between Burl Ives and Santa Clause dressed in a colorfully flowered Hawaiian aloha shirt, beige summer dress slacks and gray socked feet stuffed into leather buckled sandals. The handful of combat veterans he elects to work with three days a week all agree Brooks is a godsend. He takes notes, especially on your dreams and you know he's been thinking about you a great deal since you've visited him last.

In my sessions with him, after he gives short voice to some caring observation, he is quiet. I do most of the talking and I can tell that he is listening. I feel something about what I'm saying to him is being looked after on some level.

Brooks has finished his smoke. I sit inside myself while my corporeal form sits on a comfortable, chocolate-brown leather couch a few feet from Brooks' seat. He lies back in his commodious, custom chair. I begin talking around my state of mind and feelings…

…Two weeks after coming home from Nam I had to move out from living with my Mom. She would inconsolably stare at me across the dinner table with her sad expressive eyes that said, *"my poor son, my poor son..."* It was a motherly attempt to find and reach the boy who had left for war and returned a different child. On one occasion, I even yelled at her. *"Quit looking at me that way Mom!"* I really needed to be alone and on my own. After all I was twenty-two years old and had survived a war. These two facts said I was a not a boy but a man. *A man on edge...*for nearly thirteen years now. It wasn't that my *dis-ease* was forever present during this time. My *'events'*, as they have been called, came and went like stormy weather and were just as unpredictable. Restful sleep chiefly eluded me. I did sleep but in fits, thrashing about in my bed, quite often running in nightmares from enemy soldiers, running in fields of fire, waking exhausted, going to work with adrenal glands stuck in the *wide-open* position and natural endorphins at a *critical low*. In addition, I had an endless, nagging ringing in my ears. As my nights got longer, my fuse got shorter. I had outbreaks of anger at work and lost many different jobs many times over. My world around me seemed a cartoon prison. I was a charicature without bearing. My feelings consisted of rage, depression or numbness. Nothing else. That was it.

Brooks looks up from something he has written on his yellow note pad.

"Tell me about your first experience in seeking medical attention."

I remember this well.

I had gone to my local Veterans Administration Regional Office. I complained of not being able to sleep, nervousness and the ringing in my ears. From the receptionist to the admissions staff, from the staff to the doctor, I was treated like a stepchild. The lady who typed my onerous request for medical attention had such long fingernails she had to use a pencil to push the keys on the typewriter. One keyed letter at a time, with every push of her pencil, her breath made little tortured sounds of displeasure at having to be where she was and doing what she did.

"You're like all the rest." she claims.

"Excuse me?" I say, not entirely sure I've heard her correctly.

"Here," She says, yanking the paper from the carriage of the typewriter. "Take this to the claims division. It's down the hall. Second door on the left. Wait in the reception area there."

I walk to the Claims Division reception area. I hand my papers to a man at the counter. He looks at the form I've handed him. His face wrinkles. His eyes tighten. He looks me over for a moment and then demands more than he says, "Have a seat and wait."

I take a seat in one of the gray plastic chairs lined like soldiers along the wall. The reception area is empty except for me. On the pale green walls of the room hang several framed lithographs depicting colorful scenes from well known battles of the wars America has participated in from the Revolution to World War II. There are no paintings of the Korean War or Vietnam. An anti-drug poster is on the wall near the doorway. It displays a soldier lying in a fetal position trapped inside a capsule with the words *"Speed Kills."* Boldly written above the artwork someone has penciled in the words, '*FAST.*'

It is 1971. The war in Vietnam is still being fought. I think of the men I left there and feel a chill of guilt. I shake it off. Across from where I sit, there is a large placard tacked on the divider wall of the reception counter. It reads: *America is #1 Because of our Veterans*.

The entire office area behind the counter seems conspicuously empty. The man I presented my papers to is nowhere to be seen. There are many empty desks. A few workers, chuckling among themselves, eat doughnuts and cluster around a coffee pot. Occasionally a phone rings and goes unanswered. I listen intently to the ringing in my ears and I swear it sounds like the cacophony insects make in the jungle's night.

I have now waited for two hours. I am anxious to get this over with so I can apply for a job at the construction site of the new VA hospital being built next to the building I am now in. A person appears at the counter and calls my name. He gives me another set of forms to fill out. When I am finished he directs me to the medical center across the street. "A doctor will examine you. Come back here when you are done." He hands me the papers. A dry smirk hangs on his face.

I leave the claims area and walk across the street and into the medical center. I am immediately directed to an examination room where a doctor is waiting.

The doc has me take off my shirt.

He places a stethoscope to my chest and listens to my heart.

"A little rapid" he says.

"It beats for several people," I reply.

He checks my blood pressure, looks in my ears and eyes, hits me in my wrists and knees with a little rubber tomahawk, then sends me back to the Claims Division I just came from. Again I take a seat and wait. And I wait. Finally, several VA employees, all men of the WW II generation, file out of a door on the far wall and walk to the reception counter. They group together behind it. Their actions make my mind recall a battlefield axiom: *'stand too close together and one grenade will get you all.'*

One of them calls my name. I rise from my seat and go to the counter. I get the impression something is terribly wrong with me.

One of them speaks.

"There's nothing wrong with you!" He pronounces. "You have no legitimate claim." The other VA workers are nodding their heads in agreement.

"I'm not here for a claim. I'm here to get some help. You are supposed to help veterans aren't you?" I am getting riled. "I am in the right place aren't I?"

The employees behind the counter have folded their arms over their chests. Their eyes throw stink in my direction.

The spokesman for the group speaks again.

"You're nothing but a cry baby! Just like the others. You *Viet* vets think the government owes you something. There's nothing wrong with you. Your visit here is finished."

I feel like I've been stunned by the concussion of an explosion. I stare at the men who stand before me. They stare back. My vision skews like I'm viewing the scene through the wrong end of a telescope. The room and everyone and everything in it shrink into a distance. *The thousand meter stare.* Through the glass of the reception area entrance doors I spot two security guards coming my way. I sense they are coming for me. I hastily turn from the reception counter and the VA workers who stand fast at that position. Utilizing the focus of combat, I walk straight at the two security guards. Luckily for us all, they move aside. Using both my palms I stiff arm the swinging doors. They blow wide open with a crash. I feel my heart pound wildly in my head. Once outside, I gulp the air like a man long deprived of water. Fighting dizziness, I force march my way across a wide grassy area.

Behind me I hear the flung words, *"...and don't come back or we'll call the cops!"...*

I suddenly realize I am in Brooks' office, shouting, acting out the entire story as if someone had scripted me for every character.

"Can you fucking believe it Brooks?! Can you believe those assholes?" My anger is everything I am for the moment. I look at Brooks who looks at me and says, "What did you do next?"...

"I went to my car in the parking lot. It had been several hours since I first went into the VA. I got into my car and slammed the door"...

****

My veteran buddy Vic has been comfortably nodding on heroin all morning in the passenger's seat. He raises his chin from his chest and with his hands pushes his head of long black hair away from his goateed smiling face.

"Hey Burky. How'd it go?"

"It didn't!"

"Oh well, fuck'em. It don't mean nothing...Hey, we gonna go apply for that job?"

"Yea, let's do it. Something good has to happen today. The sign says they're hiring carpenters and laborers. Our chances are good. Let's go do it."

The job we are applying for is with the construction crew for the new VA hospital. It's directly across from the VA building I just left. Vic and I get out of the car and walk across the street to the construction trailer on the building site.

It's a busy place. The air is alive with the grinding strains of heavy machinery moving to and fro. Electric saws sing their whine through wood and hammers pound their heads against nails. We walk up a few wooden steps to the door of the office. A large sign on the door reads: NOW HIRING. I turn the knob and open the door. Inside, several men are in discussion. They wear blue hard hats and stand around a table spread with blueprints. When Vic and I enter the trailer they all look towards us.

"We want to apply for a job," I say aloud.

A man I assume is the Foreman walks over to us. The rest of the group looks on.

"We don't hire hippies." He puffs up his chest and places his hands on his hips. He looks directly at Vic.

"Were not hippies," I say. "*We're veterans.* We'd like to apply for a job to help build the Veteran's hospital. We're experienced. We can read blueprints, swing a hammer and cut a line."

Vic explains that he's been trained and certified by the carpenter's union. He pulls a union card from his wallet and presents it to the guy. The Foreman only glances at the card and hands it back to Vic.

"What kind of veterans did you say you were?" The Foreman folds his arms across his chest.

"Vietnam vets," I explain.

"We don't hire losers," the man says cocking his head and shifting his weight to one leg. "All you guys are losers and you think you're owed something."

Something inside me snaps. Without hesitation I grab a hammer from a utility belt that's hanging on the wall next to me. I experience the energetic swell of war's psyche. My unbridled intention knows its path…

The Foreman hastily shrinks away from me. I can sense his fear and doubts. I can tell by the look on his face he is about to piss his pants. I grip the hammer tightly in my hand. My arm cocks itself like a catapult.

Vic grabs me by my shoulder. "He ain't worth it Burky. He ain't worth it."

Everyone in the room is frozen with tension. The atmosphere hangs suspended like the moment preceding an explosion.

Vic's words ring true to me. I toss the hammer to the floor. We turn and walk out of the trailer. Vic takes a planned moment to slam the door extra hard behind us. He chuckles…

****

Brooks asks me, "*Do* you feel you are owed something?"

My emotions are heated. I'm animated pacing the floor in front of his chair.

"*Fuck no*, Brooks. Nobody owes me anything. *Nada!* It's not a matter of *being owed*! It's a matter of setting things right. It's about justice. How would you feel if you and your friends were conscripted, deceived and manipulated? How would you sleep knowing you killed people because you were led to believe a huge fucking lie? What would you do if you knew men schemed to make fortunes off of your blood and your friends' lives, then tossed you aside like fodder? Are you going to let them get away with it? Does a man shrug his shoulders and walk away? What kind of movie would that make? *Fuck no!* A man takes a stand and tries to make it right!"

"What would you like to do to make it right?" Brooks asks me.

"I feel there are a few more people in this world who need to be killed. I really do. But I'm not going to do that. *Never again!* I'm going to heal myself of this frightening rage and goddamnit I'll make it right! I swear to God I'll make it right."

The high charge of my emotions slowly begin to bleed off. My present world is one of disbelief. I try to detach from the psychic vibration I have just created. It's as if a blowing wind is trapped within Brooks' office. It blasts ill unable to escape the walls around it.

I look at Brooks and how quietly he sits. I sense he is there for me. *He hears me*. Like some giant sponge his large being absorbs all the ugly debris I have set loose.

The psychic wind dies down. I throw myself onto the couch. My emotions are expended. I feel like a hole.

Brooks informs me the time for the session is over and reminds me that the group therapy sessions will begin next week.

A collection of trip wire vets. All in one room. I hope the walls are made of rubber.

Why Men Fight

To be wounded is to experience pain. Pain is the root of all anger. Pain of body. Pain of heart. Pain of mind, psyche, soul…Who or what is it that wounds us?

"Ouch!" I cringe aloud to the empty interior of my VW Bus as I grind the transmission gears into high. The pumpkin-orange van surges along the concrete highway towards Denver. It is a blue sky Rocky Mountain Spring day and I am driving to Cherry Creek High School to be one of three guest speakers addressing the student body. We have been asked to lecture about our country and military service. I have no idea what I am going to say…

****

Pain is the root of all anger. Anger is the root of violence.

****

I park the VW bus in the visitor's space. I shut off the engine, lean my elbows on the steering wheel and take in the bright view rushing through the van's panoramic windshield. Hundreds of students gather on the green grass in front of the school's main entrance. They congregate in small groups and mill excitedly about like the spring fever that permeates the air. I feel a wave of dejection pass through me.

I suddenly remember that immediately after this speaking engagement I have a court hearing to attend. Mandatory. Third degree assault is the charge but I've shown evidence to the County to allow me to file a counter charge of assault against the plaintiff. At the moment I am a starving student so I can't afford an attorney. I am armed only with the bargaining chip of having counter charges entered into the court. I hope to get the County prosecutor to drop charges in return for my withdrawing of charges. Up to that point is the plan. After that it's make it up as I go…

I get out of the van and ask a student where I might find a Ms. Oppor, the high school teacher who has organized the event. The pupil extends their arm and points to a woman in the midst of a chatting throng of students. She stands on an small stage constructed for the speaking event. She is as pretty as any school teacher I ever had a crush on. I introduce myself with a handshake and pleased smile. My heart pumps a single ache. She explains to me one of the speakers is an Air Force Colonel from the Reserve and the other speaker is a man of my age who is a non-veteran and peace activist. She asks me in which order I wish to address the audience. I choose to be the final speaker.

The Colonel is first to speak. Dressed in a blue uniform he stands uneasily erect behind a dark wooden podium. Attentive only to himself, he proceeds to read directly from a prepared speech…it's several pages long…something about duty, honor, commitment to government and glory all delivered monosylabically to mostly deaf ears.

Except for a group of about fifty students sitting on the green grass directly in front of the podium and busily taking copious notes, the majority of students are totally indifferent and inattentive to the Colonel. He drones on in his dissertation and doesn't look up from his composition, but in a corner of his military mind, given the chance, he knows he could whip these youngsters into organized ranks.

The Colonel finishes his speech. There is some applause but the Spring day has captured the audience's attention. The next speaker goes to the podium dressed in jeans, Mexican serape and head band. Slung on a strap over his shoulder is a large tie-dyed cloth bag from which he removes a fistful of yellow papers and piles them on the podium. With a critical eye he takes a moment to arrange the papers differently, then directly launches into a language of ire and hostile rhetoric. He makes occasional nearsighted glances up from his writing. He skews his myopic eyes with such intensity he appears vicious, but his vision doesn't catch the Spring fever possessing the student body. Imaginative, his intellect muses without doubt that he leads these people in the coming revolution. Above him an indifferent yellow sun rotates in the abyss of a blue sky. Orator and audience create their separate worlds.

I observe the audience-turned-crowd and watch my trepidation build. Both rabble-rouser and government officer are unable to connect with the audience. The Spring-fevered crowd of teenagers carry on in the innocent joy of being juvenile while behind them, unobserved distant snow covered mountain peaks claim a piece of blue sky. It's my turn to speak.

Feeling like an actor in a film gone suddenly silent, I stand speechless behind the podium. I wear the look of a young college professor with short but riotous hair, a trim beard and wool sport jacket. Directly to my front and sitting on the lawn is the group of students who are doing their assigned listening. Their eyes hold to me. Their ears wait. They suspend their pens over their pads while the rest of the adolescent throng ignores everything but themselves.

In the center of the crowd, a band of jocks, probably the football team, grab ass and make jokes for a large group of attentive students. Except for the class assigned to take notes no one pays me any attention. *I own the element of surprise.* I pick my target and watch myself move into position.

Authoritatively I bellow into the microphone, "HEY!.. YOU!" Some students jump others turn to look in my direction. I grab the mike from its stand and in my most drill sergeant like command voice I order, "LISTEN UP!...LISTEN THE...FUCK. UP!" The expletive creates a spontaneous wave of attention. I walk from the podium on a straight target line for the group of jocks. "HEY YOU! ASSHOLE!" I raise my arm and point my finger at largest of the football players. The entire student body drops suddenly silent. I stand in front of the jock I have picked out of the student crowd. I start in on him.

****

To be human is to wrestle with change. The difficulty of enduring the pain of change. To be this and not that. To be free and not bound. The drama of need, confusion, frustration and fear, the messengers of pain. Pain the fuel of anger. Pain from fighting that anger, wrestling mentally and emotionally, conscripting oneself to the inner battle.

****

The entire student body has hushed and turned its attention to me. I push my finger into the chest of the jock. Eye to eye, my psychic familiarity of war holds him fast.

"It's guys like you, who don't pay attention to what is going on around them, who are going to end up in a fox hole with the blood and guts of your best friend on your hands and in that moment you won't have the slightest idea of how the hell you ended up in such a situation."

I take the blue-sky-spring-fever-day and cover it in the rot of war.

"Your life could be in danger. If you don't pay attention to what your government is doing, from the community level up to the federal, you may find yourself a pawn in the plans and ambitions of those who would gain from manipulating you. In the blink of an eye your life could be forever changed. All your plans, hopes and dreams could be interrupted by the authority of government. Guaranteed! They will take you from your family, your comforts, program you with skills and use you to perpetuate their ideals. And if you don't go willingly to their conscription when they call, they will harass your family, hunt you down and imprison you. *Listen up!* These are the facts of history. *Pay attention!* Will your history be written by you or will you allow someone else to dictate your life? Make life your choice. Wake up and get involved! Be cognizant of what the world is doing around you and feel how you are connected to it. Be conscious. Be aware. Be free!"

I hoped the 'be free!' would play into the Spring day. The crowd erupts in applause. The jocks are shaking my hand and apologizing for not paying attention. The students, the Spring day and my few words have resonated.

I talk with a few curious students and surreptitiously take a long look at the teacher who organized this event. She endures a come-on from the speaker in the serape. I feel a yearning. She smiles in my direction. Amidst waving hands and the smiling faces of youth I walk to the VW bus and think about teenage boys. At the age of nineteen the majority of them either want to fuck or fight. That's why the government can conscript them to war with little resistance. I fire up the van's engine, drive out of the parking lot and turn onto the highway to head to the court hearing.

****

Fighting anger is an endless war. Rather we should understand the anger is because of pain. Finding the anger's root in the pain, identifying the wound then treating it, will heal the anger. Lacking anger a human being is not likely to be an aggressor.

****

So how did I get into this situation with the courts? To be accused of assault? Yes, I did punch my ex-girlfriend's boyfriend. But this was after he had threatened and challenged me to a fight, on three different occasions, over a period of a year. I only have two cheeks.

****

Pain posits anger. First there is pain but the anger manifests so quickly it masks the pain. Pain makes us weak. Anger makes us strong. Anger is something you can war with. Pain is what we most avoid.

****

One day I joked with Dr. Brooks that if we as humans, in genesis, were all in a state of grace and we fell from that grace, we are all a bunch of wounded individuals. To live the experience of blissful existence then suddenly lose it or worse yet be cast out of it. How much can that hurt? How angry can that make you? To go from bliss to physical birth of daily existence with the trials and tribulations and conflicts it contains? It is no wonder human history is rift with violence. We have all been hurting for so long and so deeply the pain and anger are programmed into our genes. In our anger we humans strike out. We inflict pain. We fight. I fight.

****

The year is 1968. The place Fort Benning, Georgia. Paratrooper training. 'Jump school'.

I sit on the short rise of wooden steps in front of the barracks. I hold my bowed head in my hands. In the pit of my stomach hangs an uneasiness.

Here I am finished with jump school and infantry training. In less than a week, I will ship out with an airborne unit to war. *I am going to die*. It's not the thought of going to war that pains me but the idea of having to follow incompetent leadership. *Doomed by default*. A casualty by someone else's orders. I am going to get stuck under the command of one of the Army's six-month-wonders, add water, shake-and-bake, instant Sergeants, who have no experience in real combat. From my previous encounters at the hands and orders of these instant NCO's, I know I am a dead man. *Oh my god. Holy fuck.*

I sit on the barrack's steps and shake my head in lost disbelief. Around me sit and stand several other soldiers, all who have just completed jump school and have their orders for the war. It is a hot summer Sunday morning. Outside the Company headquarters' entrance hundreds of purple irises stand at attention. The flowers' fragrance fills my breath and authors future memory. *I am going to die.*

Unexpectedly, across the mental cavern of my vast internal drama bugles a command voice.

"Any of you men want to be your own boss?" *What, an angel?*

Standing in front of me is a member of the legendary Green Berets. Before he gets a chance to speak again I am on my feet my hand thrust in the air, *"I do Sarge! I want to be my own boss!"*...

After three long days of evaluation and testing I was accepted into Special Forces training. I would become a highly skilled soldier. A warrior. An elite fighter free from the yoke of shake and bake leadership.

****

Even before I was a soldier I experienced fighting. Bullies in elementary school and in the neighborhood. Wrestling in High School. But war was beyond a black eye or bloody lip. The *shock* of life or death. *Your* life or death. No winner. No loser. Just horribly dead or frighteningly alive. War turned fighting into a necessary study. Defend or attack? Do you fight to survive or do you fight to kill? They are not the same fight. Do you fight at all? As a soldier you are not supposed to question. As a Warrior you will have to.

****

The court hearing is not going well. The county's prosecuting attorney didn't care that counter charges had been accepted. Bluntly, he told me,..."I'm going to see to it you get at least six weeks jail time..."

Unprepared, doubtful and worried I sit alone behind a large wooden table in front of the judge's bench. To my left, seated at another table are the plaintiffs and their lawyer. Behind us the court room seats are filled with a host of people, an audience captive to the judicial process. The judge enters. We all rise. We all sit down.

It is absolutely amazing how we as humans experience memory as fact. Two people two views. Three people, three stories. Four people, four realities. Myself, Anna my ex-girlfriend and Mark her husband are no different. I thought I knew exactly what happened. I was surprised to hear Anna and Mark's testimony.

Mark said I hit him once. Anna said I hit him twice.

My cross examination of them was neither prophetic nor clever. I asked Mark if he had previously challenged me to fight on three different occasions. He denied it.

I asked Anna,*...why did you break my heart?what went wrong?It took me six months to get over you. Was it me?It took me six more months to get over losing your father's companionship, I fucking starved to stay in school...why did you have an affair with Mark? Do you think I could get copies of the eight by ten color photos of Mark with black eyes, broken nose and lacerated head???* Anna, "When I was sitting at your table, did Mark physically grab me and threaten me with violence?" A moment suspends between us, *is there still a connection?*

"No." is her answer.

I had no plan. I only knew what I believed to occur the night of the fight. We happened to be in the same restaurant that evening. Mark and Anna invited me to sit at their table. Halfway through our drinks and after small talk Anna started ranting at me to return a ring her father had given me. Mark threatened to kick my ass then grabbed me by the collar of my shirt pulling me up and out of my chair. I defended myself…I take the stand.

The prosecuting attorney *accuses* me of being a Vietnam Veteran and a highly trained fighter. He argues I am an equation for violence. I feel the personality of my combat sergeant speak up.

"Your Honor, this man is a fool." I point my finger at Mark whose eyes are still slightly black and blue. However, the large cut on his eye brow, gnarled by more than a dozen stitches, will forever bear him a nicely placed scar. *Remember.*

"This man is a fool. On two different occasions in the past year he arrogantly challenged me to fight him. Each time I told him I had no quarrel with him and would not fight him. Each time I avoided conflict by walking away. This man is a fool. He thinks by fighting me he can gain reputation with his wife. He thinks that fighting is a game he can play and win. Fighting has nothing to do with winning or losing. It is not a game. I am a combat soldier. In fighting you either live or you die. For this man to threaten my life with fighting reveals his arrogance and ignorance."

I turn in my seat and face the judge.

"I have only two cheeks your Honor. I turned them both. On the night he threatened me for the third time, I responded appropriately. I hit Mark three times. Once on the chin when he grabbed me by my collar. A second time in the nose when he came back at me. And a third time on the side of the head to stop him from attacking again. I knew exactly what I was doing. Like the prosecuting attorney said, I am a highly skilled and trained fighter. I could have done far worse and chose not to. I used restraint and stopped his aggression. I exercised compassion for his ignorance. I cannot help but feel sorry for him. To perpetuate a fight is foolish and deadly." The words that come from my chest feel neither angry nor justified. They just come. Like an orgasm.

I feel like I am floating somewhere between epiphany and trance. I gaze out across a court room and see an attentive audience of victims and victimizers, each here for their own justice, but for the moment entranced and eager for the denouement of my, Anna's and Mark's personal soap opera. I step down from the stand.

The judge finds my actions are in self defense. For the second time today the crowd is supportive...and there is some cheering from the street elements. The judge raps her gavel. The victory becomes even sweeter when the judge lectures Anna on the immorality of instigating a fight between men for personal amusement. I am free to leave.

But I am not free from the truth of my own pain. How difficult it is to recognize and how difficult it can be to heal. We are all wounded in some fashion. It doesn't take a war to know trauma and shock. Everyday life offers sufficient opportunities for the experience of pain. If we fail to recognize our anger is a result of our pains, our anger will lead to actions that cause pain to others.

Just what is it about us, of us, that experiences pain? There is the body. Just about every part of it is capable of aches and discomfort. Then there is the identity of self, the ego. The ego can find a myriad of reasons to be upset. By others or by oneself. The thinking mind can experience anguish. The mind of feeling, the heart, suffers when rejected. Truth is, we needn't look beyond ourselves for the causes of our pains.

The motto of the Special Forces Green Beret is: De Oppresso Liber: "Liberator of the Oppressed." I ask, "...and who is more oppressed than I and who oppresses me more than myself?"

Saving Face

When I first met and interacted with the Montagnards of my recon team they had no reservations or hesitations about expressing their feelings for the Vietnamese people. What we as Americans expect as normal social interaction between peoples did not happen in this war torn country. Vietnam has a fifteen-hundred year history of internal conflict festering between the myriad cultures that inhabit its territories. Vietnamese hate Laotians. Laotians hate Cambodians. Cambodians hate Vietnamese. Cultures in power suppress those people in the minority. Racism is a way of life. If your blood line is not pure to the Vietnamese race you are not considered a 'citizen' of the country. Your children are not allowed to attend state schools. If you are a farmer from an indigenous tribe you are not allowed to sell your crops in the business district of the city. If you are in the minority you are forced to live among your 'own kind', create your own economies and support systems. If you are a 'half breed' you are subject to ridicule and possible violent persecution without any legal recourse.

Even at our Forward Observation Base segregation was practiced. The Vietnamese forces had their own mess hall and bar and did not openly fraternize with their American counterparts. The Montagnards also had their separate living quarters, eating and recreation areas. The American personnel had their own mess hall and club that was off limits to the Vietnamese and Yards. The main reason for the separation of the South Viets and the Yards was to keep them from displaying and playing out ancient hostilities. If fights did erupt between Viets and Montagnards they lasted as long as revenge would allow. On the surface animosities might be quelled but in reality each side patiently waited until another time presented opportunity to even scores.

My own men had shown restraint because I demanded it. I was their leader and the Montagnards were fiercely loyal to us Americans. But there were occasions when ancient angers rose up and I had to swiftly intervene because rational compromise and civil diplomacy had no meaning. It wasn't a simple matter of choosing sides or passing judgment. It was a matter of playing God.

****

I and the Yards had been on local patrol near the small village of Bien Cat. It was early afternoon, hot and humid. We were walking in single file out of the sweltering jungle and onto a wide plateau of brown grass and scrub brush. Here where the jungle ended began a narrow dirt road that quickly led straight into the Vietnamese village of Bien Cat. About a mile beyond the village, across the sparsely bushed plain, lay the MACV (Military Assistance Command Vietnam) compound that was our final destination.

One by one, the eight of us, keeping a proper defensive interval between each man, filed out of the jungles' shadows. As it was a day patrol we wore no heavy rucksacks and carried only our weapons, necessary munitions and a radio. The dirt road we now followed became the villa's main street. Each side was lined with one-room, drab stucco buildings interspersed with bamboo thatched huts and tin-roofed plywood shanties. At intervals there were alleys and pathways that meandered off the main dirt strip of road. Down the pathways you could see well kept small cottages each with a yard containing a tended garden encased by neatly arranged bamboo fences. For an outlying village bordering a vast area of jungle, it seemed a little too well kept and untouched by war. Most likely the inhabitants of the "tiny town" were sympathizers with the communist guerrillas.

Usually, when we were on patrol moving through villages such as this, the locals paid us little attention. But today as we walked the street to the town's center, suspicious, judgmental eyes followed our movement. Perhaps it was their reaction to the presence of heavily armed Montagnards. Whatever the reasons, we were made to keep our guard constant and alert.

For the most part the villagers consisted of women, old men and children. The few men present that were of the age to be capable of being soldiers were disabled. Missing a limb or disfigured and twisted in body due to the wounds of war. From window and doorway quiet stern faces watched us pass. Children in the street stopped their playing and stood silent. We walked on. We had come into this small town unannounced. An air of mistrust followed us.

In the center of town were several shops open for business and active with people. The delicious smell of simmering soup wafted from a small outdoor restaurant. I halted the patrol when I came to the cookery's store front. Sitting at the open-air serving counter were several old men each a caricature of the ancient, wise Asian: lengthy white hair tied in a pony tail, a Fu Manchu mustache growing down into the long, thin, gray chin beard. They played a board game at the soup kitchen's counter, bantered amongst themselves while giving me and my team of Yards an uninterpretive glimpse.

In a dispersed line the Yards hold their respective positions, each man maintaining a watchful guard to building tops, the flanking alleyways, and to our rear and front. Yubi is the point man for the patrol. He crouches at a building's corner ahead of me and looks back my way wanting some signal as what to do next. I call Gai and Hyak to my position in front of the soup shop. Together we do a quick but careful recon around the restaurant building's perimeter. We agree that we'll stop here and eat.

Vietnamese "pho" (soup) is delicious and beats eating the soggy rice and dried veggie rations we carry. To be safe, Diu the tail-gunner and Yubi take up positions across the street to keep watch while Gai, Hyak, Bunh, Deng, Pei and myself take seats at the rickety folding tables to the store's front.

Two long-haired, pretty, but unsmiling, pre-teen girls wait on us, bringing bowls of hot broth made from beef and pork bone. In the steaming broth is a healthy portion of thin rice noodles. Another side bowl is brought to us containing cooked tendon and paper thin slices of rare steak, meat unknown. Bean sprouts and a Vietnamese basil are also placed at our tables. To this steaming delicacy the Yards and I add the condiments of red pepper paste and a smelly fermented fish sauce named nuc-mam.

The food is good. It relaxes us. Clear blue skies and sun grace us. The Yards start carrying on between themselves with their boyish cajoling. Refreshing cool breezes come playing out of the nearby jungle's shadows. An occasional Vietnamese on bicycle or foot travels the street on their daily errands. It's a pastel moment on a perfect summer day. I finish my meal and take the place of Diu and Yubi who have stood guard over us. Gai sees I have finished eating and rushes his meal so he too can stand guard as the others finish their lunch.

There is plenty of day left. We have patrolled the areas assigned to us and as soldiers will sometimes do, rather than make work for ourselves, we decide to make our time leisure. We choose to hang out at a pool hall next to the restaurant. The front of the building is open to the street. Two pool tables that have seen ages of use grace the dirt floored room. Gai pays the patron a few *piastras*. Sides are chosen, bets are made, cues are checked for straightness and balls are noisily racked. Pei and Bunh lose a coin toss and have to stand guard while the rest of the Yards begin playing pool. Laughter and friendly ribbing become part of the play. I tell Hyak, the team leader of the Yards, to make sure the men keep their web gear on and weapons close by.

For a short while I watch the Yards shoot pool. I even play a game and skillfully lose a few dollars.

Feeling a little bored I decide to visit a gold shop we first passed when we entered the town. Gold shops are a common sight in any Vietnamese town and the prices are good. I've been wanting to buy a gold necklace to send home to my Mom. I tell Gai where I am headed then leave the pool hall and walk up the street to the shop.

As a boy I enjoyed hunting. Carrying a gun afield was natural to me but here I was on a small town's street carrying an automatic weapon. Grenades hung on my web gear. Olive cloth bandoleers of cartridges in clips criss-crossed my bare chest. I wore black fatigue pants and black leather gloves with the digits cut off to allow dexterity for my fingers. A green bandanna covered my head. Camouflage grease paint, brown and dark green, smeared my face. My blue eyes took in the glances of foreign faces. *I was going shopping.* I walked on feeling like a soldier of fortune loose in an exotic land. The gold shop was the last building on the narrow street. At this end of town there was no activity. The jungle sat quietly nearby as I entered the store.

The gold shop was a well kept stucco block building. Inside it was only one room with a dirt floor. In one corner, squatted at a cooking fire, was an old lady busy stirring the contents of a boiling pot. In another corner a younger woman sat on a wooden slat bed. She breast fed an infant. Neither person paid any attention to me. To my right was a glass case that displayed many fine works of gold jewelry. Standing behind it was the proprietor.

"Good day sir!" he said smiling through many gold teeth. "I am the artist. I make everything you see." His stood erect in his thin lanky body. At his side wearing an uncertain face was a naked little boy. The man's hand lay lightly on the boy's head. "My son," said the man. The boy shyly hid his face in the pant leg of his father's black pajamas. The man spoke in soft Vietnamese to his son. The boy looked at me and smiled then ran to his grandmother's side at the cooking fire.

"Would you like to see something?" asked the proprietor in perfect English. I felt a little uneasy having walked into this family's home. I bowed my head slightly and asked to look at some gold necklaces.

"I want to get my mother a gift," I told him.

"Oh, a good young man. Thinking of his mother," was the reply.

The man's politeness puts me at ease. I feel no longer the intruding gun toting soldier of fortune but just a boy buying his mom a gift.

The gold is pure 24 karat. Each necklace has a soft yet weighted quality about it. I choose a piece that is made of tiny, inter-connected diamond shaped links. "How much?" I ask.

True to the barter culture of this country, the man asks a price that I believe is too high. I offer less and the proprietor imitates some serious thought and comes down in price. Not to my level but it is a sum I can well afford. I feel it's a good deal and begin to pull some money from my pocket. I see a wave of serious concern enter the eyes of the store keeper. I turn to see what he has focused on. Gai and the other Yards enter the room.

"Ah Burkai, what are you doing?" Gai boldly requests.

I explain to Gai that I am purchasing a necklace. I proudly show him the one I have chosen.

"What is he charging you for this?" Gai demands.

When I tell him the price, he snaps his attention to the shop owner and begins yelling at him in Vietnamese. The loud tone of his voice makes the infant and little boy begin crying.

"Burkai, this man is robbing you." Gai insists. "He is charging you far too much money for the necklace!"

I see an anger in the eyes of all the Yards. The smell of alcohol is obvious on their breath. While I was absent they must have acquired liquor at the pool hall. Gai and Hyak both are yelling at the Vietnamese man now. The women have gathered the children up in their arms and are yelling in high pitch voice back at the Yards. The proprietor spews invective and waves his arms about threatening to become more aggressive. One of the Yards kicks the boiling pot hanging over the fire. Hot liquid splashes across the floor scalding the bare feet of the women. They begin histerically crying and screaming. The Yards are pointing their weapons at them. The entire family is begging, pleading for their lives. Gai sticks the muzzle of his carbine into the face of the Vietnamese man now backed against the stucco wall…

"YOU WANT GOLD BURKAI? LET'S TAKE ALL THE GOLD!" yells Gai.

The family wails, cries and trembles. The terribly frightened little boy pees over himself and his grandmother who holds him. Hyak moves behind the counter and points his weapon at the Vietnamese man's temple whose frightened face falls destitute of options.

"All the gold, Burkai," broadly smiles Hyak.

I look at the Yards. In their eyes is the gleam of killing one's enemy. It would be no different to them than killing a dog, except for the pleasure.

Seconds tersely pass. *I have to act.*

I reach across the glass counter display of gold and grab the trembling shopkeeper by the collar of his clean white shirt. I pull him from the muzzles of Gai and Hyak's weapons and halfway across the display case. I gangster slap him across his face several times and push him to the dirt floor. I point my finger and yell obscenities in Vietnamese at him, then in my foremost command voice I bark at the Yards.

"FOLLOW ME! LET'S GET THE FUCK OUT OF HERE!" I quickly move out the door of the shop into the front street. Miraculously, *fucking miraculously*, all the Yards follow me. I shout orders for them to move out in single file. "YUBI…TAKE POINT.

DIU…REAR GUARD. EVERYBODY SPREAD OUT! MOVE OUT! MOVE IT!"

I couldn't tell the Yards to walk away from the situation they created. I couldn't rebuke them for being hateful toward their historical enemy. I just couldn't walk away. *I was their leader.* I had to do what I did. If I would have hesitated the family would have been killed. I couldn't let that happen. I had to save face to save lives…

We swiftly and quietly move as a disciplined team down the dirt street passing the crowd of people that have gathered near the gold shop. Bystanders scatter before us. Within minutes we are outside the village, alone on the dirt road that stretches before us, headed toward the MACV compound that lay a mile in the observable distance. We walk briskly. No one says a damn word. Deep inside I am trembling. Deeper still, I wonder what my Mom would think of me.

Para-Transcendental Social Departee

The Vietnam War was mother of the modern terminology Post Traumatic Stress Disorder (PTSD). Although psychological science has assigned to this acronym the observation of the effects of severe combat trauma on the human psyche, the malady this modern scientific definition represents has an ancient history and has lived by many names throughout time: 'Shell shock', 'war neurosis', 'combat fatigue', 'soldier's heart', 'PTSD.' Some of the earliest record of war trauma was written during the first century A.D. by the Greek biographer and essayist Plutarch. He kept detailed accounts of many prominent people and their lives. In the book The Lives of the Noble Grecians and Romans, he wrote about a soldier from the army of Alexander the Great, who suffered flashbacks. In understanding the human psyche, what better a laboratory of rats and men, than a war…

****

Time has stopped. It too exhausted, succumbed to the creeping void, velvet-fingered iron grip, holding and suspending me to this timeless dimension of observation only. I hear this voice where my head used to be and experience my actions in silent movie, slow motion. So painfully slow that intent is made visible. And I am powerless to affect it.

I am in motion and twenty four men, a crew of laborers, stare from a safe distance, clustered like domesticated livestock uncertain of the moment, while I stand straddling an eight inch diameter, black steel water pipe that lay on the green grass. To my front the black pipe snakes away from me, twisting its way up into the Hawaiian rainforest on the peak above me. To my rear, the pipe rushes downward, running its length for ten miles across dry dusty plain then surges five miles up the pastured slope of Mauna Kea to disappear in the mists.

Sparks dance before my eyes from the collision of the four foot, red steel pipe wrench I unmercifully beat against the black steel water pipe lying between my feet. Wham! Bam! Bam! I wield the long steel wrench in an unbroken, figure eight pattern. Crash! Bram! Crash! Bram! Hup, two, three, four...perfect cadence. Profane efficiency. Excellence of anger. Wild animal sounds stampede out of my throat.

It's me gone rage mad and the part of me that should be preventing it, is stuck ineffectual in the referenced space time has cast me. I'm beginning to feel vibrations in my hands from the wrench's bulbous metal head slamming against the serpent pipe's steel skin. Sparks explode with each strike. I see the sparks. I see the silent work crew starring as if in wait for the unknown to happen. I feel in achingly short moments my psychological control beginning to return.

From my mental suspension I hear two Hawaiian men in the work crew talk loudly to each other over the racket I'm making.

"Bruddha, da boss freek'n!"

"Loss'em Brah. Loss'em. He neva comin back!"

"Guarrans dis time."

I could guarantee them I would be back and am actually on my way back right now. But the only communication I am capable of is through the continuum of the black pipe, the red wrench, my rage and the detached frame of reference time holds me in.

****

I've worked this job of laying fifteen miles of eight-inch steel pipe seven days a week, eleven hours a day for the last six months. Each day I travel up the mountain into the rainforests above Kamuela, me ke aloha Hawaii and get soaked in the mists and warm rains as I work. I drive down the mountain to work on the windy desert plain where the blowing dust sticks to my wet clothes and body covering me in a fine coating of mud. I then drive up the cold rocky slopes below snow capped Mauna Kea and shiver as I work to complete the pipe's ascent into a man-made earthen berm reservoir.

****

My head is throbbing, but there's no pain, only pressure. I wield the pipe wrench with profane precision. Time leaks. I see clearly what I'm doing. I realize it's Friday. Shortly, I'll be able to stop the madness. The work crews standby…

I've worked every day for six months but every Friday I get the afternoon off. Not for a break but to drive seventy-five miles one way to the town of Hilo to talk to the Veteran Administration's (VA) social adjustment counselor Marvin. I often pace the wooden floor in Marvin's small office and vent this unnamed rage. But I don't believe Marvin is hearing me.

****

It's raining Monsoons. Water falling from the sky drowns the wiper blades ineffectual on the windshield of my truck. In the brief moments between the wiper blade's cyclic travel, vision is good for about five feet. Water drops big as marbles pelt the truck's metal roof. The roar is deafening. Driving on the narrow, winding, old asphalt island road to Hilo requires nerve-wracking vigilance. From the truck's ashtray, I pick up a half smoked joint of Hawaiian bud, light it and draw thick, sweet mango tasting smoke into my lungs. In my head I ponder the VA's counselor Marvin's unawareness to my predicament. I've been seeing this guy every week for a year and he's never reacted in any telling way to my ramblings about my deepest angers. I fear the rages might consume me or someone else and all Marvin ever says is, "Yes, Mister Burkins."

I arrive at his office. He greets me in the opened doorway and gives me a limp hand shake, "Hello, Mister Burkins." His face and eyes behind government-issue black-framed spectacles twist into a body language that is indecipherable. He has a small head.

"Hello Marvin." I respond despondently.

Marvin asks, "How are you, Mister Burkins?"

"I feel like I'm a trip wire. If someone touches me I'm going to detonate."

"Yes, Mister Burkins." *He doesn't believe me.* "Here Mister Burkins. Please. Sit down."

I follow him into his office and sit on the familiar gray government chair. Marvin sits in his coaster equipped wooden chair. The wheels on his seat help give him mobility to turn between looking at me and turning to look for something on his desk that he can never seem to find. It's a nervous habit of his.

I sit in the uncomfortable gray chair and wait for Marvin to turn around. He looks for something on his desk. I'm wondering what the fuck I can say to this man to make him understand what I'm feeling. *Just what am I feeling?*

Marvin can't find what he's looking for. He swivels his chair around and now faces me.

"Yes Mister Burkins?" His face is twisting again. I think he's trying to show concern.

"I'm having a bad day, Marvin. Shit I'm having a bad life. I haven't had a decent night's sleep for the last thirteen years. Restless. I'm starting to wear thin. I'm ready to explode. It's one of those days when I feel like going out and hurting somebody."

Marvin's eyes look at me but I have the feeling they aren't seeing me. I see me and I feel not the origins of the spell upon my soul.

"Damnit Marvin, do you hear what I'm saying? I'm afraid I'm going to hurt somebody or myself."

"Mr. Burkins, you are going to have to adjust yourself to the conditions of a civil society. The war is over."

"War is alive and well, Marvin. Your fucking everyday society plants the seminal seeds to war daily. Greed, envy, jealousy, desperation, fear. Everyday feelings experienced by everyday people everywhere. Add it all up as a collective society and boom! War spawns." I feel something rumbling deep in my psyche.

"You know Marvin, there are basically four powers and four powers only at work in this world. They make it turn round and round and when I say world, I mean this collective life that is made by man."

Marvin squints at me. I think it's his look of 'I'm listening.' I continue my rave.

"The first power is 'THE WORD.' Speak well enough and people will listen. Speak with authority and people will follow. 'THE WORD' is basic to everyone's survival. If you sit at a boarding house table and the potatoes are at the other end of the table, you don't get any unless you speak. 'Pass the potatoes!' If you go into a store, you don't get any service unless you tell them what you want. If you need help you have to ask for it. If you want someone to do something for you, you have to use 'THE WORD'. So, if someone in this society wants someone else to do something, they have to ask or persuade them with 'THE WORD'. 'THE WORD' is the first basic power in this world making events what they are."

"Now what if 'THE WORD' isn't persuasive or convincing enough? Example: Marvin, I've got this opportunity for you and I'd like you to become involved. But suppose you Marvin aren't buying it. You say no thank you, Mister Burkins I'm not interested. So where does that leave us. 'THE WORD' isn't working!"

"This is where the second power comes into play. I say, hey Marvin, if you do this for me, I'll give you all this MONEY! And it's a lot of MONEY. 'MONEY' is the second power. Marvin says, well, tell me again what it is you want. I think I can help you out. But maybe Marvin says, no thank you I'm not interested."

"Now the third power comes into play, 'FORCE'. I say Marvin, either you do this or I'm going to kill you, your family and your friends. Our country does this daily on an international scale. The USA wants this. The little country says no can do. USA says, hey, I'll give you all this money. Little country says, no don't want it. USA says either you give me what I want or I'll engage economic sanctions against you and if that doesn't convince you, I'll bomb the shit out of you. This is how many societies function. Check the history books. Read current events."

"That leaves us with the fourth power, 'INTENTION/SPIRIT'. Now this power is unique because it is within the first three powers. What is my INTENTION in convincing you to do something for me. Is it for personal gain or the benefit of the both of us? Or think on this: Marvin, I've got all this money and I want to share it with you. Here, have a couple thousand. On me. But later I come around and say, hey Marvin, I need a favor. What was my INTENTION in giving? Just to give or to give to get? And what about FORCE? Do I exercise physical prejudice against you because you won't give me what I want or do I knock the bodily fluids out of you because you are a threat to all decency? What is the INTENTION?"

"Four powers and only these four make the world what it is. Any other idea you or any one else might conceive falls under one of these four."

"Yes Mister Burkins."

The response of dead meat. Sudden inspiration floods me manic.

"Well listen the fuck up Marvin. You go and tell your fricken VA bureaucratic bosses that me and a bunch of other combat vets have been taking the blood out of a consenting veteran who has AIDS. We've got a couple of gallons of infected hemoglobin on ice, Marvin. *I think I'm getting through.* And you know what we're going to do with it, Marvin? WE'RE GOING TO DUMP IT INTO THE FUCKIN' WATER SUPPLY!"

I'm yelling loud enough and clearly enough for everyone in the surrounding offices to hear me. Marvin's kisser loses its twisted feature. His mouth hangs open and silent. His face drains of all vital energy. Horror seeps into Marvin's eyes and enters his brain. His glasses fog over. *Finally, I got through to him.*

I get up from my seat and leave a traumatized Marvin frozen to his thoughts.

****

Time releases its conscious grip on space and I finally fall into my recognizable senses. I'm back. The flying sparks and unnamed rage have stopped. The steel water pipe on the ground between my feet is unhurt. The wrench I hold in my hands still works as it was meant to. I realize it is Friday afternoon and that it was a week ago I stopped my sessions with Marvin. The laborers stand silent and wait for me to tell them to get back to work and I tell myself I've got to find a real doc.

Out of This World

Sitting in the soft, dim light and quiet cool of an air-conditioned windowless office, Doctor Brooks and I ponder my madness.

"Why do you think you put yourself in situations that cause you great fear?" he asks.

I sit in silence trying to find a definition for the ineffable.

"Release." I reply.

I can see the analytical mind behind Brook's sober brown eyes calculating the myriad probabilities of my neurosis.

"How is it fear gives you release? It seems more a reality of bondage." He slides a pinner Turkish cigarette from its hard pack, lights it, takes one long draw then extinguishes it. His looks at me, his eyes and face speechlessly speaking 'well?'

I ponder revealing to him what I haven't told anyone. I've kept it a secret not because it's something horrible or shameful but because it's an experience that gives me a thread of the extraordinary that I don't want to loose a single drop of by talking about it. It's a shred of reality that gives me respite from my grueling daily madness. A daydream. A desire. A home to long for. I speak:

"I had an out of the body experience in the middle of battle. I was so goddamned scared Brooks, that my mind..., my psyche..., *something* of myself leapt out of my body and hovered over the battle as it raged. Fear. It kicked me through the door and like a vehicle it drove me into the sublime."

My eyes take the position of looking deep within at a memory. The corners of my lips lightly curve upward from the rise of an inner smile.

Brooks is busily writing down notes and without looking up says, "Go on."

"It was in this bomb crater, Brooks. Myself, the team leader Kinnear and two Yards, Gai and Hyak were making a last stand of sorts. A platoon size element of NVA were doing there damnedest to overrun our position."

Brooks cuts in. "You mean kill you?"

I feel the adrenaline coursing from my kidneys to my heart. I knew its pathway well. "Yea, you could *certainly* say that." I continue…

The fight started after we ambushed a group of six soldiers who were busy digging a new bunker. I was against the attack and it wasn't the first time during this mission I questioned Kinnear's tactics. He was the designated team leader and had rank over me but we were clearly at odds.

After eight days of sneaking around in the NVA's backyard, we discovered a hidden bunker complex. We had been in this area for two days taking pictures and notes while observing enemy activity. The NVA were busy in the canopied forest stockpiling munitions in several dozens of well hidden bunkers along a network of winding, narrow foot paths. We had estimated there to be forty to fifty NVA in the immediate area although at any one time we had only observed soldiers in groups of three to six men.

Kinnear wanted to snatch a prisoner but this group of soldiers were on the opposite bank from us across a shallow but wide stream. The jungle was moderately canopied and we had no pre-determined or known area where we could be quickly extracted by chopper. Once we radioed for extraction, the slicks were more than an hour's travel time from reaching us.

Kinnear was impatient and agitated. His plan was to wound one of the soldiers in the shoulder while the rest of us shot to kill the others. After our initial fire he, Hyak and Yubi would cross the stream and grab the wounded NVA while the rest of the team provided cover. We would then flee the ambush site and keep moving until the choppers reached us for extraction.

While the Yards kept watch on the enemy soldiers digging the bunker, Kinnear and I moved several meters to the rear of the area to discuss his plan. The opposite stream bank was a mere thirty meters away. The NVA, while busy working, talked and bantered amongst themselves. Kinnear and I kneeled next to each other in the darkly shaded jungle foliage. I leaned close to him putting my lips within an inch of his ear and in the quietest whisper argued against what I believed to be a foolish move.

When I finished Kinnear cupped his soiled hands around his mouth and put them to my ear and whispered, *"Call the god-damned air relay and tell them we are about to make contact. Tell them to send the fuckin' slicks for our extraction. Now..."*

We had been on this mission for nine days, pretty much without sleep for the last two and Kinnear was fucking crossed-eyed for a gun fight. Why argue with a superior when you can fight with a common enemy? I shrugged to myself. Fuck it. Don't mean nothin.

Kinnear moved back into position and gave his orders to the Yards. I whispered into the radio's handmike attempting to establish contact with "Covey". Covey is the code name for a twin engine Cessna that overflies our area of operation. In the plane is a Special Forces member, who keeps radio contact with us, because our mission is in extremely remote, mountainous areas, where telecommunication over land is impossible.

I can't get Covey on the horn. I try for several minutes until Kinnear moves back to my position. I pantomime the fact I can't make radio contact. Sternly waving his hand, Kinnear signals me to move into position.

We are set. Kinnear will initiate the contact by shooting, in the shoulder, the soldier who is on the furthest right side of our view. Immediately after the first shot I and the Yards will place a killing fire on the other five soldiers. In the distance and high overhead, I can hear the beating drone of Covey's twin engines approaching us. The NVA momentarily cease their talk and their work to gaze upward through the quiet sunstreaks that pierce downward through the jungles' patchy canopy. I can see sweat running down the chest of the man I place my gunsights on. POW! Kinnear fires a single shot from his weapon and our teams' fusillade erupts. I place a three round burst into a foreign soldier's chest then turn my sights and fire into another who crawls his way across a pile of dark dirt. In a scant instant it is over.

"Hyak! Yubi!" Kinnear barks. He and the two Yards leap up from our concealment and splash their way across the stream's knee deep water to the other side. The smell of cordite itches inside my nose. I keep watch to the right flank. Diu watches the left side.

"FUCK! FUCK!" Kinnear is screaming. "FUCK!" I look across to his position. He is repeatedly kicking one of the NVA soldiers who lies face down in the dirt. Suddenly, a couple of hundred of meters from our position, come three repeating staccato blasts from a bugle. I can hear the loud cry of other enemy troops calling across a wide area to each other.

I yell. "Kinnear! Hurry the fuck up!"

Kinnear, Hyak and Yubi jump into the stream and hustle toward me. All the while a steady stream of swearing flows from Kinnear's throat.

"Shit! Fuck! God-damn it! They're all fucking dead. The god-damned prisoner is dead!! Fuck!!"

I'm more worried about our lack of radio contact.

****

Furiously, Brooks scribbles notes then quickly lights his cigarette and secures a swift puff. My rambling intensifies onward. Past feelings of excitement mixed with terror tremble in my nervous system.

****

We had a pre-planned route of evasion to an area of open canopy about two hundred meters to our rear. In this area a helicopter could hover and throw out ropes for us to hook to our stabo-rigs so we could be lifted out of the jungle.

We move about a hundred meters when Yubi, the point man and Kinnear open fire. I am back in the middle of the file talking to Covey on the radio. Help is on the way but it won't get here for another sixty minutes. I am crouching with my weapon at the ready. Kinnear is cussing.

"FUCK! SONS OF BITCHES!" Kinnear comes back to my position looking pissed off and says, "The mother fuckers are between us and the extraction area."

The eight of us huddle in a small circle. The situation is not good. The jungle in this area is almost entirely covered with canopy. There is no place where a chopper can drop ropes to us. We keep to our small perimeter of sweating bodies. Looking at the faces of the Yards, I notice their eyes getting wider and whiter. In the distance we can hear the enemy yelling and breaking brush.

The forested jungle area we are in is level and not very dense, but thick enough to limit line of sight to less than thirty feet. Occasionally it thins allowing a quick glimpse for thirty meters or so. We sit fast in our small perimeter listening to the commotion of soldiers obviously gathering together to begin their hunt. Unexpectedly, the roar of a what sounds like a large truck engine in the distance gets louder as it approaches off to our left. From our previous day's recon we know the Ho Chi Minh trail is about a hundred and fifty meters from our position. We listen to the truck stop. Doors slam shut and gates crash open. Anxious North Vietnamese voices and shuffling of booted feet make my imagination vivid. We've got to move. Kinnear and I huddle close and talk in whispers.

We decide to cautiously make our way upstream while keeping ourselves in the thickest of the brush. Hopefully we'll keep moving away from the enemy in the process. When the choppers arrive we'll try to find an open area in the canopy near the stream's bank and get extracted from there. The stream is a danger zone but it's our only option.

The NVA are no longer making a ruckus which means they are quietly searching for us. We begin moving. Like a meditation, we progress in slow agonizing motion. I, Kinnear and the six Yards, keep a space between ourselves that allows each of us to have slight sight of the man to the front and rear. A step isn't taken without looking where the foot is placed. No foot is moved without first looking forward, then right, then left, to the rear and all around up into the trees. Slowly, very slowly we obliquely inch our way toward the stream and away from the last contact we had with the NVA.

Like a web of lace I extend my senses of perception into every direction. My index finger rests on the steel trigger of my CAR-15 and I crane wishfully to hear distant choppers. Somewhere, close by, the enemy lie in wait for us.

Without incident we eventually make our way to the stream. At this spot it's not more than twenty feet wide with two feet of running water busily frothing around a bed of man-sized granite rocks. Winding along the opposite bank is a narrow foot path. Sprouting from each bank, tall gray-skinned trees, their tops spread like large green umbrellas, lean out over the water. There is enough gap between the tree tops to allow a chopper to drop ropes down to our position.

Suddenly, in my chest cavity, I feel the distinct resonate rumble of incoming choppers. A split second later I can hear the faint distant thumping of chopper blades beating against the air as they get closer and louder. We are in position. I click on the squelch switch on the radio and make contact with the pilots. There are two slicks to pick up our team, another two Charlie model Hueys with rockets and mini-guns and two Panther gun ships with mini-guns, rockets and cannons to cover our ass.

There is too much vegetation to physically signal the helicopters and it's too dangerous to throw a smoke grenade which would reveal our position to the choppers and the enemy. As I talk to the lead ship commander, I direct his flight path using the sound of his position as he approaches us. The chopper's flight direction is considered "twelve o'clock". The incoming warbirds are flying off to my right and still approaching.

I whisper into the radio's hand mike, "Fly two o'clock, over."

"Roger." Comes the reply.

The ships are on a dead course towards us. When the slick flies directly over us, I call into the handset, "BINGO!"

The noise of six helicopters in the air beats above and reverberates around us. The pilot comes back on the horn.

"I see a narrow river, some large boulders. Over."

"We're alongside those boulders, over."

"I'll have to make another pass, over."

"Roger. Standing by…"

The chopper makes a wide turn and heads back in our general direction. I again guide him toward us. The bird flies directly overhead.

"Bingo!

"Roger. I have your position. I'm going to maneuver down onto the tree tops and have the ropes thrown out. What's the situation on the ground? Over."

"We've broken contact but enemy is in pursuit, over".

Suddenly there is small arms fire breaking out from an area across the stream and maybe a hundred meters from our position. It's directed toward the choppers. Radio transmissions from several pilots simultaneously erupt…"Enemy in the open!"

The electronic whir of mini-gun fire spews a span of destruction down into the jungle to our front. Another ship's cannons boom and thunder. The shock waves ripple over us. We can hear the enemy yelling to each other. We sit unmoving in our location while the pilots deliver their payloads of death upon the enemy. More and more small arms fire erupts. Covey has come into the fight repeatedly releasing its load of white phosphorous rockets.

The fighting between war birds and ground forces continues unabated for nearly an hour. The pilots are caught up in a glee. They have hit and ignited several bunkers containing explosives and munitions. It sounds like the fourth of July. Many targets of opportunity keep them busy. We wait with our eyes wide open and our fingers on the trigger. Evening is fast approaching. The sun is setting. The ground fire has not decreased. I get a call from Covey. "What's your situation?, over."

"Sitting tight, over."

"We're getting low on fuel. A ship is going to come in on your position. Get your ass ready to extract. Over."

"Roger copy, over!"

The lead slick starts down to the canopy directly over us. I can hear the other ships working their ordinance around the area. I'm yelling into the handset as the ship, its turbines screaming, hovers directly over us. The beaten wind from the chopper's blades violently thrashes the tree tops and forces them to flail and separate. Looking up, I can clearly see the helicopter. One of the door gunners is waving. He has our position.

"We're taking fire! We're taking fire!" screams the pilot into the radio.

About twenty meters from our position, on the other side of the river, several NVA shoot up at the hovering chopper. The enemy doesn't see us. They are standing erect shooting upward. *We have clear shots*. Several of us open fire on them. I see a couple of them get knocked to the ground. The others disappear like mist. The chopper yanks itself out of its position above us. I yell the ship's call sign into the radio. Covey comes on the air.

"The ground fire is too heavy. The choppers' fuel is nearly spent...They are going to have to leave position...I have to refuel also...I'm sorry but we can't get you out before nightfall...we'll have to return for you in the morning...I'll be back this evening to keep contact with you...do you copy? Over."

From the pit of my pounding heart I reply, "Roger copy. *Oh Fuck.* See you in the morning. *I fuckin' hope*. Over."

"Sorry Burko. Hang in there. Covey out."

As they fly away, the thundering beat of the helicopters' rotating blades slowly and surely decays into the distance, leaving us in the deafening silence of sinking hope. Kinnear, the Yards and I must find a place to hide.

The night begins to seep into the ambient atmosphere. As the air cools, the jungle floor exhales mists up around us. The NVA in this area know we are alone and plan their hunt.

****

Brooks interrupts me.

"I hate to do this, but our time is up. Sorry, no pun intended. We've already gone a little over and I have another client waiting. I'm sorry. We'll have to continue next time."

I know I am staring blankly at Brooks. I understand but now that my adrenaline and psyche are at overload, I'm a little worried about leaving the safety of Brook's office. I'm worried for the safety of the world from me.

I nod affirmatively and get up from the brown leather couch. "Okay Brooks. See you next week." Brooks smiles supportively.

I move to the door and grab the brass knob. My hand is vibrating, the palm is oozing sweat. I swing the door open and staring a thousand meters into the distance, I walk past the receptionist and out the front entrance into Kona's sweltering summer heat and sun of day and think seriously about self medication.

Jesus Never Made It This Far

The Montagnards tell an ancient tale of a man and his wife. Their love for each other was so great it made all the people happy and the land peaceful. But one day tragedy struck and the man's wife suddenly for reasons unknown died. All the people were sad and the husband fell into grief. The wife was buried and her husband spent his entire time sitting on her grave. For days and months he wept not moving from the grave site. The gods themselves felt such pity they intervened. Where the man's tears fell on his wife's grave suddenly grew a flower never before seen. It bore fruit that the man partook. His grief was healed. This is how the Poppy came into existence.

****

It's a beautiful February morning. Nature is feigning an early Spring. The vital juices of the plants and trees seem to be anxious to rise. I have just pulled into a gas station on my new Harley Davidson Sportster. I stop at the fuel pumps, push down the kickstand and shut off the bike's engine. I stand then lift my leg over the seat and remove the crash helmet from my head. It's warm enough to be wearing a t-shirt and although it has been nearly two months since returning from Asia, my body and face are still browned from Vietnam's tropical sun. I look back up the highway and in the distance, I can see the gunshop where I work and its huge, vertical sign, red letters on a white background:

G
U
N
S.

My hair is long enough to lay on the back of my neck. I put my face toward the sun's warm light, close my eyes and shake my head slowly side to side feeling the softness of my growing hair brush the tanned skin of my shoulders. For the first time since the worst times, it feels good to be alive.

Keeping my eyes closed, I listen to a lone automobile pull up to the opposite side of the gas pump. I feel dreamy, trance-like from the sun's rays dancing reddened streaks across my closed eyelids. The softness of my hair caressing my neck soothes me. SMACK! An open palm of a screaming middle aged woman lands precisely on my jaw. My adrenaline jumps like a bullet out a muzzle. Throwing open my eyes, I am confronted with hysterical hands grabbing at my hair and flailing at my face. Connected to them is the mother of a young soldier. She is screaming, "You long-haired freak! Who are you to be so free? My boy is in Vietnam fighting for the likes of you. What gives you the right to…" I stand frozen as a marble statue, inured to the physical blows of the distraught woman's attack. Two attendants in Texaco uniforms come running out of the gas station and grab the flailing arms of the crying, at-a-break-down sobbing woman. Her justified worry for her son's life has broken her nerves. I stand numbed, a million miles from nowhere. The service station attendants help her walk to the curbside and sit her down. She shakes and sobs uncontrollably. The two attendants try gently to console her and then look up at me with angry faces.

I look to the 'GUNS' sign in the distance. Under my breath, I tell myself in a drill sergeant's command, "it don't mean nothin', troop." A chill snakes up my spine and spreads through my skull. I put on my helmet, mount the bike and turn on the key. With a sharp commanding downward kick of my jungle boot, the Harley Sportster rumbles to life and in a spirit of its own machination leaps forward and roars into traffic. The engine screams acceleration and speed courses in my veins. The highway is thick with vehicles. The machine shoots along the dotted white lines as its personal raceway, threads between cars in their lanes leaving inches of space to spare. Leaning myself forward over the handle bars, my torso stretches into the rushing air until my body and my vehicle are in repose like an image of a classic hood ornament. At one-hundred and thirty-five miles per hour the cars rush behind me to a world left in suspension. I scream at the top of my lungs. The machine and I blaze into a stretch of empty highway. When the bike turns control back over to me, I realize I should be on my way to work. I jam the gears down, the engine screams high-pitched in deceleration, the bike slows for the next highway cross-over. I turn the rumbling machine around and head for the gunshop at a legal pace.

****

I like riding the Harley. Molding my body to the machine's power. One energy. Single intention. Like an artillery round punching a hole through the sky. The relationship reminds me of riding on the helicopter. Sitting in its open doors, butt glued to the floor by centripetal forces, feet hung over the side of the war bird. The flying machine and its thundering, beating the wind into submission, harnessing the air like it were a beast of burden. To ride screaming like a Valkryie into Valhalla. War is hell. Actual combat is a motherfucker.

****

My boss greets me as I enter the gunshop. He has errands to run and leaves the business to my oversight. I see the regular customers gathered around the coffee pot. George, a millionaire executive of the chemical industry, has the ears of a rapt audience of would-be great-white-hunters. George has just returned from a tiger hunt in India. The entire group acknowledges me with a quick, quiet glance. I move to behind the sales counter and sit on a bar stool. George continues the-great-white-hunter tale in his Harvard Yard accent.

"Waell, as I sat on my elephant, forty bush beaters from the local village walked on-line through the thick brush. In their hands they held short sticks they used to poke into the thickets. They raised and pitched their voices in a most peculiar shrill vibration. Hopefully, their movement and clamor would drive a tiger into my view from the elephant I rode. The elephant's back was saddled with a small wooden platform bordered with short sides, something resembling a box. In it, I and my arms bearer rode. I carried a Winchester bolt action, .458 Magnum. The elephant lumbered slightly ahead and to the flank of the hired natives. Before long a good sized tiger bolted from a reed covered area. It was mid-day so we probably startled the beast from sleep. It was a beautiful cat. Not a record breaker but trophy quality." George pauses and dips his pipe into a cured leather pouch. Pushing tobacco into the bowl, he continues, "The creature did not quite get the gist of the entire situation. It made the mistake of stopping and turning to look at the noise that stirred him. I shouldered my rifle and snapped off a quick shot. The round blew fur and dust off the cat's hip. I bolted a second round and fired again. I knew I had hit him from the sound this bullet made. Nothing can duplicate the sound of a bullet striking a large animal. It's sharp when the bullet strikes a limb and a smothered thud when it enters the larger part of the torso. The sound was definitely sharp."

As I listen to George's story I feel my pulse quickening and a growing anxiety stirring in my heart. George continues. His voice raises slightly indicating a tense turning point in the hunt.

"I clearly wounded the beast. But before I could take another shot the tiger leapt up and ran faster than I've ever seen an animal move. The cat bounded into a thicket of large bamboo ahead of us. The villagers on the drive line yelled hysterically, pointing to the thicket in which the cat now lay."

Beads of sweat perforate my brow. Perspiration drips from my armpits into my shirt and coldly runs down the sides of my body. Vibrations deep within me want to leap out and scream.

George's tale mesmerizes everyone else. They look like a photograph to me. Life without animation. George's mouth is moving but I can't hear a voice. My breath has disappeared. My mind tosses like a boat on stormy sea from the vibration escaping from somewhere in my psyche. George is deep into the zest of the hunt that tingles pleasantly in the hunter's blood…he continues.

"The bush beaters have the hiding place of the great cat surrounded. It roars defiance at its predicament. The wounded cat is cornered and I find myself facing a most dangerous situation. I shout for the arms-bearer to…"

"A DANGEROUS SITUATION!" My words rip from my lungs and out into voice. Everyone in the shop is jolted to my presence. "I'LL SHOW YOU A DANGEROUS SITUATION!" I rage. Quickly I move to the racks of rifles in the gun shop. I continue yelling. "BIG GAME HUNTER, HUH!"

The customers are bewildered. The look on their shocked faces says which way do I run but fear keeps their feet glued in place. I take a box of 30/06 ammunition from the shelf and grab two M-1 Garands from the military section of the gun racks. In a blur of precision I lock and load both weapons. "OKAY MISTER BIG BRAVE GAME HUNTER!" I walk toward George and toss one of the loaded rifles at him. He looks shocked but manages to catch the heavy weapon with both hands but the muzzle lightly scratches his forehead. A single drop of blood appears and trickles its way down to the tip of his nose and hangs there.

"HUNTING DOWN A WOUNDED ANIMAL WITH FORTY MEN AND AN ELEPHANT. THAT AIN'T SHIT. YOU WANT DANGEROUS? HOW ABOUT I GO OUT BACK AND HIDE IN THE BUSHES AND YOU COME HUNT ME DOWN, MOTHERFUCKER!"

I turn and make a crouched run for the shop's door. In a blink of an eye, I am out the door and have darted into the field behind the shop to conceal myself behind one of the many clusters of scrub bushes. I lie in unreasoning anger and hunger for the fast, taut pulse I would feel in my throat after killing a man.

The morning's bright warm sun is being assaulted by deep purple clouds. Shadows swiftly slash the sunlight to pieces. Grayness grows over the field I hide in and the wind begins a cold blowing. No one is leaving the gunshop.

I don't remember how long I lie there before I see my boss drive his truck into the gunshop's driveway and park next to my Harley. He walks into the shop and I realize there's nothing more for me here.

I stand up from my prone position and fire the Garand from my shoulder in rapid succession into a nearby berm until the hammer clicks on an empty chamber. Satisfied in the moment, I turn and walk back toward the gunshop.

My boss Joe and several others have cautiously come around the building and stand staring. I walk up to Joe and hand him the rifle. His mouth is silent but his eyes say his mind does not comprehend. No one else says a word. I walk to my motorcycle, climb on, kick it to life, drive to the highway's edge and stop. I reach back into one of the saddlebags and retrieve my jungle fatigue jacket to put on. Rain drops and snow spit from a darker growing sky. I remember that a high school friend was supposed to return from Nam a couple of days ago. I point my scooter in that direction and gun the throttle.

****

When I reach the front street of Vic's apartment, the weather turns mean. Sleeting rains and it's getting colder and darker. I hope Vic is home.

Vic and I first met in the woods. I was sixteen. He was fourteen. We loved hunting. Unknown to either of us, we both had been keeping a watchful eye on the same family of nesting crows in a local wooded area. Each of us wanted a crow for a pet. The day I had chosen to remove one of the newly hatched chicks from its nest was the same day Vic had decided to do the same. On a crisp Fall morning, we simultaneously arrived at the base of the crow's family tree. The karma of such a meeting began a long friendship of hunting and fishing and bird-dogging girls together.

****

Vic was drafted into the military two years after I had enlisted. I was in Vietnam about to rotate to the states when I got a letter from him saying he would be in Nam attending an army school for forward observers. The school was in Nha Trang where I was currently assigned and the letter told me Vic had already arrived for the training. He had no idea I was in the area. That same afternoon I jumped in a company jeep and drove down to the school. I convinced his company commander to let Vic off duty for a night so we could spend the time together. After combing the company area I finally found him in the latrine taking a piss. He was focused on shaking out that last drop when I yelled, “Lieutenant Stevenson! The company commander wants you ASAP!” If he had been sitting on the john he would have shit from the unsuspected visit.

“Lee! Where did you come from?” He zipped his fly and shook his right leg for minor adjustment.

“Out of the bush, Vic. And you are coming with me.”

“I can’t get away.”

“Already taken care of, troop. Company commander has given you permission.”

We went back to my company’s area of operation and sucked some beers down at the Recondo School bar. I made arrangements to have two of Mamasan’s girls visit us before the camp was secured for the night. We finished our brews.

“I’ve got a surprise for you Vic. Two of the trickiest girls this side of Saigon are waiting for us outside my hooch.”

He stops and gets serious. "Can't do that. I'm married. Have a little girl, Tenna. Check out the pictures." Like a man living on pride he displays the photos he has carefully removed from his wallet.

"Nice. Nice to have someone waiting for you. A reason to live, Vic."

The call-girls are waiting for us. They do a good job of acting disappointed when they learn we won't be enjoying their company. They know they get paid anyway. I give them a twenty piastra note and a see-you-later-pat on the buns. "Check out at the gate girls." They giggle gleefully and leave Vic and I to ourselves. We walk between the hooches to the camp's perimeter and sit on top of the fifty caliber machine gun bunker. Inside the sand bagged fortification, a South Vietnamese soldier sits on guard and smokes his stinky tobacco.

Vic talks at length about the great hunting trips and good times we shared as teenagers. He is full of the infatuation a new and strange world brings. It's been three years since we last saw each other. I look him over, listen quietly and wonder if he will make it home alive. He has just arrived in country. I am about to leave…

****

It rains. I park at the curb and leave my Harley covered by a tarp I carried in the saddlebag. I don't hurry as I walk to the front door of the apartment complex. The rain soaks my clothes and me. Just like Nam I thought. I swing open the front door and stand in a small foyer lined with gray mail boxes set in the peeling paint of yellow walls. I scan the names and locate Mr. and Mrs. Vic Stevenson, Apt. 3A. I push the little black button to ring his place. Over the intercom I hear Vic's voice, "Yea, who is it?"

"Front and center Lieutenant Stevenson!"

"Lee! Come on up." A raspy buzzer rings releasing a metallic lock. I open the security door and head up the wooden stair case to #3A.

I see Vic's head emerge from the door of his apartment. A shit eating grin spreads across his face. I greet him at the threshold. We grab each other in a manly hug then look into each other's eyes. For a moment we experience pure joy and laughter.

"You made it dude! You fuckin' made it!" I congratulate him on being alive.

"Yea, I fuckin' made it back to the World. Got all my parts too."

"The World." Terminology soldiers in Vietnam used to refer to the reality outside of the war's. The place they had left. The idea each man defended. To return to the World of peace, civilization and friends. The one ticket for the ride every soldier wanted to get on. Hopefully in one piece. Hopefully not riding in a pine box.

I look beyond Vic into a messy apartment. Dirty dishes, trash needing emptying and the smell of stagnant air. We go into the flat.

"Where's the wife and kid?" My tone has changed from elation to concern.

"Gone. Both gone." Vic's energetic greeting has wilted. He turns and walks to the kitchen table plopping his slouched body into a chair.

"Beer?" Vic asks swigging from a long neck brown bottle.

"No, gotta keep alert. Clear headed you know."

"Yea, you never know what to expect." He gulps another swig.

"What happened?" I ask.

"I came home two weeks earlier than I was scheduled. Looked forward to surprising the wife and got surprised myself. Big time. You know I could live with that. The affair, I mean. I was gone for eighteen months. I know how lonely it can get. Hey, I should've taken you up on those girls in Nha Thrang that night! Shit I can't believe it."

Vic takes a couple of gulps from the beer bottle and sighs heavily. "It's my fault."

I interrupt him. "It's not your fault, man. You were conscripted."

"Yea but I signed up for two more years for Officer Candidate School."

"You didn't ask for the fuckin' war."

"I volunteered to go."

I'm not helping. "Well, you can't take the entire blame."

"Yea, I can. Six months ago the company I was assigned to got into a big fire fight. It was the first time I ever killed a man. Right in front of me. The bastard dropped at my feet. The battle was still going on, I don't know why it possessed me but you remember how as kids we use to cut off the antlers of a deer. Well in the middle of all that friggin' noise and chaos, I bent down and cut off the fucker's ear."

"You aren't the first soldier to do that. The ancient Romans used to dismember their enemies and scatter the pieces over the battlefield."

"Yea, but they didn't send the pieces home."

"What?"

"I sent the ear home in a box with some other mementos. My wife wasn't supposed to open the box. She was told to put it away until I got back! She thinks I'm a sick person. She said she could never let me touch her again. She's gone. But…I'M BACK! BACK IN THE WORLD!" Vic's depressed state has launched manic.

"And I have a surprise for you, buddy! We are going to soothe our souls if the mailman comes through today." Vic dances up from his chair and does a little jig across to the door.

Downstairs in the foyer, the local mailman stands dripping the rain he has braved and stuffs the letter boxes with mail. Vic leans his head out his apartment door and shouts. "Hey mister postman is there a letter in that bag for me?"

"Looks like you've got a book or something of the kind here, Vic."

"Hot dog!" Vic cheers and disappears out of the doorway. He bounds down the steps to pick up his mail. I hear him taking leaps back up the stairway. He jumps through the doorway and slams the apartment door shut behind him. He clutches the package to his chest and smiles like a mischievous boy at me. "Are you ready for this?" he asks.

Vic tears away the brown paper wrapping letting it fall forgotten to the floor and presents with outstretched arms a photo album held in his hands.

"Pictures?" I ask.

"Dreams." He replies.

"More like nightmares," I say.

Vic spreads the album open on the Formica kitchen table. I scoot a chair alongside him and watch the pages turn. Each shot presenting faces of men I do not know, jungle I want to forget and images I had forgotten. Like a guide on a tour bus, Vic intently explains each photo's meaning.

I feel nostalgic. I need to make a phone call. My mind and attention drift from Vic's tour and I reach to my rear pocket and remove the little red book I carried for the duration of my service time. In it are the addresses and phone numbers of people from around the world I have gotten to know. Civilians as well as fellow soldiers.

There are two men in particular I have to call. Bill Bent, my buddy and sidekick during my time stateside and in Germany with the 10th Special Forces Group. And Sam. Poor fuckin' Sam. Last time I saw him was when he was medevaced by helicopter from our compound. He did write soon after that. Life in Japan was good. The phosphorous burns were healing. The docs said there is a little gangrene but nothing to worry about. He wrote one more time giving me an address and number in Utah he could be contacted at. I never returned a letter. That was over a year ago.

"Hey, Burkai. Snap out of it." Vic has sensed my departed interest. "Now for the best part." Using his fingernail he lifts and peels off the clear plastic covering protecting the page of photos. He gently lifts a photo off the page, looks at it sadly and tosses it carelessly to the kitchen floor. Beneath where the photo had lain on the page is a cellophane packet of China White Heroin. Beneath every photo is a clear cellophane packet of China White. I swear he's looking at me with the eyes of a devil.

"Where's your phone? Vic."

"Phone?"

"Yea, the telephone."

"Hey man. I said we had dreams here. Don't you want to..."

I cut him off. "Nah. Gotta stay clear headed…"

"Yea, yeh, yea." He cuts me off and points to the phone within my reach behind me. He returns to busying himself removing the white packets from the album. Without concern, one by one, he carelessly tosses the pictures to the floor. I put the phone in front of me on the table and paging through my little red book, I look for Bill Bent's number.

Bill was a wild man. An explosives expert on the A-Team. He owned a motorcycle when we were at Fort Devens. More than a few times I rode through the city of Boston on the back of that bike with Bill drunk as a skunk. Together we endured the thrills and hazards of mountain climbing school in Alaska. We helped instigate the riot at the Newport Jazz Festival. On a three day pass, we went to Woodstock. He stayed at stateside duty. I went to Nam. Through the phone's receiver I hear a connection being made, then a ring. I look over at Vic. He has opened one of the packets and with concentrated attention is pouring it into a little pile. "Look Burkai, it's snowing! Right here on the friggin' kitchen table."

"Yea, and it's snowing outside too." I reply and point to the window. On its pane, little flittering white spots dance in the foreground of a darkening day. On the phone, I hear a click then a hello.

"Hello. Is William Bent there?"

"Just a minute," comes the reply. As I wait, I see Vic has his face nearly on the kitchen table's surface and a short straw in his nose. Using his thumb and forefinger he aligns the other end of the straw with a small match head size mound of white powder. His face contorts and his eyes are thrown wide open. I hear his lungs reach through his nose for the air on the other side of the room. The noise it makes sounds like a high school bully trying to bring up the biggest hocker known to mankind. The small pile of heroin disappears into the straw. His right eye waters heavily down his cheek, his face turns red. "It's all in the technique," he says. "Want some?" I wave him off. Bill Bent answers the phone. "Who is it?"

"It's Lee, Bill. I made it."

"LEE!" I am surprised at his jubilance. "Lee! Thank God you made it. Thank God! I'm so happy to hear you." He really is. Too happy, I puzzle.

"Lee. I'm not the man you remember." *Neither am I, Bill.* "I'm a changed person. I'm working for the Boys Club and the YMCA. I don't drink, do drugs or harass anyone anymore." *Bill was a good harasser.* "I'm so happy Lee! I found Jesus! *Jesus!* Jesus is Lord. Jesus is my company commander. Praise the Lord."

Bill goes on for awhile about his job and his new found self and how Christ is his savior. I listen and *I wonder what Bill will do when that doesn't work anymore.* Bill is exuberant about the possibility of us getting together again. Sadly I feel it'll never happen. We make a little small talk and say our good byes.

"Burkai, Burkai, how are thy? That is your frickin' name isn't it?" Vic squints and grins at me. "Want some?" he smiles, his face now smooth from the analgesic in his blood. "What did Bill have to say?"

"He said Christ is his company commander now."

Vic giggles to himself as his eyelids all but cover his vision. His chin settles into his chest. His breath sighs a long slow relief. He nods and dreams of saints and pussy. I take a deep breath and dial Sam's number. It rings. There is an immediate answer. I recognize Sam's voice.

"Sam," I say. "It's Burkai. It's Lee." Dead silence answers me. In the receiver, I hear only the wheeze of air through a nose. "How are you Sam? How's the arm?" Silence. Then…

"They cut off my fuckin' arm!"

My heart falls in a cold black hole.

"It's your fuckin' fault!"

The cold black hole falls into my gut.

"I can't even hold my camera now."

****

Sam was the camp photographer. He ran the photo lab and was responsible for developing all the pictures we took on the secret operations my unit conducted in Laos and Cambodia. Sam was a rear-echelon type and not a combatant. We had made an easy friendship when he arrived at the forward observation base. He taught me how to develop my own pictures and how to shoot a camera. I taught him how to shoot exotic weapons. The last time I saw him, my recon team was preparing for being one of the lead elements for the invasion into Laos. I invited Sam to tag along with me, Hein the team leader and the recon team while we drew extra ammo from supply. He wanted to take some photos of us as we prepared for the mission.

Out on the helicopter pad the Hueys' jet turbines started their slow whine climb to operating speed. Blades rotated swishing the air, then beating it.

In the staging area, all our gear and rucksacks lay ready for us, only so was something else. A white phosphorous hand grenade lay carelessly on the ground next to our gear. It was not supposed to be there. All of our ordnance was accounted for. "Shit," exclaimed Hein. He had the look of *I don't like this.*

Cautiously Hein and I squatted down near the grenade for a closer look. It looked benign. The pin was in. But the grenade shouldn't have been there. Hein moved his hand toward it.

"Don't touch it," I declare. "Don't touch it Hein. Let's do this by the numbers."

I stand out of my squatted position and step opposite Hein on the other side of the WP grenade. I look down at Hein. "Don't touch it." I say again.

Hein picks up the grenade…It's harmless. Hein stares up at me with a pissed look. In my head there is a scream: *LOOK OUT!* I ever so slowly start to turn away. Before my eyes break contact with Hein's I see he is holding a small brilliant ball of light in his hand.

In an instant, white phosphorous blew and spewed and exploded in all directions. I was blown through the open doorway into a small hallway of a hooch I stood near. Sam was blown in on top of me. Sam's right arm from his shoulder to his fingers was saturated with burning phosphorous. I had been made groggy from the concussion. I came to my senses lying on my back in a hallway. Above me Sam stood screaming, his outstretched arm ablaze. I got to my feet and hurriedly took off my fatigue top, wrapped it around my hands and was able to pull the burning phosphorous off of Sam's arm. He was deep in shock. He seemed to be holding his arm as far from himself as possible looking at it in horror and screaming sounds I never heard a human being make. I slapped his face and got the attention of his wild eyes. I pointed to the doorway at the other end of the hallway and yelled, "GO! GET TO THE DISPENSARY NOW!" Sam turned and ran. I turned to the open doorway the explosion had thrown me through. I could hear more ungodly screaming. I stepped out the doorway. Before me stood Hein. He was totally engulfed in flames outstretching his hand to me for help. His face was melting off his head. I didn't know what to do. Tear gas grenades in among our gear detonated from the fire. The gas kicked me in the lungs. Another explosion. The concussion hit me like a brick wall, blew me back through the doorway, unconscious. Others were hurrying to help…

When the horrific fiery event had finally ended, Hein had been burned over his entire body. His face was burnt to a crisp, his fingers seared together and his eyes burned out of their sockets, but he was still alive. He would live for twelve hours. Sam was immediately medevaced with his arm burnt to the bone. That was then. This is now and Sam is on the phone and my guilt feels like lead in my blood.

"They cut off my fucking arm!"

"Sam, I…"

"It's your fucking fault."

I don't know what to say.

"Fuck you!" The slam of a receiver in Utah stings my ear in Delaware. I hang up a dead line. I look over at Vic who nods peacefully.

"Vic. VIC!" I yell. Vic lifts his chin off his chest and slowly opens his watery, bloodshot eyes at me. "What?"

"Give me some of that smack."

"Havin' a bad day, Burkai?.. Me too…"

He hands me the straw. I cut a small line out of the white powder and snort it through my nose, deep into my lungs trying to reach down to the cold black hole in my guts. Within a minute or so, I begin to experience the release of thousands of tiny, warm, liquid pins and needles of ecstasy flowing under my skin, up over and around my skull and swimming deep towards my soul. The black hole in my gut turns to warm liquid light. Outside it is cold dark. The kitchen's single ceiling bulb chooses this moment to expire itself in a bright flash. The room is momentarily bathed in a passing car's lights reflected off thickly falling snow. Vic and I merge with our chairs, nod our heads ever downward into our chests and dream of other worlds. Outside it snows it snows it snows.

Vested in War

During a lull in heavy fighting at Gettysburg a young Union soldier noticed a foreign national wearing a strange uniform and fighting alongside him. Puzzled why a foreigner would be fighting in a civil war in the United States, the young soldier asked him, "What are you fighting here for?"

"One U.S. dollar and thirty two cents a day," came the reply, "Which is about twice as much as you are fighting for son."

****

When soldiers train for war the military tries to make the experience as real as possible. In the 'gas chamber', nothing more than an air tight little shack, small numbers of troops take their turn being exposed to chlorine gas and tear gas.

Out of the doors of the chamber soldiers stagger into fresh air. Their eyes burn with blindness, their stomachs wretch, they choke. It is an exercise in intimacy. A soldier must become familiar with the afflictions of combat, including getting shot at.

And you do get your chance to be shot at. In the final week of basic infantry training there is the "infiltration course", an exercise in penetrating a gap in enemy fortifications while coming under fire.

****

Basic Training: 1967.

It is a frigid, wet winter afternoon in North Carolina. And for some act of God it is even colder and wetter where soldiers train. I slide on my back in the mud. I cradle my M-14 weapon against my chest and belly with its barrel and bayonet passing over my face. The rifle's muzzle hits against the brim of my steel helmet whose leather strap tightens across my jaw. Precisely eighteen inches above my face the red tracers of a .30 caliber machine-gun crack the sound barrier. While trying to make myself as small as possible, I dig my heels into the muddy ground and push my body forward. I slide into a large icy puddle. Cold water floods down the back of my neck and into my ears. I shudder and focus on the fact that bullets are flying closely over my body. I roll to my stomach and cradle my weapon across my folded elbows. Using my elbows and knees I low-crawl like a lizard through the cold mire.

Across the miniature no-man's land concussive explosions repeatedly erupt. Three M-60 machine-guns spray wide fields of red tracer fire over our heads. And then there is the booming voices of the drill Sergeants' screaming from the sidelines into their bull-horns. *"Get your fucking ass down unless you want a bullet up it!...Move it! Move it! Move it!"* and the more personal kind of encouragement: *"Brown, if you don't get your dick moving I'm gonna personally kill your sorry mutha fuckin ass!* Preparation for war must be relished.

After a period of several hours three hundred of us have completed the course. It is four in the afternoon, the temperature hits freezing. We stand in ranks, our bodies wet and muddy, chilled to the bone. God looks down on us and sends a messenger in the form of a drill Sergeant. *"There will be no evening meal before your night trip through the live fire course! Platoon Sergeants! Dismiss your men to the immediate area!"* Ours is a god of war…

We are allowed to be at ease, as much ease as is possible considering we are all fighting the bitter weather. It'll be two hours before it is dark enough for the night time portion of the infiltration exercise. It is frigid. Really fucking cold.

In hushed tones soldiers are bitching. Smoky breaths blow into freezing hands. Boots stomp and stamp numbed toes against the ground. I'm starting to question how much longer I can take this when an unfamiliar voice asks, "How's it going men?" Standing in front of us is the Captain of the company. I am suddenly humbled for he too is just as cold, wet and muddy as the rest of us. For some reason seeing our leader in the trenches with us moves us to find a deeper inner strength. I watch him move about the platoon quietly strengthening men's spirits with nothing more than his presence. The commonality of suffering.

"Burkins. Burkins?" A familiar voice turns my attention to Robert James a member of my platoon. "I can't take this anymore!" he exclaims.

"Hang in there Robert. There's a warm bed waiting for us."

"No. No. It's not the cold. I can't take THIS! I'm not meant to be a soldier. I'm a school teacher not a fighter. I'm twenty six years old. I have a wife and two kids. Why did they ever fucking draft me?" I've never heard Robert cuss until now. "I want to run away from this madness. I could never kill anyone! I am against war!" He looks off into the woods around us. "Do you think I should just leave?" Robert's face hangs agonized with his personal truth.

A time for every purpose and for all of us standing in the cold that time is not far off. At least it will be warm in Vietnam. Darkness falls and the temperature follows. Robert stands shivering and shaking down into his boots and soul. "What do you think I should do, Burkins?"

"Go Robert. Make your statement. A man is only free if he can choose. That's what I believe. That's what we as soldiers are supposed to be fighting for. To make men free. Be a free man Robert. Make the choice you want."

I can see the mind behind his eyes solidifying. "Thanks Burkins. I never would have believed you would say something like that. Thanks."

A sudden cheer rises up out of the ranks of men. A truck bearing several large metal containers of hot coffee drives up. The gods of war are too kind. After drinking our fill of the hot bitter liquid we are sufficiently dosed to look forward to one final trip across no-man's-land. Hoooo Ya!

We get the call to fall in. Hundreds of cold bodies align themselves in ranks. Finally, no more waiting around. We are all eager to get this over with. Warm bed and the comfortable oblivion of sleep, a crawl in the mud away.

But there is a delay…A man is missing from the formation. It seems Private Robert James has declared himself a freeman.

****

The darkness of night descended upon us hours ago. The coffee is all gone. Our wet fatigues have stiffened in the freezing cold. The night exercise will not start until Private Robert James is found. Soldiers stand around and bitch. I look off into the dark wood around us and wonder how the school teacher is doing.

Around midnight a jeep races into the training area and skids to a halt. Two drill Sergeants pull Robert James out of the vehicle. His face is filled with fear and a pained look of loss. We are called into ranks again. The exercise begins. The machine-guns fire. Detonations shake the earth. We get down in the mud and begin our crawl towards the warm bunk that awaits us.

The next morning Private Robert James and his personal belongings are gone from the barracks. I never knew what the exercise of his belief cost him.

****

What was it in the beginning that gave men the right to impose their beliefs on others? Was it the false information that governments were God ordained? Whose right is it to sit in judgment and dictate who will kill whom?

****

Vietnam: 1970.

Yesterday I was minding the government's business of destroying other human beings and today I am being questioned about and charged with lying on my application for a top-secret security clearance.

"You mean to tell me that because I was arrested at a party for possession of pot that I can no longer do my job? Heaven forbid I might smoke a little weed and have second thoughts about killing people." I sit under the heat and bright lights of what is supposed to be an interrogation…Ugly faces surround me. I feel amused.

"It says here that you were also arrested for disturbing the peace! Why didn't you put these facts on your application?" A member of the military criminal investigation department drills me.

"Disturbing the peace? Isn't that a pre-requisite for murdering peace? The charges were dropped," I reply. "I was guilty of nothing." I knew when it came to being selected for the job of doing cloak and dagger work for the government that only those individuals with the utmost record of morality and ethics would be accepted.

"You Sergeant Burkins are a security risk!"

I look into the overly serious faces of the men that sit and stand around me. I see the innocence of power that has never been questioned or tested on a real battlefield. I've spent the last eleven months exposed to death in all its forms. I saw it. I felt it. I dealt it. These guys are not about to faze me. "Fuck you ass holes. I've got less than thirty days left in the military."

"How would you like to spend those last thirty days in the bush with a Vietnamese unit?" Perhaps there are some things more frightening than death…

They let me off with a simple written explanation of why I failed to list my trespasses and made me sign several papers that threatened me with ten thousand dollars in fines if I spoke about the work I did...

****

There is a rule of work among the Special Forces fighting soldiers: Once a defensive perimeter has been established the next immediate priority is to begin the construction of the camp club. A place for the gathering of warriors to eat, drink and be merry...

****

Voices in Valhalla attach in song:

"I had a dog and his name was Blue...best damn dog I ever knew...Hey Blue...you were a good dog too!..."

Fifteen members of the recon company sit around a table in the FOB 2 'club'. We carry on in a ritual of song lamenting our loss of comrades and saluting their lives, their fate. One by one we stand, drink and sing our personal renditions of 'Blue' for the friends we've lost...*"I had a friend and his name was Grand...lost his life in a foreign land...Hey Grand you made a good last stand..."*

During our singing we have drank sixty bottles of wine for our fallen. It is near noon and our mood is metamorphosing from intoxication through oblivion and into animality. We become the creatures humanity claimed we rose above. Our singing has degraded into grunts, groans and bellowing. There is a spontaneous group mentality of primate madness. We screech and bound around the NCO club like baboons alerted to disaster.

In the club door walks a stranger. He stops just inside the room unsure of the world he has entered. We freeze postured in our animal frenzy. From across the river Styx our dilated eyes lock onto the visitor. He smells of discomfort and fear. Attack!!!

The visitor is one of the newly assigned engineers here to help rebuild the damage caused by a recent sapper attack against our base. It is Sunday afternoon. He has just finished attending a service of faith and comes seeking a steak dinner. In he walks wearing the comfort of civilian clothes: leather sandals, PX polyester pants of unnamable color and a clean white shirt unbuttoned to his solar plexus. His hair cut is fresh and his face smoothly shaven. Around his neck hangs a linked gold chain. At its end dangles a large peace sign. Several curious apes in our melodic group descend upon him.

"What the fuck is this?" demands one of the recon members. He grabs the necklace of the visitor. Several other team members seize the shocked guest by his arms and legs. Others quickly align several long tables end to end to fashion a runway. Booze is poured over its surface. A couple of men piss on the tables' tops. "Okay boys, bring our guest in for a landing!"

The guest hangs in the hands of eight men. Two on each leg. Two hold each arm. They raise the spiffily dressed struggling visitor about chest height and start a run toward the aligned tables. "Ready or not coming in hot!!" screams someone.

The visitor is held spread eagle in the air. His carriers pass on either side of the long length of tables and bring him 'in for a landing'. They slide him belly down across the length of the tables. Hoots and hollers fill the room as the clean wardrobe of our visitor soaks up booze and urine. When he has been slid to the end of the 'runway' his captors pretend he is taking off and lift him into the air again. "Touch and go. Touch and go!" cheers someone. Across the room they 'fly' him banking around for another 'landing'. Down onto the tables he crashes and bounces. "Hey! A little bumpy that time. Better fly 'round and try again. Ha!" The fun of scarring someone near to death continues for twenty minutes until the reluctant human plane is stood on his feet. Still clamped by unforgiving hands he stands disheveled, stained and bruised. The animals around him close in.

"What are you some kind of peace faggot?" Someone grabs the peace symbol and physically rips it from the chain around the man's neck. It is held up into the frightened guest's face. "Peace you motherfucker? If there was peace I'd be out of a job!" The words crack open a silence filled with immeasurable anger. The brutality of war looms like an illness and those who fight know not that they are infected.

In a moment's pause heavy with the dreariness of excessive drink and mourning the abused visitor rips free from his captors and flees the enterprise of Valhalla.

****

If war is a business it will not soon end. The expense of war knows no confines and extends beyond currency. The costs must be made prohibitive.

One For All / All For One

Once upon a time there was a government of men who lived their fears and saw profit in war. To obtain their goals they created false vision and legislated patriotism. By the millions, they conscripted boys to actions that filled their coffers and made their economy strong. For many long years ambitious men spoke with righteous pride. To all the innocent people in the land they lied and too many boys who played their game came home in coffins.

One by one over time, the boys who survived returned. They were changed, judged guilty and discarded by these false men and the innocent people who had been deceived. Ultimately the trickery wore thin. After loss of innocence, the country moved to end the game. The men lived happily ever after. The boys disappeared into wilderness...

****

Brooks asks me again, "How do you feel Lee?" Again I don't answer.

It is a monsoon kind of day. The golden coast of Kona, Hawaii has alchemically reverted to lead in sympathy with my mood. Above my head I listen to the rain pour down on the roof of Dr. Brook's office. Brooks sits in his custom crafted chair uncomfortably. Like a fine perfume, the sweet smell of his Turkish tobacco reluctantly reveals a hint of itself. My undisclosed frame of mind hides behind my steady silence. I sit, externally quiet and internally bound up. In the torturous space of a time standing still I hear Brooks' question, "What are you feeling Lee?" I can't bring myself to speak. The protracted seconds and minutes pass without dialogue. On a rainy day, in the confines of his office, the two of us sit as statues in my hour of individual weekly therapy.

What am I doing here? I question. I'm sick of talking about the war, the seemingly endless loop of reliving a life that won't stay hidden or go away. Talking about events is becoming like salt to a wound. Memories stand still like photographs yet I experience the momentum of struggle. If the greatest battle is within the self then I have arrived.

In the beginning, undisciplined, I fight. Then through discipline, I learn how to fight. Then I discover why I fight. Then I study how not to fight. Then I learn how to heal myself. And finally I perceive how to heal others.

At present my healing is slow. I stand before a wound and gaze into it not knowing what to do next.

Brooks looks at his watch. On his face and in his sigh is an acknowledgment of his own inner difficulty at trying to get me to reach myself. "Time for the session is up Lee." he says standing up from his chair. And trying one last time he asks, "What are you feeling?"

Greater and greater the question and the answer squeeze me. The tendrils of my thoughts entangle my emotions. I gaze at Brooks like I stare into my undefined wound. He turns his back to me to open the door. Like a wild stallion roped for the first time, an emotion that war embodies thrashes inside me wanting out. I silently come out of my chair and unknown to Brooks I sneak up behind him feeling like I were a beast and he were my prey. At the moment he turns to face me I attack throwing my body and face to within an inch of his.

"Rrrrraaaaah!!!" I scream. Out my mouth, out my eyes and out my pores. A scream out of the floodgates of war. It pierces Brooks on every level of his existence. His body locks rigid with shock. His face drains of all color. I see horror in his eyes.

"There!" I exclaim. "THAT'S HOW I FEEL!"

I leave Brooks standing in his momentary shock. I make a focused path to the door of his office and exit out into the pouring gray rain.

Estranged from my sense of self I walk slowly through the downpour. In my heart it rains. With my clothes soaked and my soul drowning I open my truck's door and sit my wet ass into the seat. The rain falls without abatement filling the inside of the truck with a resonant roar. Within the roar I hear my troubled thoughts pour out of a deep sickening silence. What an ass I am. I have just scared the shit out of someone who is kind, helpful and dear to me. What is wrong with me? *What are you feeling Lee?...That's how I feel!...how I feel...how I feel.*

Reality grips me like a sorely needed breath. It is *fear* that I feel. I live in constant fear. It lays on me like my skin. It follows my sinews deep within me to my glands, organs and guts. It is an ever present background noise shading my every function. Fear. I am afraid.

Perhaps that is it. During the war I experienced such degrees of fear that the switch that controls it was blasted open and is forever stuck in the open position?

****

"It's a medical fact!" states Robert the helicopter pilot in our rap group. "There is a lack of the body's natural endorphins and an excess of adrenaline in the blood of combat veterans. It plays a role in restricting a sense of well-being and fueling a sense of anxiety." There is an immediate muttered response of consensus from the group.

"That's a fuckin understatement!" scowls Dale a former crew chief of a Huey helicopter. He twists his face as he sucks long and hard on his cigarette.

It has been nearly a year since the rap group was formed. Initially there were just four of us then quickly within the first year several other combat vets found their way into the group. Now there are twelve of us. We meet one night a week. It's about healing, which you want to believe feels good, but as a group the realms of personal pain, masked by ever present anger, dominate the sessions.

The illnesses of war. These afflictions were salved with recognition of the soldiers' service. Early Babylonian soldiers were rewarded with spoils and tribute from conquered lands. The Greeks saw war as a necessary evil to support democracy. Land grants and stature in citizenship were received as entitlements. Care was provided for the disabled and the family of those killed in action.

The returning combatants who were "afflicted" were given small plots of land to farm outside the city. The government understood the need to distance these men from society's antagonisms. Besides they could serve as a hardened defense should an enemy come to the city's gate.

The Legionnaires of these ancient times demanded no less. In a letter from a commanding centurion, written to the rulers of the Empire of Rome: "...Make haste to reassure me, I beg you, and tell me that our fellow citizens understand us, support us and protect us as we ourselves are protecting the glory of the Empire. If it should be otherwise, if we should have to leave our bleached bones on these desert sands in vain, then beware of the anger of the legions!" (Veterans of Foreign Wars magazine, 11/96)

We in the rap group have been labeled by our society as suffering from the 'Vietnam Syndrome.' In the early seventies thousands of combat veterans sought medical help with sleeping disorders, uncontrollable rage, anxiety, panic attacks, depression, suicidal obsession...The government and the military denied there was truth to the claims. The veterans were turned away.

In antagonistic circles within veteran's groups and the government, we were called crybabies. The terminology Post Traumatic Stress Disorder was new and argued against. Crybabies! They failed to see that these were tears of rage. Men pained by the war, angered by the hypocrisy, and in fear of their reaction to that world that claims its truth the only truth. So much cannon fodder for other men's purposes. Tears of rage. So we meet to try and understand what our healing is.

The first several months the meetings were rough for us all and I suspect it was especially hard for Doctor Brooks. The intensity and realms of emotions that were driving each one of us out of control were all crammed into an elbow-room-only session space. We were strangers to one another. We came from environments of seclusion, each of us living the belief we were alone in our insanity. Chuck, a Marine vet who got shot in the chest during his tour, once stated,…"I just want to thank you guys for being here and being so fucked up. I don't feel so bad now."

****

As is the nature of powerful people who declare war, they do so at a cost while doing their best to keep their expenses down. Giving the soldier status or recognition can be expensive. Only so many land grants can be made. Only so many hands can reach into the money pot. For the powers that be, cannon fodder must be abundant, made less expensive, and have the ability to make money for those who make enemies of others. Governments claim to be moral if it is in their favor to do so.

****

My first direct experience with government was when I was nineteen years old. I was told to report within thirty days of notice for military service. If I did not report, as ordered, federal officials would come to my home and arrest me and imprison me. If I did not agree to go and kill human beings on the other side of the world I would be 'deemed' a criminal. Essentially, the government kidnapped me and forced me to kill for them.

Rather than be legislated a criminal by my country, I enlisted in the military, became a member of a top secret organization and a killer of men and collateral damage operative.

My second direct experience with the government came a few months after my return from the war when I went to the Veterans Administration seeking help with sleeplessness, anxiety and rage. *"Crybaby! Nothing is wrong with you. If fighting wars was mentally unhealthy the government would surely know. Go away..."*

Having nowhere to turn, I began self medication for sleep and anxiety control which led to my third relationship with the government. I was arrested for drug possession. For doing no harm to anyone but possibly myself, I was put in prison and faced twenty years of incarceration.

Hmmm, let's see: a man tells me to kill other human beings because he doesn't agree with their ideology. If I don't kill for him, he makes me a criminal. After doing what he wants, I feel ill and because I medicate myself to be able to function at life and continue working, I am faced with a twenty year prison term. Morality is deemed what the government wants. Go to hell.

My story is typical of the vets in the rap group. We feel victims of moral and ethical injustice and ill at killing. The lives of soldiers become the serum for the power junkies' injection. So much cannon fodder.

As a group we've now reached a stage of maturity, thanks to the bond we began to form and to proper medication. When one or more of us were in what we called a "trip-wire" situation, (if anything touches me I am likely to explode), the others in the group were there to help.

At present, David the wound tight officer from the 101st Airborne unit, is struggling to exorcise a pain. He speaks with great effort having to fight for his breath as he reaches into his past. In each one of us, there is a resonance with his battle. We listen. Completely.

"...We had already had our asses chewed. The platoon had been ambushed in thick jungle. Dozens were killed outright. Many more were wounded and crying for help. Incredibly my radio man and I were not hit. We managed to escape a short way from the ambush. We found a wounded squad leader, William. His abdominal muscles had been ripped apart and he was opened up like a gutted animal. Hinder, the radioman and I dragged William with us. We took cover behind a large tree. I was trying to bind up William's guts so they wouldn't fall out of his torso. He was crying like a baby. Hinder was on the radio calling for support when he was shot through the chest. I crawled to the radio. William was screaming at me to help him. We were pinned down. On the radio, another platoon leader was calling *us* to come help them. They too were under heavy fire taking casualties. There was no *us* any more. Just me. William was pleading with me to save him... *"Hang in there! I told him. Hang in there."* I was able to direct gun ship fire against the enemy. By the time reinforcements arrived, William lay dead. His motionless hands lay in his guts as if still trying to hold his life in."

David's tale wretches from his soul but he talks as if it happened to someone else. There are no emotions to go with the horror. Sitting hunched in his chair he looks up from the floor and says with tears stuck behind his eyes, "I feel like a goddammed piece of shit."

The group huddles round him. Hands, seeking to give comfort, go to his back, head, legs and arms. In silence needing voice, a thick numbness bonds us all.

Out of This World II

It's that time again. Open the wound and pour in some salt. Psychological protocol says talking about traumatic events lessens their emotional charge. The charge may ease but its psychological and psychic imprint, the identity created during the trauma, is encumbered by being a prisoner of its own existence. Certain defined parts of me are not happy in chains. How can I deny being all things?

I want to be alone. Left alone mostly and where I live provides that setting.

My flower farm is located on the upper slopes of the world's most massive mountain, Mauna Kea, which is surrounded by the world's biggest body of water, the Pacific. I'm twenty-five miles from the nearest town, off a secondary road and behind three locked gates placed along five miles of an extreme four-wheel-drive rock path that leads home. Home is a weathered wood, single-walled cabin with a corrugated tin roof, lichen-rock fireplace and windows everywhere you look. There is no furniture. There is no phone. No electricity. There is: propane lighting and fridge. Catchment water. Old lava flows. Ohia forests, brush, scrub oak, Proteas, me and as the Hawaiians' say, "The Aina, brah! Without the Aina (Earth) beneath your feet you would be in da water." No matter how alone your existence is, some day you will have to reach out.

Because of my living in such isolation someone once asked me, "What will you do if you have a medical emergency?"

"Lie down and calmly die," I answered.

Pain is an indicator of being alive and I am on my way into the world of the living, Kona town, on the Beeg Island of Hawaii. Me Ke Aloha Hawaii. I love Hawaii. Hawaii loves me as I drive my pickup truck, its bed loaded with exotic flowers looking like an ikebana on wheels, down the narrow winding road from my mountain farm to the blue seaside and the good Doctor's office.

It's been a week since I've seen Doctor Brooks. In my last visit, I was attempting to tell him my battlefield experience of dimensionally fractured reality. Induced by fear, my out-of-the-body Death experience.

Fear is fear, no matter who it attends. How we react dictates our life. And Death, what is that about?

Have you ever heard the tales people tell about having a near death experience of being propelled through a long tunnel toward a bright light? A light they found themselves being 'spiritually' bathed in? Their lives forever changed?

I had a near death experience in the thick of combat and I'm not sure if I can truely remember, admit to myself or let alone reveal to someone else this moment of *transcedence?*

After making my deliveries of life affirming Proteas to the local flower stores, I drive my little blue truck into the gray gravel parking lot behind Brooks' office. I park the truck and retrieve from the water buckets in its bed a nice bouquet of Kings, Pink-minks and Eximea Proteas I've created for the receptionist.

I enter the office waiting room, hand the bouquet to the receptionist who, unable to resist the power of my flowers, breaks into a big smile. I return the smile, turn to take a seat, wait and contemplate the ongoing journey into myself.

My therapy sessions with Brooks have become like an expedition into an unknown land. That land is me. With an outdated map, I keep a faith that no matter how unnerving, painful, frightening and dangerous the mental and emotional terrain seems, the overall journey will be exciting and rewarding. Some simple questions will be answered. Who am I? Who are we as human beings? And why do we fight? Simple.

Usually, when I arrive for my appointment with Doctor Brooks, his small waiting room is empty. But on this day there are two other people, a man and woman, quietly sitting in leather cushioned chairs across from a coffee table covered in magazines. I immediately recognize the pair as the owners of a local restaurant in town. My entrance gives them a slight startle. I take two steps and sit myself into a chair directly opposite the couple.

The room is uncomfortably small and the sum of the receptionist's desk and chair plus four other chairs, a lamp and lamp stand, and a coffee table, makes the waiting room space shrink. Adding the three of us creates an unpleasant closeness. We all sit in the awkward silence of the receptionist's keyboard tapping until I verbally acknowledge the couple's presence.

"Hi Tom. Hi Mary."

They don't respond in voice but nervously nod in recognition then quickly look away as if they have been caught with a secret. Living on an island makes for little privacy. Finding your neighbor in the psychiatrist's office makes you wonder.

There is a really big silence in the small room. I sit with my legs crossed, my hands on my knee. Across from me, Tom and Mary fidget in their seats. They look like they want to jump up and run out of the room. Tom tries several times to clear his throat but struggles with each attempt. His congested efforts contort his face. Finally, he manages to acquire his voice and asks, "Uh, uh, whatare*you*doinghere, Lee?"

I intentionally pause for several moments before I answer. Tom hangs suspended in this awkward vacuum. *Why am I in the psychiatrist's office? Because I am fucking disturbed! And you?*

"I'm a Vietnam veteran." I answer.

"Ohhh! Okay. Of course!" He and Mary shake their heads and shape their eyes in agreement like this is a reasonable and acceptable answer. "Of course."

And why are you two here?…

The door to Doctor Roads' office opens. He's a partner in Brooks' medical practice. A bespectacled face attached to a bald pate sticks out of the door's opening. He smiles at Tom and Mary and cheerfully proclaims: "It's time!"

Tom and Mary promptly get up from their chairs and announce to me: "We have to go now!"

I smile, give a short wave of my hand and intonate as if the future is uncertain, "Good luck."

At that moment, the door to Dr. Brooks' office opens. His eyes and face beckon me in.

****

Once inside Brooks' office and sitting restlessly on the couch, I am ready for the excursion.

Brooks begins by recalling our last session. It ended with me talking about darkness…

"Darkness?" Confused, I'm caught off guard by Brook's claim that the last session ended…with me talking about darkness? My confusion begins me doubting. My doubt starts to worry. My worry turns to fear. My fear turns to…

"Darkness," says Brooks as he reads from his notes. "Meaning nighttime. The battle was going on. Ground fire was heavy. The helicopter pilots told you they were running out of fuel and had to return to base. They left you and your recon team alone in the jungle. Night was falling. Your team had already killed several NVA soldiers. You were being pursued."

Brooks created an opening catapulting me into telling the story of having an out-of-the-body-experience in the middle of battle...

My voice is measured.

I remember this mission beginning portentously. First off, another American had been recently assigned to my recon team. For several months I had solely commanded my team of Yards. We worked together well and functioned as a seasoned unit. Now the Yards and I found ourselves under the leadership of a First Sergeant Kinnear.

Kinnear was no novice to war. He was on his third tour of duty with about half of his service having been in combat. He had spent the first few months of his present tour assigned to a "B" team that functioned primarily as a support group to the men on operations in the field. He recently itched to return to combat operations and was assigned to lead me and the Yards on this mission.

Our target area was a section of the Ho Chi Minh Trail in Southeastern Laos, a known stronghold of the North Vietnamese Army. The word "trail" is a misnomer. The Ho Chi Minh Trail is a dual lane, well maintained dirt highway that starts in North Vietnam, runs through Laos and Cambodia and branches several roads into South Vietnam. The highway is rich with by-passes, canopy-hidden, winding stretches of roads that are always being successfully repaired no matter how often they are pounded by one-thousand pound bombs dropped by B-52 aircraft.

****

The Ho Chi Minh Trail snakes through the jungle far below our single engine, high-winged plane. I sit in the tiny, cramped back seat of a light observation aircraft. The plane bucks. The back of the head of the pilot is only a few inches from my face. The engine roars. The pilot yells over his shoulder to me.

"We're nearing the mission area!"

I am on a mapping flight.

The mapping flight helps me to get an overview of the terrain our team will be operating in. I also visually locate possible landing zones for the helicopters that insert and extract us within the mission site.

On this flight, the pilot maneuvers the small plane through bumpy air, over green mountains and up into numerous valleys while I work to identify points on the ground with those on the map I hold in my lap.

This is no easy task. The pilot rolls the aircraft so I can look straight down out the side window. An endless mosaic of textured green jungle races by. The pilot does a sharp leveling maneuver and flies lower to get a good visual on a possible LZ.

The air bounces us unmercifully. The pilot steadies the lunging controls and yells, "YOU GOT IT YET? YOU GOT IT YET?"

The plane bucks in the air while I try to land my shaking pencil point on the correct spot on the map I hold in my hands.

The plane's wings are nearly perpendicular to the ground. At tree top level we fly in a tight circle around an open area of forest. I see several muzzle flashes and gun smoke in the treeline we fly past. The pilot sees it too.

"COCKSUCKERS! COCKSUCKERS! he screams defiantly.

I am pushed into my seat by the plane's sudden vertical flight. We clear the treeline and fly away unscathed. We continue looking elsewhere to find other possible insert sites.

The boundless jungle below has few openings in its canopy where a helicopter could set down. Everywhere the jungle ground is open, level and there are possible landing areas, we encounter small arms fire. We keep looking…

Finally we did find several "holes" in the jungle canopy the team could rappel down into from a hovering chopper. This would do.

We fly back to Kontum airfield. The next day Kinnear, the Yards and I would try to insert ourselves into the area.

****

No such luck. Every time the helicopter tries to hover over one of these openings in the jungle canopy we receive small arms fire. The choppers we ride in flare off from the sector and the two Cobra gunships covering the insertion fire up the area with rockets and miniguns. Because of our mission being compromised, the air ships take us back to the launch site. In a couple days we try again. Then again. And again. Over a period of thirty days, a dozen attempts to start the mission are stopped by ground fire.

****

Despite the fact we have the firepower to overcome the few soldiers we encounter at these sites, we don't make it an issue. The point is to successfully get into the area of operation without being detected. We need to observe what the enemy is doing there. If the team is discovered the mission is compromised.

So thirty days later, after a dozen failed attempts at insertion, the decision is made by higher command for us to walk into the mission area from a remote radio relay site in Laos code-named *'Leghorn.'*

****

Leghorn is a relic outpost from the French Indo-China war. Like a sharp black tooth sticking prominently out of a long row of green molars it stands erect above all the jungled peaks along an extensive North-South mountain range.

Multiple man-made bunkers all but cover Leghorn's confined apex. There is only one approach to its peak. It is a narrow, heavily mined, denuded field, sloping up to the base of the crest. Strung across this no-mans-land is a tangle of barb wire. The bleached bones of several soldiers' skeletons hang a portrait to past failed attempts at siege.

I sit on Leghorn's pinnacle, view the surrounding land and think it like a fortified final position from a fantasy time of good versus evil. I wonder whosc sidc am I on?

On several of its sides, Leghorn's cliffs are a shear drop of several hundred feet. I sit on such a cliff's edge and look downward and out across a low land valley sprawling westward and to the North for many miles in each direction. Across the valley on its western border, another long line of mountains stretches north and south parallel to the range Leghorn sits in.

****

This is my third day on Leghorn and today something looks different about that mountain range across the valley from me.

Last night at dusk, B-52 bombers began an Arc-light. The dropping of bombs. From their silver bellies', they disgorged massive amounts of ordinance on a mountain's peak across the valley from us. All night long the pinnacle of Leghorn shook and vibrated from the distant, ceaseless rain of high explosives. On the mountain top directly under the destruction, beautiful explosions of burgeoning orange-yellow rosebuds danced to their own wild beat.

It is zero-three-hundred hours. An inky black, star-studded sky blankets Leghorn. I lie on my side, on a bunker roof's sandbags, a soft pancho liner wrapped around me for comfort. I stare dreamily at the pyrotechnics playing on the far-off peak. The distant explosive rumblings vibrate the Earth and Leghorn's shaking gently rocks me to sleep.

Come morning a mountain no longer exits…

That's what's different. Last night's bombing obliterated the entire fucking mountain. It's gone. Man destroys earth. My jaw hangs open. My head softly shakes in disbelief.

****

The following night Kinnear, the Yards and I silently rappel off Leghorn's precipice, descend ourselves to its sloping shoulders and begin our walk down into the valley.

****

In a time far removed from emotional content, I observe myself in a psychiatrist's office spinning my story to Dr. Brooks. Darkness. He said I was talking about darkness…

****

Mists are growing out of the jungle floor. I listen as the last beats of the departing helicopters' blades leave their resonance in my chest cavity and leave Kinnear, the Yards and me behind. Darkness moves upon us. Insects begin their nightly cries. In the distance a wounded soldier moans. At our hand, the enemy has suffered losses. They are going to want their due. We are in some deep shit. Time to move.

There are crisscrossing foot paths throughout the maze of underground bunkers that are in our immediate area. Movement without being detected is going to be hard to achieve.

Kinnear, the six Yards and I begin moving perpendicular to the stream where we had made our last contact with the enemy. The brush here isn't thick enough to hide us. We move meditatively keeping an arms distance between us. It is dark enough for us to be nothing more than the shade of a shadow. In the distance, away from our direction of movement, we hear a truck start its engine and the taut voices of soldiers. Slowly the gradual whine of the truck's gears disappear from our ears.

We halt our movement after we have found a thick patch of heavily leafed briar and vine. We scout and study the area, then determine pathways of escape. We make ready for this spot to be our overnight position.

First we silently tape CN gas grenades to the faces of four claymore mines. Then we crawl, one man behind the other, into the concealment of the tangled vine and brush. The last man in, our tail-gunner Diu, covers our tracks. We then place the claymores at four corners around us such that each mine faces at a right angle to the other. This will provide an exploding perimeter of steel shot to ring itself entirely around us should we have to detonate the mines. It also redirects the mine's back blast away from us. The gas from the grenades will add to the confusion should we blow the claymores at the enemy.

In the tangle of vine and brush, Kinnear, the Yards and I, keeping an arm's reach between us, lie in a tight circle. We have removed our gas masks from their packets and keep them along side us for immediate use.

The night is pitch black. I can see nothing. I jiggle my unseeing eyes in every direction and for a moment I lose spatial orientation and do not know where I am or if I am. Without realizing it, I fall asleep.

****

I wake to the feel of a hand shaking my shoulder. I am suddenly awake and in the dark I see two flashlight beams drawing near our position. I can't believe my eyes. Several NVA soldiers are combing the dark!

As the flashlight's beams meticulously cut tunnels in the night one of the enemy is calling out one word again and again. "Vun! Vun!."

I lie on my belly and keep my eyes on their movement. Gai, my Yard interpreter, whispers in my ear, "Burkai, they are looking for their friend."

The NVA must think us long out of the area. Otherwise it would be suicidal to look for us with flashlights.

I can't make out how many of them there are. They move toward our position and stop not more than forty feet from us. They stand in a tight group and talk in regular voices. One voice sounds worried. Another sounds angry.

BOOOM! Kinnear detonates his claymore.

BOOOM!BOOOMBOOOM!

Following protocol, I and the Yards detonate our mines. I am made night-blind from the brilliance of the first explosion. Before I can think I get a whiff of tear gas in my nose. I immediately put on my gas mask.

My night-vision is impaired. The ringing in my ears is deafening. I reach around and feel for the Yards lying next to me. I crawl my way around each Yard feeling my way along until I reach Kinnear. My vision slightly improves. A very pale and diffuse moonlight dimly reflects the outline of Kinnear's head. Wearing his bug-eyed, rat-faced gas mask makes him look like an alien.

Using hand signals, we communicate that it is necessary for us to quickly move from the area. We are intact as a team. No one is injured. The atmosphere is completely silent. We quietly snake our way out of the thicket.

We take a quick minute to investigate what the detonation of the claymores accomplished. Using our red lens pen-lights we find four NVA soldiers lying on the ground. Their charred, twisted bodies smolder and bleed. An AK-47 lies next to one of the soldiers. I pick it up and immediately drop it. It is hot as a coal. Quickly searching the dead we only find personal effects. We orient ourselves and quickly move out of the area.

My face sweats under the rubber of the gas mask. Due to the humidity and heat the lenses of our masks begin to fog up. Forming a human chain, each one of us holds onto the backpack of the man to our front. With concentrated effort, Yubi leads the team away from the area.

After a few minutes of stealthy progress we stop to remove our gas masks. My skin itches and burns. My eyes sting. My body perspires. My mind can't comprehend what it sees…

In the dark ahead of us, suspended in mid air, I see what looks like a ball of bluish light. Goose bumps crawl under my skin.

"Hole." whispers Gai.

"Hole?" I ask under my breath.

"Hole in the jungle roof," whispers Gai.

Quietly the team moves toward the faintly glowing, growing apparition.

Blue moonlight pours through a 'hole' in the splayed canopy above a large bomb crater. Violently formed by a massive explosion is a huge pock mark on the face of the jungle floor. Ringed by a perfectly packed dirt berm it is twenty feet in diameter and four feet deep. A huge dirt bowl. The trees and vegetation around and above the crater have been shredded into non-existence.

I stand in the crater's center and look up to see stars and a moon at near full phase. We will set up a perimeter here for what remains of the night. It is zero-two-hundred hours. In three or four hours, weather and enemy permitting, we will get our asses lifted out of this 'hole.'

We set out our claymores and position ourselves into a perimeter within the bomb crater. The jungle seems quiescent. Not even an insect stirs. We don't sleep. We sweat. We wait. So does the enemy.

****

I pause in my story and Dr. Brooks looks up from notes he is jotting down on a yellow paper pad. His look says continue, so I do…

****

Darkness slowly dies in the pathway of coming dawn. The night relinquishes the forms it hid of the jungle around us. I lie in the dirt on my belly just inside the crater's edge. My weapon is at the ready. The other members of the team do the same at different intervals around the crater's berm. I wonder what this morning will bring.

Up in the twilight sky I can hear the drone of Covey's engines approaching our position. I turn on the radio and make contact. He says help is on the way and I can hear and feel the air-beating-blades of the incoming helicopters.

Suddenly the air above and around us is alive with the roar of two F-4 Phantom jets, two Spad A1-E Skyraiders, six Cobra gunships, and two Charlie Model gunships. The pilot's voice from the lead Huey, our extraction ship, comes over the radio. I lead him to our position. Kinnear is lying on his back in the bottom of the crater with a large orange marking panel spread across his body. The pilot calls out, "I've got you spotted. I'm coming down. Get ready to hook up to the ropes we drop."

While the chopper descends to hover directly over the hole in the jungle's canopy, the Cobras, Fastmovers, Spads and other gunships sweep in many different diameter circles around us. Then the extraction helicopter hovers at tree top level, about sixty feet above us and drops two long ropes out each side of the ship. Hooked at one end to the chopper the falling ropes unroll dropping their other ends down into our crater.

Buffeted by whirling wind from the chopper's spinning blades, Kinnear and I quickly assist four of the Yards in hooking up their stabo-rigs to the ropes.

Suddenly a barrage of small arms fire erupts from a position fifty meters from us. It is directed at the hovering chopper and us. I yell into the radio, "We're taking fire! We're taking fire!"

The Huey surges forward and upward jerking the four Yards up and out of the crater. Diu, Yubi, Boon and Deng are momentarily drug through the tree tops. The helicopter lifts up and away with the Yards dangling at the ends of the hundred foot ropes.

Kinnear, Hyak and Gai are firing at the NVA. I get on the radio and begin directing fire from the Cobras flying above me. They begin shooting their mini-guns, cannons and rockets. The Spads are dropping cluster bombs on enemy in the open. A huge secondary explosion erupts.

The enemy now knows where we are. Half a dozen NVA are trying to maneuver on us directly to my front. The terrain is sporadically covered with tall, slim trees, thick brush and open areas.

Other elements of NVA are moving to our right trying to get into flanking position. They are darting across a small swath cut in the jungle. I momentarily drop my radio handset and start firing at this group. I throw several hand grenades at them then get back on the radio.

I'm talking to the pilots of the two Skyraiders. The Skyraider, a World War II vintage aircraft with a monstrous single engine, carries more armament than the modern F4 jets. I give them the enemy's positions. Both brightly painted yellow planes fly one behind the other and make a diving pass parallel to our front firing their 20mm cannons. They swoop by with guns blazing then make a long looping curve to turn back in our direction and again open up with their 20mm Vulcan cannons.

To our front, a pathway of destruction is cut by the exploding Vulcan rounds. Trees are pulverized at the point of impact. Like thunder, the atmosphere condenses and vibrates all around us. Hot bullet fragments whir and whistle in the air. For the moment the NVA attack is stopped. The roar of multiple aircraft fills the air as they fly back and forth above us like pissed-off hornets.

Suddenly our position comes under heavy weapons fire. Six feet above our heads rounds from a fifty-one caliber machine gun cut, rip and explode through the trees surrounding the crater. The deep sound of the incoming fire rattles in my chest cavity. My adrenaline flow increases. My heart sinks into my stomach. *Fuck!* The incoming fire drops closer to us.

I kneel on the berm and spot the gun emplacement. It is set on a low ridge line and behind a large mound of freshly dug dirt about one hundred fifty meters from me. I have a clear line of fire. I align the sights of my carbine at the head of the soldier firing. I let loose a single shot and the gunner falls. Two other soldiers jump up out of a pit next to the gun emplacement. They grab the fallen soldier. I fire twice more and knock both of them down. I can see several soldiers firing at us from a trench next to the machine gun. AK rounds are kicking up dirt on the crater's edge. I look to Kinnear. He and Gai are busy firing to our left. Hyak has his attention focused to our rear. I turn my attention back to the ridge and concentrate my fire on the entrenched soldiers. My firing keeps them from operating the fifty-one cal.

I pull out my compass, get a fix on the gun's location and get back on the radio. From more than one area there is heavy small arms fire cracking in the air. The Cobra's and the Charlie model chopper's mini-guns scream their deadly electronic whir. I hear the fusillade of bullets shredding the vegetation and ricocheting through the trees. Covey's voice rattles out of the handset of the radio, "What's going on? What's going on?"

"STAND BY! STAND BY!" I reply.

I catch movement out of the corner of my eye. I see what looks like a flying blue watermelon with a smoking tailpipe streaking toward the crater. It's a B-40 rocket round and it slams into a large trunked tree and explodes with a BOOOM!!! Shrapnel sprays across the crater. No one is hit. Suddenly another rocket round comes towards us. It glances off the same large tree, takes an errant flight path to the right of us and violently erupts. Again shrapnel rains across the crater. Again no one is hit. Once more the fifty-one cal. machine gun starts firing at us.

Once again I get on the radio.

"Covey. They're firing B-40 rounds into the trees above us. I've got a fifty-one cal. shooting at us...Hold on!..." I drop the handset and unload a magazine at two NVA running through the trees off to my right. Under my breath I cuss to myself...*Shit! Shit! They're going to flank us.*

I hold to my position on the crater's berm and pull out my PRC-90 hand held radio, turn it on, press it against my right ear and make contact with the F4 Phantom pilots. I hold the handset to the PRC-25 radio in my left hand, press it against my left ear and make contact again with Covey. Amid all the barrage of bombs, rockets, cannon fire and small arms cracking, I can't hear myself think but I am crouched on the crater's edge and yelling at the top of my lungs into both the radios…

"Covey! Covey! I've got a machine gun emplacement firing at us. It's one-five-zero meters at an azimuth of…"

Suddenly I am slugged by a shocking pain in my left jaw. Dazed, I look up and see a heavily camouflaged NVA soldier not thirty feet away firing his AK-47 directly at me. A fusillade of bullets strike the berm within inches of me and kick dirt up into my face. My slung weapon hangs inert around my neck. I have only radios in my hands…Stunned, I freeze in disbelief…

****

I sit on the couch in Brook's office, nonplussed, frozen in a moment of the past. Brooks sits quietly in repose, waiting.

"I don't know how to describe it Brooks." My eyes internally scan for the right words. Brooks says nothing. He waits.

"I was so god-damned scared, Brooks. So fucking…incredibly scared. It was as if all the fear that existed in the universe…suddenly welled up inside my being faster than the speed of light and annihilated every trace of my existence."

****

Where am I? Where am I?? In a jungle setting below me, tiny soldiers run to and fro, black smoke pillars and flying machines toil in noiseless battle. *I'm hit! I'm hit! I feel for my jaw. It isn't there. I'm not even there. I have no body, no form…I'm dead! I must be dead!* From a three-hundred and sixty degree, three dimensional perch, I see up. I see down. I see everywhere. *I must be dead! But wait a* *minute...How can I be dead. I'm talking to myself!..*The chaotic battle below me grows distant and I grow peaceful. *The quiet feels good. A great warmth soothes me. The warmth is me. I am not separate from it. I am the warmth.* Recollections of every worry, every concern in my entire life perfectly appear perfect. *There was never a need for them, only an illusion of it. I am totally unburdened.* Slowly, pleasingly, the warmth *I am* turns to darkness. *I am the darkness.* And in great joy, *I laugh and laugh becoming laughter...*

****

"What are you laughing at? What are you laughing at?" screams Kinnear as he shakes me by my shoulders. "You almost got killed!"

I am back. The two of us are in the bottom of the bomb crater. The noise of the battle surrounds us.

I am perfect, feeling calm and in total control. I smile at Kinnear's puzzled face, calmly move to the crater's edge and get on the radios. I press both radios on simultaneously and talk with Covey and the F4's.

"Covey. We are taking fire from a fifty-one caliber machine gun. The target is one-hundred and fifty meters on an azimuth of three-seven degrees. There is a large mound of freshly dug dirt on a ridge at this location. Look for the dark brown dirt in the middle of all the green! Over."

A pilot of one of the fastmovers answers, "I see it! I see it!"

Experiencing more calm than ever before in my life, I look around the crater at Kinnear, Gai and Hyak. In a sentimental slow motion they fire their weapons. It seems each one of us have our own targets of opportunity. The four of us, fighting for our lives, are a portrait of tranquillity.

An F4 Phantom screams a wide turn to fly directly at us on a gun target line. From a distant point high and away from me the Phantom jet begins a run at the machine gun emplacement.

Its twin engines in a deafening roar, the jet descends close to tree top level flying directly at us. I lie on my back watching the rapidly approaching F4. Before it is over us it releases a two-hundred and fifty pound bomb. The jet peels off its flight path. The bomb flares its fins and slows to a wobbling descent. In noiseless slow motion the bomb comes directly at our position, barely passes over us and strikes the ground far short of the machine gun emplacement. The concussion sweeps over the crater like horses over a race track. The booming fifty-one caliber machine gun keeps firing on our position.

In the radio handset the other Phantom pilot is yelling, "Ready or not coming in hot! Coming in hot! Get your heads down!"

The F4 streaks past our position releasing a long canister that is pointed on both ends. Tumbling end over end, it falls from the belly of the jet. It strikes the base of the green forested ridge where the mound of fresh brown dirt protrudes and the enemy gun fires from.

Napalm explodes and washes like a wild liquid wave up and over the entire ridge and the enemy soldiers on it. The immense yellow pyre sucks every drop of atmosphere from around us causing the winds to whip in a torrent. Thick black smoke broils and rolls in conflagration. The soldiers and the fifty-one cal. burn in hell.

For a few moments there is an overall lull in the frenzy of the battle. The enemy is demoralized. I am swelled with satisfaction.

Then in a new fury, the NVA concentrate an assault on our position. Kinnear and Gai are shooting and throwing grenades off to the left of me. The helicopters are busy shooting at soldiers in an open area far to our front. On the right of me, out of my sight, I hear dozens of small arms open fire at the helicopters. I direct the Spads to the general area of fire and the planes drop canister bombs in that section.

The NVA are moving far around us to eventually attack our flank. Quite suddenly the peace and well being I experienced earlier leaves me. I am getting worried. Our ammo is getting low.

The continued fighting is eating up the fuel of the F4's. They unload their remaining bombs and leave to refuel. I get word from Covey more jets are on the way.

AK firing erupts from heavy jungle vegetation on my right side. I can only catch glimpses of the enemy squad's maneuvering. *Shit! This is not good.*

I heave my rucksack onto the berm's edge and try to give myself cover behind it. I peer out to the side of the rucksack. I'm thinking the radio should be able to stop a bullet should it get hit. I can see two NVA in pith helmets stealthily moving tree to tree toward me. I wait until they are less than thirty feet from the crater then blow my claymore. KA-CHA-WOOM! A huge cloud of gray smoke billows in front of me…

"Burkai! Burkai!" Hyak screams and opens fire at two more NVA who are running up the crater's side off to my right. I see their faces full of sweat and their blood shot eyes seething purpose. On my face I feel the concussion of their rifles' continuing muzzle blasts. I empty my remaining clip full auto at them. My and Hyak's fire hits them and for a flash of a brief moment I think I see the life that animated them depart like a wind. Their bodies, left lifeless, drop like sacks of mud.

Firing comes at us from our rear. *We are taking fire from three sides!*

Hyak is firing clips as fast as he can load. Kinnear and Gai are firing to their front. I'm firing in yet another direction. *This is it!* I grab the radio handset and scream into it. Hyak blows his claymore. *This is it!* I am firing and trying to talk on the radio at the same time.

"Covey. We're taking fire on three sides! Put a ring of fire around us. Bring everything you've got down onto us." *This is it! THIS IS IT!* "You have my permission to bring the fire on us! Do you copy? DO YOU COPY?"

"Roger copy. Get you heads down. Incoming on the way!"

I yell at Kinnear, Gai and Hyak that the ships are going to bring the fire in on us. Gai and Kinnear blow their claymores then scramble down into the crater's bottom with Hyak and I. We huddle with our backs against each other, our asses on the ground, our weapons at the ready and brace for the onslaught.

The Cobra's begin their attack unleashing cannon fire, mini-gun fire and flushette rockets all around us. Spads drop cluster bomb canisters and fire their Vulcans. Again and again and again. Over and over the earth around us is being torn asunder. Trees are being uprooted and fly through the air. Dirt and debris fall from the sky. The sky falls. Blistering shrapnel buzzes whistles and whines. The noise is ungodly and fucking overwhelming. In it I hear the screams of men and I am praying to God-anything-anyone-even-the-Devil to get me out of here alive...*THIS IS IT! THIS IS IT! I'M GOING TO FUCKING DIEEEEE!!!*

The Earth is falling apart. Chaos reigns and I succumb to its glory. My freedom torn from me, I surrender my resistance. *Take me. Take me. I am destruction*...yes, *I am all this.*

After several minutes of all-hell-breaking-loose, the fire abates and Covey's voice comes over the radio.

"Burko. Are you there? Burko? Over."

The gunships and Spads have done a textbook job of bringing their fire right up to us. The area around our crater is chewed to shit and shreds...

"Covey. This is Burko. You've suppressed the attack. I can only hear a distant firing of a few AK's. Over."

"Get the team ready. We're coming in to get you out. I'm turning you over to the pilot of the extraction ship. Over."

The voice of the pilot of the Huey comes on the air.

"This is Leader Two-niner. What is the situation on the ground. Over."

"Two-niner. This is Burko. We've got a few lingering AK's shooting up at you guys. Over."

"This is Two-niner. We're coming in to drop ropes to you. It's now or never. We are getting low on fuel. Over."

"Two-niner this is Burko. I love you. I swear to Christ I love you..."

The Cobras are making wide circles around the crater and firing up the ground as they fly. The extraction ship appears directly over us. Its blades are beating the air like a giant drum. Ropes are thrown down to us. The four of us, Kinnear, Hyak, Gai and I lie in the dirt of the crater's floor and hook our stabo-rigs up to the snap links at the end of the ropes. Over the radio, I give the pilot the ok...

"We're hooked up. Go! Go! Go!."

The chopper starts a slow, wobbly ascent then begins moving forward. We are pulled up from the crater and slightly across the shredded tree tops. The door gunner of the extraction helicopter starts firing down past us. I look down and see three NVA troops standing in the crater and firing up at us. A Cobra swoops beneath us and fires them up. As I am ascending I empty my last clip down into the crater at the NVA and scream obscenities.

Up, up and away we are carried. Below us more F4's have arrived and are bombing the shit out of the area we have just vacated. Several secondary explosions ignite. Towers of black smoke reach upward. Kinnear, Hyak, Gai and I are on our way back to Dak To. Flying at three-thousand feet I cannot contain my elation. Adrenaline courses through my every pore. My nervous system vibrates like an afterburner…

****

I sit in Brook's office on a comfortable couch and vibrate like I just left the battlefield. I look at him. He looks at me. "Whew!" is all he says.

Now that I've told my tale, I begin thinking back on the darkness. Those moments I thought for sure my life was over. I prayed. My prayers seemed answered but I realize now that there were moments, some really long moments when it appeared that my prayers to a God went unanswered and I reached out to a Devil for help.

The atmosphere in Brooks' office seems filled with a charged haze. There is an expansive moment of great empty space then I wonder and ask.

"Is it possible Brooks? Have I sold my soul…?"

Beatific Beast

The time was moments after twilight. I experienced my body as lighter-than-air floating upward above a company of soldiers bivouacked below on the hard dirt, bare but for scattered thorn bushes. Warriors, men in arms, whose forms in the fading light moved green and shadowy below me.

Receding faces full of white eyes and teeth tracked my slow ascent. I looked down upon the faces and their elevated eyes visually disbelieving my divorce from gravity. I floated like silk on rising air. Life's warm electric currents gently oscillated like a liquid love flowing smoothly, unrippled, from the eternally reaching core I know as my self. My eyes rested half-open viewing the life forms below through a sweet feeling of freedom from earthly bounds. I yearned to return to the men with whose lives I was entwined.

The night was quickly consuming my visions below me, so with a heartfelt longing I acquiesced to a feathery descent. Down, down I drifted into and among the soldiers and the thorned earth we shared as stage for battle.

When floating upward I had felt sufficiently filled and ever expansive, but now in descent, my inner lightness of being, densified and waned. I embraced the weight of gravity as a feather would the air.

My eyes opened from half-mast. I felt the leather of my black battle boots touch the hardened brown earth. Soldiers surrounded me, their eyes wide in near disbelief with what they had just witnessed.

I was a leader of these men, animistic warriors, all great spirits interred within diminutive physiques donned in mahogany skin. I returned to my earthly senses. Many of the soldiers reached to touch me. Other faces pressed closer in wonder.

"We never knew," they said. Held in awe, some of the men held my hands.

"You, always the quiet one. Why didn't you reveal your abilities? We never guessed. We silently thought ourselves respectfully like you…"

Amongst the attention given me came a voice of question: "How do you do it?"

"It is love," I reply. "Like a vast consciousness burgeoning inside me, reaching for heaven. I surrender to it and my body follows".

"How high can you go?" came another question.

I look to my left. There stands a group of ten tribesmen, quiet and smiling proudly in my direction. I am made warm by their attention.

"How high have I gone?" I repeat. "Once…I traveled to such altitude I lost sight of men and found ecstasy in the complete stillness of my breath. I lost my ego and discovered beauty."

Night spread itself inky. Many soldiers dispersed to their assigned guard posts. A few men remained. One approached me. He touched my elbow and placed a hand on my chest. "Do it again!" His intent was that of a curious child. "Of course" I replied.

I focused my vision inward on a glowing ember of love, fanning it with joy like a fire by bellows. Lighter my being became. I experienced gravity as an internal caress soothingly saying good-bye so I would not "fall up" too quickly. Rising, feeling pleasure, I perceived an awaking awareness approaching like a dream.

My body lifted and rose above the darkening armed camp. The stars above me whispered, "come, come…" I felt love flowing in my veins and seeping into my nerves. My expansiveness neared omniscience. Pleased with myself, I momentarily suspended my ascent then floated downward. Reaching earth and the warrior who asked me to rise, I could sense his satisfaction in knowing me. We smiled at each other then went our own ways.

I went to a large hootch where many men slept. I entered and crawled onto my cot. Sleep fell into me.

In the pre-dawn gray I woke in a panic. My nervous system overdosed with adrenaline, electrified and shocked my being. A voice repeatedly stabbed inside my head, screamed throughout every atom of my body…"GET OUT! GET OUT! RUN FOR YOUR LIFE! MOVE!!" I grabbed my weapon and tried to race out through the hootch's doorway but a laborious slow motion was all I could achieve. My mind rapidly screamed "Danger, Danger!" The dirt beneath my feet painfully gave up its lengths. As I dove toward the ground I quietly wondered if I was far enough away to escape the explosion I knew was about to happen.

The detonation blew the soldiers' sleeping quarters to smithereens. The blast stabbed like knives into my ears. The concussion slammed my twisted body to the ground. My head cracked against the hardened earth. Like a discarded rag I flopped into unconsciousness.

I regained partial awareness as several soldiers' hands pulled me from under splintered, burning debris. My eyes opened to blurriness. My hearing rang like hammers against steel, crippling my equilibrium. Slowly my wits gained cohesion. Smoke, dust and cries hung in the air. Around me soldiers hurried about the business of reaction to chaos. I lifted heavily to my feet. My ears came alive to the screaming of the wounded. Soldiers silent in task darted left and right amongst those who howled.

In places blood puddled. Bloodied torn torsos and twitching limbs littered the dirt, debris and thorns.

I screamed. Raging! Raging! I screamed…"NO!!" and fell into action. I helped other soldiers gather the guts and appendages ripped from life and lives of men I loved. In the dirt, the puddles of red blood coagulating black at their edges drew fat flies.

The explosion had occurred underneath the sleeping quarters. One giant blast. No incoming. Only a blast from within. Booby-trap!

Then I remembered…

I recalled yesterday eve seeing someone's face starring mute at me from under the building now reduced to fragments. It was only a moment of my eyes meeting another's peering out from under our sleeping quarters.

It was routine to have someone check the company compound for hidden explosives and booby traps, there being men of two faces. This was my thought as our eyes met as I hurried to other duties. But I remembered his face well. Stuck on it was a smile of guilt. I assumed this man was checking to clear the area of threat but it was he who planted the bomb that woke us with death's toll.

The man with the sickly smile. He grimaced because he worried in that moment I had caught him in his deathly, devious act. This man was the saboteur!

A quiet rage grew ugly in me. I swung my slung weapon to my hands and pushed off its safety. My mind set in its intent I started screaming. "I know who you are. I know who you are!"

The other soldiers, busy in their bloody duty of cleaning up, followed me with puzzled eyes as my feet kicked the earth, moving me among the many men and smoking carnage. My eyes hunted for the man with the sickly smile. I found the face it belonged to…

I focused my eyes on him, and drove my anger sharply into him. My inner rage alone held him fast. The other soldiers moved silently away. The remnants of sabotage smoldered. The moans of victims hung heavy. The atmosphere ceased to breathe.

My growing rage fell into a hole of omniscient quietness within me. Standing in stillness, I pointed my weapon at the shirtless, sickly smiling man, frozen in his brown skin by the discovery of truth. I fired a single shot into his right side. He is violently knocked to the ground. A black pea-size hole surrounded by a doughnut-sized purple ring branded his abdomen. His kidney blew out his back like a tomato slapped against a wall.

He screamed. His eyes pleaded, bleeding fear. I yelled and yelled, "You mother fucker, You son of a bitch!" and shot him in the throat. The bullet ripped the cry from his voice. Death snatched his life. His body lay silent but for frightened eyes reaping an invisible horror.

I stood trembling, anchored in disturbed silent screaming at heaven.

My feelings fled…and I turned to stone.

Sin Loi Ma Noi
(sorry about that my love)

In the preparation of, in the midst of and in the aftermath of war and fighting, man must find a time to fuck. And fuck he must. And better he keep fucking and forget about ever fighting again…

I've survived six months of war. Still alive. Somewhat intact. Looking for oblivion. I ride in the back of a cab in the city of Bangkok. It's night. The smooth air coming through the open windows is warm and sultry. In the breeze waft all the perfumes and reverberations of an exotic Far East. My driver Tex, a short heavy-set Thai-Polynesian man, wears a cowboy hat and asks me in broken English what the cowboys are like in the USA. He tells me he would like to be like one of them. "Jon Wain" he says broadly smiling. "Opera Hotel. Right away!"

A huge benefit for having survived combat for six months is to be afforded a vacation from it all. Every soldier in the war who makes it to the six month mark is given what the Army calls an 'R and R'. Rest and Relaxation. One week for me of not having to sleep with a weapon.

…In this hand is my weapon (note: M-16). In this hand is my gun (note: penis). This is for shooting (note: M-16). This is for fun (note: penis). Repeat…

Leaving behind my weapon and bringing my only gun, I have come for the deep softness of women. That feeling of being welcome and secure in the complimentary sharing of flesh.

War is hard and cold. It penetrates you. The love of a woman is soft and warm. It suckles you. There is no greater escape from war then the exercise of hedonism. The fun of flesh.

And it is fun I am after, in Bangkok, at the Opera Hotel. Tex maneuvers his pink cab into the hotel's black crescent driveway. The hotel, a blue and white painted concrete three story structure, laced with wrought iron balconies and sliding glass doors, is surrounded and partially hidden by a fusillade of palm trees. Under their canopy Tex and I are met by a smiling young Thai man who is full of friendly energy.

"Hello. I am Billy. What is your name? *Lee.* I see you are a Sergeant. Sergeant Lee, Welcome to the Opera Hotel. Hotel of the 'Special Forces.' I can get you anything you may want. Let me be of service." He takes my partly filled duffel bag from Tex. "Come! I will show you to your room."

Suddenly I am exhausted. My body involuntarily spasms and a chill runs through me. In my nervous system the pensive stickiness of combat anxiety reluctantly loosens. I realize I am no longer in a war zone and the feeling is strange, foreign, unsettling. *Where have I been?* I follow Tex and Billy to my room. *Where am I?* Billy enters a door and turns on a light.

My room, on the second floor, is replete with bed, dresser, table lamp, and a large velvet painting of a beautifully naked Asian woman. Billy sets my bag on the dresser. Tex slides open the glass door of the balcony. Its parapet overlooks a colored light lit swimming pool. I give Billy the bellboy money for my stay and a generous tip for himself. "You like girl?" he asks. "You like whiskey? You like marijuana? Anything you like, I get!"

"Nothing now. Maybe tomorrow. Right now I want nothing but sleep, Billy."

He nods and leaves the room to go register my stay with the front desk. I pay Tex and negotiate the services of his cab and himself for the week of my stay. I hand him enough American greenbacks to cover a month of work. His wide face broadens into a smile. His eyes twinkle. "Be right back, Sergeant Lee." He exits the room and closes the door behind him.

I am alone. My whole body becomes like an ear. Like a vacuum I suck in all the sounds that fill the night air. I listen to: No explosions...No crackling of weapons fire...No thump of mortar rounds...No vibrating earth...I take a deep breath and exhale in a long release of exhaustion. I sit down on the king size bed and remove my beret, boots and jungle fatigue jacket. I lie back on the soft bed and feel myself fade into the existence of a hole...

"Sergeant Lee. Sergeant Lee!" I hear a distant voice softly calling my name. I instinctively feel for my weapon and can't find it. My mind struggles. An acute message belays an oncoming panic. *Bangkok! You're in Bangkok!*

Reluctantly my heavy lidded eyes peek outward. Through the thick lens of sleepiness I see Tex and Billy standing at the foot of my bed. They are giggling. Their smiling faces suggest they are up to something. I teeter on the edge of sleep and uncomfortable dream.

"Sergeant LEEEEEEEE!" Hidden female voices of glee and giggles permeate the room. My sleep-drunk mind cannot register what it cannot see. I rub my fitful eyes. Suddenly my mattress jerks and bounces. Abruptly my eyeballs open to see two beautiful Thai girls, identical twins bouncing up and down on the bed I lie in. I sit up. *Am I awake?* Tex and Billy bend over in laughter, holding their sides.

"See you tomorrow Sergeant Lee!" Feeling satisfied and gay with their surprise, they leave the room to me and my gifts.

I indulge my presents. One girl works her nimble fingers with surprising speed and unbuttons my pants and pulls out my swelling penis. She pauses a moment twisting and bending it this way and that for a close inspection. She smiles up at me then wraps her moist lips around my dick and sucks and sucks. Surrendering to the bliss of pleasure's promise, I lie back into the bed. *I must be dreaming!* The other dark hair beauty quickly removes her blouse and shorts then proceeds to rub her succulent breasts over my chest and across my face. I close my eyes and suckle pleasure into my every pore…

Before I entered the Army, I had no idea sex could be purchased almost anywhere soldiers were stationed. It was beyond the imagination of a suburb teenage boy that he would someday walk into a nightclub and have the option of choosing from a group of girls, any one (or more) that he wanted for sexual adventure.

****

Even though the Special Forces compound, FOB 2, south of the city of Kontoum was in a war zone, directly on the north side of the camp along the highway that led into the city and the country road that winded west, was a thriving collection of small businesses and homes. Soup shops, tailors, fruit and vegetable stores, gold jewelry shops, furniture shop, laundry and a bar and whore house known as Hazel's.

For a long time Hazel's was without competition. Her and her girls knew every swinging dick at FOB 2. But one day a bar and brothel named Suzi's opened just up the street. A reason for war.

All the girls from Hazel's (which numbered about ten) some in high heels, some in bedrobes and others in short shorts and halter tops, marched to the front of Suzi's establishment. There they stood in the dirt street and shouted insults and challenges to the girls inside. A small crowd of onlookers gathered. From a safe distance I and some other soldiers watched. And waited for denouement.

Suddenly, the double swinging saloon doors of Suzi's flew open. Nearly a dozen girls rushed out of the building and directly into the group of women from Hazel's. The fight was on. Fists flew. Cussing and screaming filled the air. Girls kicked at each other. Hair was pulled and female bodies rolled and wrestled in the dusty street.

Two members of the Vietnamese Special Police roared up in their jeep and jumped out. They yelled for the fighting to stop while they ran back and forth around the contingent of women furiously swinging fists and wrestling on the ground. One of the police pulled out his .45 and fired a shot in the air. For a moment, everyone froze.

Then, as if in planned unison, every fighting whore, Hazel's and Suzie's alike, turned and attacked the two military policeman. Within seconds the girls managed to get the pistols from the officers. Tiger, a girl from Hazel's fired the weapons in the air until they were empty. The girls tore at the policemen's uniforms eventually leaving them in nothing but their underwear. Under a continuing barrage of fists, feet and shouts from some twenty relentlessly pursuing women, the officers made it into their jeep and hastily drove away. All the girls cheered in shared victory. Tiger threw the pistols after the fleeing jeep and defiantly screamed, "Du mame!"

The tumult over, the two groups of girls stood and eyed each other with uneasy suspicion. There was tension in the air but the fight was over. They backed away from each other then turned, some walking, some limping back to their perspective brothels with only a few snide remarks made in the withdrawal. Life went on in the war. Suzie's remained in business. Hazel had the prettiest and toughest girls. There were enough dicks to go around.

****

At the Opera Hotel, somewhere in a pause in the midst of all the love making the Thai twins pleasured me with, I dropped into a heavy sleep. I didn't wake until noon the next day when the backfiring of a car had me unconsciously throwing myself off the bed to the floor. My hands groped for my weapon as I tried to remember where I was, *again. Was I dreaming? Eh?*

I stand up and scratch my balls and give a good morning shake to my gun. The pleasant fragrance of mixed perfumes and female body sweat rises from the bed sheets and my body. Bangkok. Bang Cock.

City of Angels. I sigh a relief so huge I crumble back into the sheets and don't wake again until the following morning when Billy the bellboy knocks on my door and helps himself into my room. "Sergeant Lee! Killing communists must be hard work. You sleep for two days! How can I help you?" He easily wears a pleasant smile on his thin face. He goes to the balcony windows and draws back the curtains. In comes sunshine. He sits on the edge of my bed.

I get up and ask Billy to bring me some breakfast. I go get in the shower and recall the dream-like joy of the twins. Was it a dream? I'm really not sure for my life nowadays seems as if it all is a dream. A strange one. Seamless realities. While toweling off my body, I feel a strange tightness across my face. I raise my hand to it and feel myself smiling using muscles long forgotten. I tell myself, *this is good!* and for a moment I am comfortable. I grab my olive drab clothing bag and dump the contents of it on the bed. Out of it falls my wardrobe, a pair of bell-bottom blue jeans (compliments of the Navy), Ho Chi Minh sandals and a brightly flowered Hawaiian aloha shirt. I dress and the bellboy Billy returns with a breakfast of papaya, toast and scrambled eggs. As I eat Billy sits with me and again asks if I am in need of anything.

I tell him I want to buy some civilian clothes and have a pair of shoes made. He tells me he will arrange with Tex to take me where I can have these things done. By the end of my breakfast Tex has arrived and is smiling and ready to chauffeur me around Bangkok. "You like more girl?" he asks with a broader grin.

After running my errands with Tex, I have him drop me off in a busy store district near the hotel. I go into a streetside fruit-drink bar. I am looking over a display of postcards opposite the serving counter when my eyes catch sight of a day-glow painted pair of tight black jeans on a female customer at the counter. Hand painted stars, galactic spirals, flowers, symbols of peace and red hearts of love adorn the pants. Fitted into them is a beautiful Thai girl. I stare. She speaks. "Hey, whatsa matter wit you? You fucked up?"

"No. I was just admiring your legs. I mean your pants." She laughs and kisses me on my cheek.

"My name is Jerry. What is yours?" she asks.

"Hey Lee. You like spend time with me?" What young man's innocence I have left in my life is amazed at the way women suddenly seem intent on giving me sex. Jerry buys me a fruit smoothie. We walk hand in hand to the hotel and my room. For the next two days it's room service and sex, sex, sex.

On the morning of the third day I thank Jerry for her company and pay her well. I tell her I want to spend some time alone. *Lie.* There is a moment of sadness in her eyes but she quickly smiles and cheerfully says, "hokay."

Really what I am interested in is more sex with more women. Never in my teenage years could I have had such illusions of grandeur. I begin to think the last six months have been worth it. Again my face tightens. A spreading smile feels like it is going to crack my jaw…

I get together with Tex and ask him where a great night club for girls could be found. He pushes his cowboy hat back from his brow, grins with his entire face and says, "You stick with me partner."

Later that evening Tex drives me to a bar that is the size of a large warehouse. Inside, under red lights, there is a live band playing "Johnny Be Good". Out on a sprawling dance floor there are hundreds of dancers and almost all of them are girls! An older woman wearing an elegant black dress escorts me to a table at the edge of the dance floor. She motions to a waiter who takes my order for a margarita and quickly returns with the drink. The madam in the black dress hands me a pencil and small piece of blank paper.

"You write numba on paper," she commands me. I am confused. She sees this. "Look," she says and grabs by the hand one of the girls from the dance floor. “Look here. Numba!” She points to a round red button, printed on it is the block white number seventy-two. It is pinned on the blouse of the girl. “You look around. See girl you like. Write numba down on paper. Give to me and I get you girl. See?”

Wow! A warehouse full of girls all wearing a number. Pick a number any numbers. Man, is this the easiest time I’ve ever had picking up a girl? I gulp down my drink, ask for another and head out on the dance floor. After many drinks and many dances later, I’ve written a number down on the slip of paper given me. I signal to the maitre d’ of maidens and give her the slip of paper. After a short while she returns with my pick-of-all-the-girls for the evening. I am grinning like a teenage boy satisfied with myself and all the world. The muscles in my face pull only a little tight now. I think my face is getting used to the grin on it.

Faithfully waiting cowboy Tex taxis me and number sixty-nine back to the Opera Hotel. The ride back was a blowjob away.

I and my date laugh, giggle and wobble drunkenly outside the door of my room. I search my pockets for my room key when suddenly my door is jerked opened from the inside. *What?* Next, someone grabs me by my hair and yanks me inside the room. The door slams shut and I am left standing alone in the foyer of my room. Directly outside the door a loud voiced argument starts between two women, then there is what sounds like a short scuffle. Then more yelling. A final thud. The door reopens.

The door opens and shuts. Jerri, the girl I met in the fruit bar puts a wad of money in my hand.

“Here is your money back. You don’t know that girl. She has five kids and a pussy that big!” She holds up her hands miming the shape and size of a cantaloupe.

She takes me by the hand and leads me to the bed. “Hold me,” she says. I put my arms around her and fall asleep. Grinning.

****

Next morning we sleep in. Wake to sex. Eat. More sex. Eat. Sex. Fall asleep. Dream sex. Wake. Sex and eat. Sometimes simultaneously for the next two days.

On the last day of my R& R, Jerri was waiting for me to wake up. She ambushed me when my eyes were barely open.

"Hey! Lee!" You have to take me out. Take me on a date. Take me to dinner. All you want to do is have sex. Always sex. I want some love. I want boyfriend."

There is a sudden deep sinking in my chest and a feeling of an age too old for a young man.

"Jerri, I can't be your boyfriend. I can't love you…" her large brown eyes swell with tears…I feel the psychic mail armor of war drape across my shoulders, chest and arms. "Tomorrow I have to return to war. I may be dead next week."

No response. I feel dead inside. I tell her:

"I'll take you out today. A date. Sight seeing. A movie. And a great dinner. Okay?"

"We'll go and visit the great statue of Buddha," she answers and smiles at me. I wipe her tears with the back of my hand. She kisses me and asks, "would you like to fuck?"

Obscenity of War

Nothing is More Noxious. More toxic.... More septic...More poisonous...More destructive...More Obscene...than Hate.

"Welcome to War!" I announce.

My words have the ears of the eager head of the newly arrived troop, who stands at voluntary attention, clean shaven and freshly equipped with the standard (meaning once belonged to a dead person) tactical gear. Moving their bodies behind him, the Yards of the recon team quietly spread themselves, their weapons, their gear, their sleeping bags and blankets across the sandbagged roofs of three perimeter bunkers.

Tonight our recon team is on "bunker duty". Every night the bunkers are manned with personnel to stand guard against possible sudden enemy attack from outside the camp's perimeter. It's the 'new guy's' first night in the combat zone. He is a new addition to our camp's support personnel and not a member of the combat ranks. But his duties will occasionally include manning the defensive perimeter.

Everybody's got to be 'new' at one point or other in their life. And in death. Newly dead. It's the gate of encounter, the rite of passage and in war the molestation of innocence.

The new guy doesn't know that he's already been pegged with the odds of five-to-one that he's going to end up dead within the first three months of his tour. Not that he's incompetent, it's just a perpetual 'worry' that some guys, this one included, carry around their neck. They worry about their girlfriend back home, their mother, their car, booby traps, getting maimed...things like that. The worries border on fear. Little thoughts that are a perpetual mental nagging that leads men away from the moment at hand.

I hop up onto one of the bunkers and stand hands akimbo in the middle of the Montagnards as they prepare for the night watch.

"Listen up!" I address myself to the new guy. "And stand at ease."

The new guy lets his torso relax, shifts his weight to an opposite leg and exhales as if his breath is under some great weight.

"At ease, Galt!" I use his name to feign personal connection. "At ease for Christ's sake."

Using the bunker's roof as a stage for preaching, I dramatically sweep my arm across the space between me and the new guy and point at the perpetually growing jungle beyond the perimeter of bunkers, rows of concertina wire, claymore mines, trip wire, more mines, foo-gas canisters, more wire and a hundred foot strip of denuded earth.

"Out there is Charlie! Whether you want to believe it or not, he's out there right now." The Yards, without a pause in the animal-like comforting of their physical positions, all nod and grunt in agreement.

"Are you a believer?" I ask the new guy whose head tilts to a level of slight confusion. I'm not looking for an answer. I'm here to act out. Ritual.

"What was your name again?" There is some disdain in my tone. It's not personal but only the exercise of the truth that after months of combat duty you tend not to get close or personal with anyone. The contempt is for the death they will befriend despite your half-ass attempt to educate them otherwise. I give the orders for the night.

"Okay, Gile. Here's how it is. Two hours on. Two hours off. You, Yubi, Deng, Diu and Boon take the first watch. I, Gai, Hyak and you will take the second shift. Any questions?" The new guy makes no mention of the fact that I scheduled him for double shifts. Not a good sign. Either he didn't pay attention to what I just said or he is too passive to speak up. The odds against his survival just increased. Six to one.

The team is distributed and settled on the sandbagged roofs of three bunkers. The eight of us sit upright and crossed legged, holding a weapon in our lap to protect us from Charlie and a blanket wrapped around our backs to insulate us from the chilly Central Highland air. Our backpacks are secured inside the bunkers along with hand detonators that have been connected to the wires of the claymore mines and foo-gas barrels to the front of our position.

I look down the line of bunkers to my right and to my left. Transforming out of the invisible cool air, ghostly pockets of fog drift silently along the line. Soldiers seated in repose on the bunker's roofs, appear like apparitions of monks seated in meditation. We wait. The sun passively sits in its star seat while the earth rotates and turns its back on the remaining light. We watch. Dusk spreads like an unheard sound. We listen. Twilight's gaseous envelope blurs the lines of men and earth, truth and reason. Then the cussing starts.

"Phuuk youuu!" Clear as a bell the expletive discharges out of the depth of the jungle before us and lands soundly in our ears.

"What the hell was that?" The new guy tightly grips his weapon at the ready and cranes his neck and eyes toward the jungle.

"Ssshhh!" I admonish him to be quiet. "Shut up and listen."

We sit in motionless tension. All our ears reach across the battlements to the thickening jungle. The amorphous mist congeals along the bunker line. Darkness slowly sucks away our ability to discern shape and form.

"Phaaak Yoooo!" Another clear curse, from a position different than the first, rips across the perimeter. The Yards' stern faces whisper among themselves. Hyak points a gnarly finger in the direction the shouting is coming from.

"Who is that? Who's doing that?" The new guy is working on an anxiety attack. Odds: seven to one.

"This is it Gill. You are about to lose your cherry. That's Charlie out there," I explain with the utmost seriousness.

"Shouldn't we get into the bunker?"

"No! Hold your position, Grit. We can't let Charlie think we're afraid."

"Phuuk Youuu!...Phauk Yooo!.. Phuk Yu!" Emanating from several distinct sites, more obscenities are launched our way.

"Fuk you, fuk you, fuk you!" The barrage continues.

The new guy fidgets with the safety on his weapon. The Yards lie on their bellies and train their weapons towards the haunted darkness. The cannonade of Charlie's unclean cries array themselves from gravely deep throated to squealy high pitch.

"Fouk yuu! Faaak yoooo! Fuck you! Fuk Fuk youuuu! "Fouk yuu! Faaak yoooo! Fuck you! Fuk Fuk youuuu! "Fouk yuu! Faaak yoooo! Fuck you! Fuk Fuk youuuu! "Fouk yuu! Faaak yoooo! Fuck you! Fuk Fuk youuuu!!!!!!!!

"What should we do? What should we do?" The new guy is ready to shit a brick. Odds: eight to one.

In the chaos of cussing, I take a moment to really connect with him. I place my best concerned face a few inches from his and ask, "What was your name again?"

"Grims! Grims! My name is Grims!" He pleads desperately for understanding. Make it nine to one.

"Okay Grins. Follow my lead." The staccato of Charlie's threats flow unabated. I throw the blanket off my shoulders and stand straight up into the fusillade of expletives.

"FUCK YOU TOO CHARLIE! FUCK YOU!"

The new guy looks up at me like I've lost my mind. I scream at him.

"GET UP GOD DAMN IT. YELL BACK! THAT'S AN ORDER!"

I grab him by the collar of his jungle fatigues and yank him to his feet. The Yards and every other soldier along the perimeter are on their feet screaming. Back and forth across the battlements, 'FUCK YOUS' fly like shrapnel through an insane air. The new guy stands paralyzed. Odds: ten to one.

Bombarded by unabated obscenities he finally realizes there is nowhere to run, nowhere to hide. Deep in the rational gray matter behind his eyes that are locked into a stare, a forgotten prehistoric neural pathway of survival lets loose a bellow: "FUCK YOU CHARLIE! FUCK YOU!"

Along the line of perimeter bunkers soldiers are jumping up and down, shaking their fists, waving their weapons, spewing spit and screaming at the top of their lungs. Adding to the melee are short bursts of automatic weapons fire that quickly crescendo into a mad minute of nonstop shooting until the lone lingering of a few single shots reveal a quietness only definable by its opposite. Everyone along the perimeter busies themselves with reloading and then calmly return to their previous meditative sittings. In the newly created stillness there is a lone weak cry that expends itself in its attempt to retaliate.

"PHUCK YOOOOOOOOOO!"

"FUCK YOU TOO CHARLIE! FUCK YOU, FUCK YOU, FUCK YOU…! The new guy screams alone. He is jumping up and down. He froths at the corner of his parched lips. The veins in his neck bulge like a river on a relief map. His string of obscenities flow like water burst from a dam. Every word he flings carries the pain he experiences at having been conscripted from his home, deprived of his mother, girlfriend and possessions to be planted in a place where only fear, death and destruction grow.

In a quiet moment of fury, Grims realizes that the echo of his screaming is the only sound in the jungle's night. He stands as if caught naked before the world. Short, fast, heavy breathing oscillates between his clenched teeth. The adrenaline of anger undulates in his molecules. Exhausted, he drops his ass to the bunker sandbags. No one pays him any attention. He is alone with what he is destined to become…

A symphony of insects harmonize in the night's void. On another day, the new guy will figure out the reality of what has just come to pass. As always, the first casualty of war is Truth. Odds are it affects us all.

Shrouded in the darkest parts of the respiring jungle, choruses of apolitical amphibious reptiles, affectionately known as the 'fuck you lizards' because of their peculiar roosting clamor, descend into their dreamless sleep.

Fly Away Home

I lie in the mud. Shivering and wet I draw into a fetal position. The energy of my life leaks and wanes. It is warm only where my blood flows and my bowels escape me. Others run by me forward across the denuded plain of trench, wire, mire and live fire. Sighing heavily in my chest, I notice a seamless song hidden in the cacophony of war. So this is peace. I'd thought it to be more for the living. Suddenly upon my brow a touch. No. More than that, a gift of being unalone. Winged beings clad in radiant armor replace the emptiness of my veins with comfort. They kneel about me spreading their countenance and strength. In their faces the all knowing. So this is death.

****

I ride shotgun as Kinnear slowly drives the jeep along a solitary footpath that weaves through an open canopy tropical forest. The jungle closes behind us and reluctantly gives way before us. Sitting in the back seat is Gai. He is turned to our rear keeping his weapon at the ready. I too strain to see into the jungle around us. One hand holds my weapon. With the other I brush aside the thin limbs of saplings and other vegetation as our jeep creeps pushing its way toward the Montagnard village of Plei Krek. This is an area the enemy is known to operate in. Still we drive on like we are the ones to be feared. Our mission is to deliver a member of the village home. In the rear of the jeep with Gai is Than. Than lies absolutely quiet in a dark green body bag. We are bringing Than home.

Yesterday, Than was shot through the neck...The chopper was hovering several feet off the ground to avoid the tall grass. I had to help boost the Yards up into the helicopter. Than was the last Yard up. I interlaced the fingers of my hands making a sling for him to put his foot into. When he put his weight into my hands I lifted him upward into the chopper. As he sprung up and cleared my hands an AK round caught him in the neck. I neither heard the firing nor knew that Than had been struck. The door gunner returned fire with the machine-gun. I grabbed onto the slick's landing strut and heaved myself up and into the belly of the warbird. I landed on top of Than. He lay limp. Blood from the shattered spine in his neck streamed across the metal floor of the chopper. His jaw attempted to mouth words I couldn't hear. His eyes looked beyond the seeing. *There it is.* Up, up and away we all flew.

****

Gai speaks. "Kinnear, we are close to Than's village. Stop here. We must leave the body outside the village."

Kinnear halts the jeep and turns off its engine. There is a breeze coming through the jungle. It is warm and soft. Gai, Kinnear and I take a long quiet look to all sides of us. The color green, soft and light, dark and obscure, patterns the forest vegetation around us. Ahead in the direction of the path we follow, the trees thin and reveal blue sky. Not much further to go. From the back of the jeep Kinnear and I pick up the olive drab bag that shelters Than and place it off the path. We cover the bag with brush and grass then lay a long bare wood branch on the path to mark the location. We get back in the jeep and cautiously drive towards the village.

The jungle thins and abruptly ends at the edge of a large flooded field. We have arrived near the end of a wide peninsula. On the peninsula's end is an encirclement of several dozen thatched huts built on raised platforms. To our front, left and far right rice paddies stretch for several hundred meters. In a wide arch bordering the brown water fields of emerald rice shoots, is a forested green mountain ridge line. We motor our jeep into the center of the village. Kinnear shuts off the engine. Only the breeze can be heard. The village is empty of life.

Kinnear, Gai and I get out of the jeep with our weapons. Gai motions us to walk down to the rice fields. There we are greeted by a young Montagnard woman. She stands shin deep in muddy water. On her back, slung in a piece of woven cloth, a child peacefully sleeps. Gai speaks to the woman in their native tongue. Slowly her eyes widen in concern then horror. The conversation is brief. She hurries herself into a shallow long boat and poles across the muddied water paddy. "Than's sister," says Gai. "She will tell the others. We go back to the jeep and wait."

We linger in the dirt courtyard of the village. Kinnear sits in the jeep. I sit on the hood. Gai patiently paces back and forth in the square. The village is empty but for us. Suddenly a woman's wail slices the air. Then the sound of sobbing. The sound of many people sobbing and crying precedes the people themselves. It is as if the forest itself is crying. Then by one's and two's people appear out of the forest around us. Old men, women and children come walking, crying and wailing into the courtyard. Before long more than a hundred tribal members moan and lament around us.

The crying and sobbing climb in timbre. Yards are throwing themselves on the ground. They hang on each other. They hang on the jeep. They hang onto me. The crying is all there is. Kinnear and I sit likes stones unmoved by a flood of personal grief. Silently I feel lost and ashamed at my inability to relate to their anguish. Numbness is a blanket I pull around me.

****

When humans lose loved ones through violence, love itself becomes another victim. As humans we are born into the world *wanting* and *needing* love and affection. Undeniable magnetic urgings pull at the life around us in desperate need to feed us with more than bread alone. Do the dead feel no mourning? How is it the living feel dead? No one can remain an island.

****

After what seems an eternity of crying, a village elder calls for everyone to gather round and listen to the story of Than's death. The villagers sit on the ground and draw themselves together, each person laying a hand on another. Gai takes the role of storyteller and like a father relating a tale to children he speaks softly and directly to all. In the subtle accompanying intonations and whisperings of the tribe, the spirit of Than comes home.

A Moment of Memory

Time pulls us into the world, pushes us, moves us without our asking, embroils us, then eventually leaves us behind. A string of spells spanning our lives with too little, too much, too soon, too late, perfection. Embrace the occasion and there will be life without measure. No duration for the pains of fear or loss. No season for desire or judgment. Great measure is indeterminable…

For the moment I am without knowledge of the world's activities around me. *Just like I want it.* Hiding in my work in an experimental physics lab at the Department of Commerce, mentally immersed in the sub atomic universe, I focus on trapping a single electron I have ripped from an atom of Tungsten. If successful, the charged lepton will be held prisoner by an extremely strong magnetic field that pierces the precise center of a machined ceramic sphere, two centimeters in diameter, with a hollow inner chamber whose inner walls are coated in pure gold. The magnetic field falling through the sphere's center serves as an axis around which the electron will be captured and maddenly spin in a precise circle near the speed of light. Across the electron's path I will focus the beam of a ring dye laser and measure each time the electron crosses its path. Simply put, I am making a clock that measures not minutes, seconds and hours but billionths of a second. How much life can so minute a moment hold?

I pursue the microcosmic to escape the larger world of complex human interaction. I want nothing to do with the reality that is human. The reality of desires that drive societies to war. In the blink of an eye humans can alter the course of life.

Peering into the smallest world of atoms there is suddenly a glitch. Time stands still and out of the infinitesimal I clearly see a human hand reaching out in my direction. *What?* I rub my eyes, shake my head and feel *something* deep, deep within me rupturing my psyche. I pause. Suddenly again the image of the outreaching hand flashes and its reality wave rushes through my consciousness. The image of the hand appears and disappears rapidly, pulsing faster and faster until it becomes like the spinning spoked wheel rotating so quickly its center becomes solid. Solid is accepted as reality.

My eyes are wide open and filled with blue sky and sun. *I'm no longer in my lab.* I struggle to keep my eyes from rolling far back into my head as I hurriedly walk toward the University's Memorial Center. *The hand reaches for me*. There is screaming. *I am scared.* I fear losing consciousness to something unknown.

As a growing mental and emotional instability attack my control of reality, I uneasily weave my way through the loud, crowded throng of students in the UMC's hallways. *The hand reaches out for me*. I reach the door of the Veteran's Association office. In less than a moment I am inside.

The office is empty but the space that contains it is in flux. The furniture, the desks, the walls have lost the solidity that binds their atoms. *On the bulletin board!* I strain to focus on the many papered notices tacked to the announcement board. *There it is!* I continue fighting to keep my eyes from rolling backward towards the hand that reaches out to me. *Dr. Sternberger...Psychiatrist...784-2442*

I dial the number. I wait an eternity. It rings. It rings...a voice from the void.

"Dr. Sternberger's office."

I take a really deep breath..."Dr. Sternberger. This is Lee Burkins. I met you at a talk you gave to the Vets at CU about war trauma.... I need to talk to you."

"Where are you Lee?"

"At the University Memorial Center."

"What is the problem?"

"I'm fighting to keep consciousness. My eyes want to roll back into my head. My world seems to be deconstructing…I'm scared."

"Can you get to my office?"

"I'll be there in a few minutes."

"Are you driving?"

"No. I'm running."

The Doctor's office was downtown Boulder, about a mile away. I toss the phone's receiver on the desk and bolt out of the office. *Run Lee run!* I burst into the crowded hallway of students forcing anyone in my way out of it. I hit the exit doors with a crash and run across the sunny, green grounds of the campus like a man on fire. *A hand reaches out to me.*

Dr. Sternberger is waiting for me when I arrive in the tiny space of a small room filled with walls of books, a desk and two wooden chairs. My breath is heavy from running, my chest heaves, I gulp the air as I explain to the Doctor, who sits suspended above the edge of his chair.

"I saw a movie last night *breathe*…in it, during a storm, two brothers capsized their small boat *breathe*…one brother clung to the overturned boat, the other brother, floundered in the rough water *breathe*. They reached for each other in the storm…but their hands never reached each other…nothing could be done but for the brother to watch his brother's hand slip beneath the sea…nothing could be done…*breathe*…In Vietnam my friend reached out to me…A white phosphorous hand grenade, a booby trap, exploded in my friend's face. He was totally engulfed in flames…He outstretched his hand towards me…*there was nothing I could do.*"

I watch myself tell a tale, relive the past and simultaneously notice Doctor Sternberger shaking. His eyes water and his face looks tortured. *He's crying and it's freaking me out!*

For a moment there is a compassion that fills the room. It cuts my root, breaks my rock, breaches my defenses and I begin to sob. Snot-out-of-the-nose sobbing. The Doctor cries with me.

****

I fly in the belly of a war-bird. In the open door of the helicopter, I sit on the metal floor, my legs dangle out and down to the air-ship's landing struts. The wind, rushing by at a 'hundred and thirty knots submits to the rotating, beating blades' desire. We fly to the hospital at Pleiku airfield. Beneath me passes an appearance of a large red cross painted on a building's white tin roof. The pilot sets the helicopter down in front of several rows of medical buildings. The turbine unwinds to a lowering pitch while the blades turn their beating into a long cutting swish. I step from the chopper and move into the nearest building's front doors. In the foyer sits a nurse behind a desk.

"Can I help you Sergeant?" she asks poker-faced.

"Hein. I'm here to see Sergeant Hein."

She looks at me as if we've known each other for hundreds of years.

"Follow me."

I walk behind the nurse as she traverses a long, wide hallway, gray tile on the floor, pale green paint on the walls. The hall is empty but for us. The nurse pushes open two swinging doors on her right. We enter a large, square shaped room. In it, lined on each side of the room are two long rows of hospital beds. They are all empty except for one.

At the far end of the row on the right one bed is occupied. At its side, hung on racks are several bags of fluids, their long tubes running down and attaching themselves to a mummy, a person totally wrapped in greasy gauze.

"Here is Sergeant Hein," announces the nurse. "I'll be at the front desk if you need me."

I stand at Hein's bedside. His throat is tracheotomized. In the gauze that wraps his head is a hole for his mouth. *His lips are burned off.* There is a hole for his nose that is now only a hole. *Burned away.* There are no holes for his eyes. *There are no eyes.* Cooked. Covered in gauze.

I lean down next to Hein's head and for the god of me I don't know why but the only thing I can think to say is, "I'm okay Hein. I'm okay."

Hein tries to speak. It's inaudible. I lean my ear to his mouth. In a soft, shrill rush of air he says, "Waterrrr…" He moves his arm in a motion that mimics raising a glass.

"Water! Water!" I talk out loud to myself. I look around the empty room and see no faucet or other source of water. I yell out. "Nurse! Water! We need some god-damned water in here!"

The nurse comes running in. "Where's the water?" I demand to know.

Hein is lifting his arm up and down, up and down. The nurse grabs me by the shoulders.

"He's not allowed to drink through his throat. It's too badly burned."

I'm not believing what I hear. What I see. Hein is rocking back and forth in his bed and flailing his arms in every direction. His movement tears the iv's from his arms. I start yelling and push the nurse away. A couple of doctors and an orderly rush into the room, grab me and wrestle me to the floor. I am screaming, screaming, "Get him some god-damned water!" The nurse desperately wrestles with flopping-like-a-fish-out-of-water-mummified Hein. She fights to restrain him to the bed. A medic administers a shot. Morphine blessingly draws Hein from consciousness.

I am hit with a snap of calm. Not that from understanding but that of separateness. Dead spaces. Detachment. I stop my struggle with the men holding me down. I look them in the eye. "I'm okay…I'm okay." They loosen their grip on me. We get up from the gray floor. Other medical staff have entered the room. They put the I.V.'s back into the mummy. A nurse sits on the floor and weeps. I take a last look to Hein's bed. He is surrounded by caregivers. I turn and walk stonily out the doors.

****

The next morning I catch a helicopter ride back to the hospital. I go into the room where Hein is. I push open the swinging doors and stop. The room is empty. No Hein.

I go back to the reception desk. Sitting there is a very pretty nurse. I think her beautiful and ask, 'Where is Sergeant Hein?'

She lifts her pretty face from a paperback book she reads. Expressionless she looks at me and answers, "Sergeant Hein died this morning" and goes back to reading her book. Time releases me. All frames of reference disappear.

****

An electron races light in a circle. Particle. Energy. Vegetable. Human. I wonder what I would see if I could be perfectly still, unmoving with respect to all else.

Peace in Pieces

My calculus tutor Barruk is busy explaining the theory of the infinite within the finite. I sit on a high stool and listen to his teaching but today my heart is somewhere else. Barruk sees this and brings it in the open. Interrupting his lecture he sternly says, "Your mind is wandering. What is it?"

Barruk, stocky, middle aged and bald, is a veteran officer of the Israeli Six Day War. No nonsense. An original 'just do it' person. An engineer, he's working on his Ph.D. and tutoring me twice a week. Today my attention falters from the lesson. My focus wavers from my thinking mind and falls into the feeling mind of my heart.

"What's it all worth, Barruk? I mean why am I doing this?" I raise my hands palms up and extend my arms toward the mathematical equations on the chalk board. Equating requires great focus at the distraction of everything else. Time unhinges and floats me for hours and hours in the exact fitting of numbers and their calculations. It's as if the process of computation becomes a god and I am one with it. Is the value only in my personal experience at the exclusion of all else? And when I fail to compute is not my suffering like that of every counted soul? Where has god gone?

"What is the value in what I am doing? I feel this melancholy is not my own but belongs to the world. Some tendril of my humanness feels pulled to the lack of peace in the world"...*and more so in myself.*

I look Barruk in the eye. "The world is in dire need of peace."

Barruk's brow tightens, his eyes flame. "THEN DO SOMETHING ABOUT IT!" he yells, turns and stomps off. "The lesson is over."

****

Overhead the shrieking sound of a 122 millimeter rocket passes above our position. Hearing the rocket cutting through the air lets you know it will land somewhere behind you. BARRROOOOM! It detonates a hundred meters or more behind us. The more lengthy the screeching sound of the rocket above you the further it lands beyond you. When the jagged lines of vibrating air get shorter in duration that indicates the explosives are dropping closer and closer to our position. BBBAROOOOOMMMMM!...that one I didn't hear. It hits out to our front. The rocket's heavy load of shredded metal plates tear the air indiscriminately. Our bunker vibrates from the initial explosion and the impact of shrapnel waps and thumps into the sandbags. At impact a plume of thick black smoke vertically shoots two hundred feet into the air.

Hyak, Gai, Yubi and I each squat in a corner of the bunker. Our teeth grind and we grin at each other for the moment. There is nothing to do except wait for the attack to cease and pray our bunker doesn't take a direct hit.

Explosions from the incoming rockets steadily shake the earth and our bones. I look up at the bunker's roof. It is made of ten inch square timbers. Stacked on top of that are sand bags piled three feet thick. If one of these falling rockets lands on the roof, we'll be disintegrated.

BBARRROOOOOOM! Another rocket explodes off to our left. Shrapnel whines and buzzes. Debris drops from the sky. In my mind I'm trying to picture what the round could have hit to create so much falling rubble. The rocket must have struck the Vietnamese compound next to ours. Large quantities of splintered wood and twisted tin roofing rain down to the ground. The Yards and I compress our bodies ever tighter into the dirt floor of the bunker as the incoming rockets shake our world.

****

It is night. The rockets no longer fall. It is cold and dark at the Dak To launch site. The Yards and I sit on the bunker's roofs. We are wrapped in wool blankets and quietly eat our cold wet rice, dried mystery meat and canned fruit. Suddenly there is a noise overhead. It is friendly. It is the sound of an artillery round fired from many miles distant now cutting its way through the atmosphere above us. Like a stereo sound crossing between speakers, the projectile approaches from the east and increases in volume. As it passes our position the *zzzusshing* sound fades off to the west, then silence, then in a few short moments we hear a faint…*BOOM!*

Night trains in the sky,
passing high overhead.
When they get where they're going,
Someone will be dead.

****

The rocket attacks started seven days ago. Each morning for the last week dozens of rockets are fired when the operations helicopters arrive at the airfield here at Dak To. The barrage usually starts after the pilots have landed and shut down the choppers' turbines. Then it rains. Steel. Red fiery explosions and tall columns of black smoke start dotting the landscape while everyone runs to their ships and restarts their engines to fly away as quickly as possible. Sometimes the rockets begin falling even before the choppers land. On occasions the gunships will make a run directly at the ridge line where the rockets are launched but the enemy has avoided being sighted. When the rockets cease falling and the ships try and return to the airfield, the rocket attack immediately begins anew. After the helicopters leave, the shelling intensity lightens to only a few rounds an hour.

Like a small pimple, our little Special Forces launch site butts itself up against the larger perimeter of a Vietnamese artillery unit. Within that circular bunkered perimeter is a company of South Vietnamese soldiers who crew several one-fifty-five millimeter howitzers. A hundred meters or so on the other side of the Vietnamese compound there are two massive rectangular aviation fuel bladders that lay surrounded by large dirt berms. Oriented East-West and running along side the fuel site and fortified compounds is a crater-pocked, thousand meter long airstrip. Running from North to South on the West end of the airstrip are several jagged ridge lines of defoliated mountains. From North to South on the East end of the airfield a large dirt plain of scrub and bush prevails. The fuel storage containers and the big guns in the Vietnamese compound are the targets of the rockets. Our unit's operations are also hindered by the daily barrage.

My team and I are on what is called Bright Light duty. Our compound at Dak To is a launch site for operations into Southern Laos and Northern Cambodia. Should one of the teams on operations in the field get into trouble or should an aircraft get shot down, the Yards and I load into a helicopter and fly into the heat of battle to rescue those in trouble. At other times we assist the helicopter flight crews with loading ordinance on the gunships. Lately, because of the rocket attacks, we've spent most of our time hunkered down in the bunkers.

****

The Yards and I have finished our evening meals. I assign the order of guard for the night. Pe and Bhun will be first watch. Every two hours we will rotate the guard. Slowly the Yards and I settle ourselves into the bunkers for the evening. The moon is new and swallowed whole by the darkness. Before turning in I take a last look out the firing slit of the bunker. A faint starlight illuminates the runway to my front. For a moment my mind envisions hordes of enemy soldiers running across the tarmac towards us. I shut my eyes, shake my head and shiver at the thought. Shaking off the illusion I lie down on my ground cloth on the dirt floor of the bunker, pull my wool blanket and pancho liner completely over my body and head and fall asleep to the scurrying sound of the rats that live in the bunkers with us.

KABOOM! The explosion's vibration lifts my body a foot into the air and raises me out of a dead sleep. I twist my body and turn around in mid-air before my body drops back to the floor of the bunker. KABOOM! Another out-going round erupts from the 155 howitzer in the Vietnamese compound. Again my body bounces a foot off the ground. I stick my fingers in my ears and fall back asleep while the howitzers behind me fire again and again into the long dark night toward Laos. With each round fired I awake for only a rising moment then fall to the ground and back into sleep. Eventually the fire mission ceases and except for the ringing in my ears all feels quiet.

At zero-four-hundred hours Gai and I get up to stand the last watch before dawn. We keep our blankets wrapped around us, pick up our weapons and walk out of the bunker up into the cold night's fresh air. A million stars twinkle brightly through an inky heaven above us. Gai steps down into a small fire pit and lights a golf ball sized piece of C4 explosive with a match. It burns furiously hot. Gai squats in the hole and holds his metal canteen cup of water over the hotly sizzling ember. Within a minute the water is boiling. "Coffee Burkai?" he asks looking up at me. I decline.

Gai and I move to sit on the sandbag roof of the bunker that has the fifty caliber machine gun emplacement on it. I throw off the tarp that covers the weapon then sit myself behind it in firing position. I peer out into the darkness toward the barely visible mountain ridge line that the enemy rockets are launched from. Gai sips his hot black coffee. "Ah, Burkai. Here. Have some coffee." He reaches toward me with the canteen cup. A gossamer steam hangs over the black fluid. I take the cup from him and sip the warm bitter liquid. We smile at each other. I hand the cup back to him. Wrapped in our brown blankets we sit like quiet-minded monks waiting for the dawn. After a great while of silence Gai speaks.

"Burkai, did you know that a Montagnard man went to your country and learned to fly an airplane?"

"No I didn't Gai."

"Ah yes! And he is going to teach more Montagnard men to fly. Soon we can have our own air force. I too would like to fly."

I listen to the hope in his voice and feel saddened and slightly ashamed. Gai has known only war in his life and chances are he'll die knowing only that life. Yet he is quick to smile and eager to know of other's lives. He and his people put so much faith in the United States winning this war. He and the rest of my Montagnard team members put so much faith in me. While I am here, I am here for them. But I am only passing through. This is not my country. Not my life. Naively I believe the war is a temporary event for me, *if I live.* If I die it will certainly be temporary. Gai interrupts my thoughts.

"Burkai, I do not think today will be a good day." His brown face lit with wide sad eyes expresses his worry. I do not reply. He continues. "I know this because there are many wandering lost spirits out here." Gai points out across the darkened air strip and denuded surroundings. "To die violently leaves one's spirit lost. Many lost spirits here. Evil spirits."

I let his words pass through me allowing them no meaning and think on my morning ritual while Gai continues to talk as if something has found itself within his body and speaks from another dimension.

"I wish I had an animal."

"Why is that Gai?"

"We must appease the evil spirits. If I had an animal, especially a pig, I would make it scream and scream. Evil spirits like to hear the yell of a dying beast. They would be appeased and the day will not become evil."

His words move unquestioned into the night around us. Soon it will be dawn. I prepare for the morning ritual of fire. “Gai, help me with the ammo belts.”

When the gray light of morning reveals the ridge line seven hundred meters in the distance, I will begin firing hundreds of rounds of .50 cal into its slopes hoping to hinder or kill the enemy as they sight in their rockets for launch at us. Gai and I toss off our blankets and prepare the belts of ammo for loading into the heavy machine-gun.

Gray light begins to leak out of the black air of night. The other Yards are waking up and coming up out of the bunkers. The radio in my bunker crackles out my call sign. It is the pilot of one of the helicopters back at Kontum. They are preparing to lift off for our location. They should arrive in about thirty minutes. I tell the pilot the weather is overcast, ceiling at about two thousand feet with an expcctation of rocket rain.

Pe and Bhun are crouched down in the fire pit boiling water for coffee. Boon, Deng, Diu and Yubi sit quietly on the edge of another bunker’s roof. They wait for the java. In their eyes and worn on their faces is the strain and blankness of a life lived under siege. Or perhaps they are just waking up…

Linking together the belts of ammo Hyak and Gai ready themselves along side the .50 cal. I kneel behind the weapon and set the bolt for the first round. I then sit on my ass with my knees up and grip the gun’s handles. My thumbs lightly rest on the butterfly trigger of the tripod mounted machine-gun. Hyak looks at me with smiling expectations. I look to my left and yell, “Ready on the left!” I look right and yell, “Ready on the right! Ready on the firing line!” The gray of pre-dawn claims the air around us and reveals the ridge line clearly in my sights. I press the butterfly trigger down. The bolt slams forward.

Boom!…boom!…boom!…boom!boom!…boom!boom!boom!…

With delight, joy and malice I fire in steady rhythmic cadence. The slamming of the weapon's bolt, the clinging of the brass, the metal belt links tinking and the muzzle's booming are a morning's symphony to a new day. *Shoot fucking rockets at us will ya! Take that du mame! Take that motherfuckers!* Gai and Hyak feed the belted ammo into the weapon. The other Yards mix instant coffee into their tin cups of hot water. Up, down and across the ridge line in the distance bullets dance up dust. I keep firing until several hundred rounds of ammo are expended. Morning arrives otherwise unannounced.

The daily flight of helicopters are probably still fifteen minutes out from our location. I tell the Yards to stay close to the bunkers. Several men are already back inside them. I take the machine-gun off its tripod and put it inside one of the bunkers. Gai puts the tripod in with it. Hyak collects a remaining box of unfired .50 cal ammo and stores it away. Pe and Bhun are standing in the fire pit. At their feet is a small fire. They are heating up a can of ham and egg c-rations. I walk from the bunker over to the fire pit. "Let's go men. Be done. The choppers will be here any minute." Pe and Bhun give me the thumbs up.

Over the radio I get a call from a pilot on the incoming choppers. In the air I can already feel the thump-thump-thump of chopper blades. *Here they come.* I turn to go answer the radio call when suddenly…KAABAROOOOM! A concussion wave the size of a truck hits me from behind. The blast slams me face down to the ground. I immediately spin around on the ground to look back towards the fire pit. Pe and Bhun are gone from sight. Other rockets start falling up and down the airfield and around us. Frantically, I crawl up to the fire pit. In the two-foot deep hole are Pe and Bhun. Pe is like a bug on its back his arms and legs flailing upright in the air. Bhun's body lies like a heap of burning rags. Rockets fall. Explosions shake the world. I grab hold of Pe by the arm and drag him up out of the burning hole. Gai and Hyak have crawled out of the bunker over to the pit. They pull Bhun out and drag him to the back of the bunker.

Pe is conscious. The biceps of his right arm has been ripped open exposing the bone. His artery has been cut. He bleeds profusely. The back of Bhun's skull is smashed and bleeding. He is alive but unconscious.

The rockets continue to fall. Unable to land, the helicopters circle high overhead. I quickly wrap Pe's arm with two ace bandages then get on the radio and call to the choppers above us. "...I've got two men severely wounded. I need a medevac. Now!"

"We can't land with all the incoming fire. Too much incoming. We can't get to you!" comes the reply. In a zone of queer separation from all the turmoil around me, I squeeze my mind for a plan of action.

There is a doctor and dispensary at the MACV compound near Bien Cat. It's five miles away by dirt road. There is a three-quarter ton pick up truck that belongs to us sitting just outside the compound on the runway. I yell at the Yards to help me load Pe and Bhun into the back of the truck. Although rockets continue to explode around the area there is not a moments hesitation from the Yards. We get the wounded into the truck bed. I cradle Bhun's head in my hands. Through the makeshift bandages his blood seeps. I yell to Gai to get in and drive...*but he doesn't know how!* None of the Yards know how to drive a truck! Shit! *Shit!*

The aim of the enemy has drifted. Several rockets fall into the river far to our rear. "Gai. Hold Bhun's head like this." Gai takes my place of caring for Bhun. I pick up my weapon and run over to the Vietnamese compound. There are two Americans there whose only job is to refuel aircraft when necessary. Most times they keep to themselves hidden in an elaborate bunker. I have only briefly met them once. I jump into their bunker. I can't believe my eyes. The inside of the large bunker is decorated like it were a dorm room. Beads. Curtains. Posters! Beds!?

The two Americans, both Texans, hide under their bunks. Outside the roar and explosion of the incoming fire continues. "I need help!" I scream at them. "Come with me!"

"Are yuu fuckin' crazy? We're not goin' anywhere!" comes the Southern accented reply from one of the refuelers.

"God damn it. Either you two get up and come with me or I'll fucking shoot you myself!" I know I look crazed and the eyes of the men from under the bunks look at me in bewilderment.

"MOVE. FUCKING MOVE IT!" I point my carbine at them. The two enlisted Air Force men scurry out from under their bunks. I push them out of the bunker's doorway and into the reality around us all. The rocket attack is in full swing. Several land simultaneously up and down the tarmac. The three of us run for the truck.

Running in a squat behind the two Air Force men I shout out orders. "You!" I point at the tall heavy set sergeant. "You, get in the cab and drive!"

"Drive where? Where?" Panic is in his face and voice. But he climbs into the cab.

"And you!" I yell at the thinner, shorter fellow. "Get up here in the bed with me. Here. Hold Pe's arm like this. Apply pressure to the wound and keep the arm elevated."

Pe lies on his back in the truck's bed. Fear exudes from his face. The Air Force private follows my orders precisely. I jump into the truck bed and take over holding Bhun's cracked skull from Gai. Bhun lies on his back. I am on my knees and cradle Bhun's head gently in my hands. Rockets continue to hit the area.

"Gai. Hold down the fort." He and the other Yards run back to the bunkers in the compound.

"Hey Air Force!" I yell at the Sergeant in the driver's seat. "GO! GO! Head across the airfield and intersect the dirt road. Make a right and hurry the fuck up. Don't wreck us either!"

The truck lurches forward. It zig zags across the airfield between the black plumes of rockets that have already hit the ground. Within a minute we are out of the danger zone. We turn onto the dirt road to Bien Cat. I look behind us. Up and down the airfield, dozens of tall black plumes stand verticle in the air. Bright red fiery explosions dance in the distance around our compound. The truck speeds onward. The scene behind me grows smaller. I look down at Bhun's face. I cradle his head gently in my hands. He has regained consciousness and his open eyes are filled with a deep desperate pleading…*SAVE ME!*.

Our truck pulls up to the MACV compound. "We've got wounded!" I yell. The gates are opened. Several soldiers come quickly to our aid. We carry Bhun into the dispensary. Pe is able to walk with assistance.

We lay Bhun on a gurney. "Where's the Doctor? Where's the Doctor?" I shout.

A thin faced Vietnamese man enters the room. "I am a Doctor." he says.

"Doc. You gotta help me. My men are severely wounded."

The Vietnamese doctor stands at Bhun's head and begins to unwrap the bandages I have applied. Suddenly the doc stands back. "This is a Montagnard!" he exclaims. "I'm not going to work on him!" The doctor looks at me defiantly. I unsling my carbine and put the muzzle in the doctor's face.

"Either you help him or I'll kill you where you stand!"

Unbelievable. The Montagnards, despite the racial bias the Viets have against them, give everything they can to help defeat the communists. But still they are treated like 'savages' and lesser human beings.

Reluctantly and cussing me under his breath, the doctor begins to remove Bhun's bandages. I hold my weapon pointed at him. Another doctor comes in. This one is an American Major.

"Sergeant. At ease. Cool down. I'll take over. Don't worry, we'll take good care of your men." He lays a reassuring hand on my shoulder.

In a breath of exhaustion I lower my weapon and move to help an enlisted medic with Pe's shredded upper arm. "No need Sergeant. I've got it under control. Why don't you go outside now."

Reluctantly I leave the dispensary and return to the truck. The two Air Force personnel sit in the cab. They look dazed, angry and afraid all at the same time.

"I want to thank you guys for your help." I tell them.

They sit silent for a moment. A look of disbelief bleeds from their eyes then one of them says, "Shit. Did we have a choice?"

"No. I guess not…" I look off into the distance toward Dak To. I can faintly hear the rockets still falling there. I look down at the blood on my hands. I smear it over my face and wonder why the hell we can't all just live in peace.

****

Everything and everyone in the universe is a part of a continuum. Despite the seeming separateness of things, I am a seamless extension of everything else. There is no point I can define as the beginning of me and the end of the universe. Or the end of the universe and the beginning of me. Dividing everything up into parts is arbitrary, a product of convention. We cannot know something by isolating it and defining it with words. It would be like severing my foot from my body then holding it up and exclaiming this is me. Fragmenting the world will lead to our extinction. Peace lies beyond the need of differentiation. I lie fragmented. A piece of the infinite within the finite.

Fishing for Compassion

We have been on local patrol to the West of our operational base for the better part of the day. Kinnear, six Yards and I now follow the dirt country road that parallels the Dak Bla River. It is late afternoon, puffy cotton clouds float like silent airships in the cerulean sky. There is no thick jungle here, just amiable open woods and fields. All along the country road, shade from tall thin trees heavy with broad green leaves, cool the air about us. Quaint white stucco homes covered in thatched roofs dot the meandering road. Here and there banana and rubber tree farms thrive. The fragrance of hardwood cooking fires waft a call for the coming evening's dinners. The voices of children playing echo among the trees and resonate along the river's bank. A group of two dozen Montagnard women naked from the waist up prattle while they do their laundry and bathe in the river's brown waters.

Our patrol walks in a staggered double file along either side of the road. We keep an interval of many meters between us. An old woman leads an ox-drawn cart laden with firewood and banana stalk slowly by us. Two old men laughing and smoking pipes ride their bicycles abreast. Their eyes give a glancing smile at us as they proceed along the peaceful road. We are less than a few hundred meters from our base camp when I get an idea.

"Hey Kinnear! Let's walk down to the river and do some fishing before we return to the compound."

Gai quickly speaks up. "Ho! Fish! I am so hungry I could eat a hundred fish."

All of the Yards laugh and start chanting, "…feesh, feesh, feesh…" Kinnear gives the point man Yubi a hand signal to lead the squad down towards the river. We leave the road and walk along a small stream that flows towards a massive banyan tree that sits on the river's bank.

The Dak Bla river, meandering like a big brown ribbon, varies in width from a hundred to several hundred meters. It is the dry season, so the water is shallow except where the channels run. We reach its bank. Below the majestic banyan tree a channel of ten meter width and two meter depth flows slowly to our right.

I have the Yards stow their web gear and weapons together at the base of the banyan. Kinnear and I also lay down our gear but keep our carbines slung over our backs. I assign Deng to guard the weapons and keep a lookout while we procure our "fishing equipment." The Yards strip down to their underwear.

"Gai, tell the men to each grab two hand grenades from their web gear. Have them line up along the river bank." I gesture with my hands as to the position I want them to take. Gai, Hyak, Diu, Boon and Yubi align themselves adjacent to the river bank's ledge and separate themselves by several meters. Every man holds a grenade in each hand. Kinnear and I stand to the rear of the line the Yards form.

"Gai, tell everyone to pull the pins from the grenades and to keep the handles secure until I give the order to throw. And for Christsakes don't anybody get any butterfingers." Yubi starts chuckling. *"Butterfingers…butterfingers… "*, he goofs. The Yards pull the pins on the grenades. They outstretch their arms to their sides holding an explosive device in each hand.

I bark. "Ready on the right! Ready on the left!

"Reedy on right! Reedy on leff!" the Yards lampoon me. I give the command…

"NOW! Throw the grenades!"…*pling-pling-pling-cling-bling!* The spoons from ten grenades fling themselves free of the explosives…*blomp-blomb…plop-plop-plup…*along a length of fifty feet the grenades drop into the channel of the river…there are a couple seconds of silence…then…*BOOM!BOOM!*

BOOOMBABOOMBABOOMBOOM!! Columns of water surge into the air. The Yards leap from the bank into the river's channel.

As they splash into the water gleeful cheers erupt. "Feesh! Feesh!" they yell.

Killed by the grenade's underwater concussion, four golden carp, each over a meter in length, bob to the water's surface. The Yards wrestle with their catch. Kinnear, Deng and I reach down from the bank and help hoist the large fish onto dry land. For a moment we forget we are soldiers and behave like a group of boys excited with their trophy. We are all smiles.

Kinnear and I lay the golden scaled carp on the green grass of the river's bank. The Yards climb up the dirt bank and out of the river.

Suddenly Kinnear makes a dash toward the banyan tree. He shouts, "You goddamn little fuck!" A Vietnamese boy, not more than fourteen years old had snuck up behind the banyan tree and attempted to steal a weapon from the team's gear. During our preoccupation with our catch of fish we became careless. Even Deng, who was supposed to guard the gear, dropped his vigilance.

Kinnear tightly grips the boy by the wrist, draws out his .45 pistol and points it at the kid's chest. The boy desperately struggles to free himself. Kinnear cocks the weapon…

I scream with all the intent of war at Kinnear, "NO! NO! Don't you fucking dare Kinnear! Don't you fucking dare!"

Kinnear turns his head to me. His eyes are filled with anger and threat.

"He's just a kid! He's just a kid!" I yell.

There is a moment of tension. Kinnear pauses then holsters his weapon. He drags the boy towards the river bank, picks him up over his head and throws him into the river. The kid can't swim.

I watch as the boy flails in the water and drops beneath the surface and bobs back up choking. Kinnear and all the Yards stand on the bank's edge. The glare in their eyes pushes the boy back under the water a second time. I look to the boy. He coughs and gags. His strength is leaving him. I look back at the Yards and Kinnear. Their hardened faces have passed final judgment.

The boy goes under a third time and doesn't resurface. *Jesus Christ*! I leap into the river where the kid last went down. My hands find him and pull him to the surface. I tread water to the river's bank and pull him up with me. As the kid coughs and gags and vomits he struggles on his hands and knees to get away from us. Kinnear and the Yards stare and say nothing.

"Let him go!" I command.

"He'll go on to kill someone…" declares Kinnear.

Still coughing and laboring for breath the boy makes it to his feet and staggers towards the country road. Deng breaks the icy moment.

"Oy! Feesh. Feesh…"

Deng has cut a long bamboo pole to carry the fish on. The Yards go back to being their cheery selves and begin lashing the large golden carp to the pole. Because of the size of the fish the Yards aren't tall enough to carry the bamboo pole without the fish dragging on the ground. Kinnear and I shoulder the pole. It bends under the weight of the swaying gold carp. We walk our catch back up to the road. The Yards are very talkative. They slap each other on the back and start singing and laughing *feesh, feesh, feesh…*Once we reach the dirt lane people and children come out of their homes and exhibit delight at our catch. By the time we reach the compound more than twenty people trail behind us. Like the Yards of our team they too are in a jovial mood. I ask Gai, "Who are all these people?"

"Oh Burkai, my cousins." he replies smiling. "They know there will be a feast of fish tonight and they are making sure to be invited.

A Drink on Me

My interpreter Gai has invited me to his home to meet and have dinner with his family in the Montagnard village of Plei Krek. The hamlet is several miles from our Special Forces base camp and lies in an area of known enemy activity.

Moving briskly along in our jeep through an open wood, Gai, Yubi and I ride down a cart-wide dirt path leading to the village. Gai and Yubi keep an alert watch with their weapons at the ready while I drive. In our jeep under the cover of a green tarp are several cases of .223 ammo and a case of baseball grenades. I have commandeered these munitions for Gai's village and the secret Montagnard Army, FALRU.

It is unspoken but the truth is known in whispers…some day soon the United States will leave Vietnam and the Yards will have to fend for themselves, against the Communists and the Vietnamese. I and other members of the Special Operations Group clandestinely supply the Yards and their furtive army for that coming time.

"Not much further, Burkai." says Gai. I look at his quiet face and see a proud man behind his bloodshot eyes. It is an honor for me to be invited to meet his family.

Suddenly the narrow route the jeep rides upon opens into a large area of low rolling hills sparsely covered with scrub brush and scattered tall palms. The village sits at the base of and between three small hills. A total of a few dozen huts, each constructed with a combination of bamboo, wood sticks, palm fronds and large poles stand raised several feet off the ground. Beneath the huts pot-belly pigs and goats lounge in pens and chickens roam freely about.

The village is fortified by a log fence perimeter. Attached to the fence are several tiers of sharpened bamboo poles that point menacingly outward forming an enclosed ring of thousands of spear tips around the hamlet. I pull the jeep up to a large swinging gate made of giant bamboo. A thin, leathered old man wearing a loin cloth stands guard with an M-16. Gai calls out to him and then tells me to turn off the jeep's engine. We stop, get out of the jeep and stretch our legs. Gai speaks with the guard who nods and then leaves. Several children, naked but for the open shirts they wear, run up to us and latch onto my hands. I kneel down to greet them. They are probably two to six years old and look upon me with wonder. They play with my blond hair, pull at my nose and point to my blue eyes. They try to sit on my knee and climb up me as if I were a tree. They giggle at the strange foreign sight my presence makes. I let their curiosity explore me.

The gate guard returns with several women dressed only in colorfully woven skirts. Gai gives them orders to remove the crates of munitions from under the tarp. They steal glances at me while they transfer the wooden boxes from our vehicle. "They will secure the goods, Burkai. Thank you so much for the supplies."

"My pleasure Gai. It is the least I can do for your people. I'll get more for you next month." I reply.

He grins broadly and nods affirmatively. Children hold onto my legs as I stand up. In the crook of my arms I hold two little girls. They perch there comfortably and rub their hands across the stubble on my face. Their eyes explore mine infecting me with my own wonder. A boisterous little boy hangs on my back with his arms around my neck. I feel the rich warmth their comfortable affection affords me.

"Come," says Gai, "We go to my family's house."

Several women, children and older men have gathered at the gateway. Gai tells some of the younger girls to take the children from me. Everywhere I look the eyes of the villagers hold fast to me. In their gaze is an innocence and acceptance that is entirely meant for me. I am slightly embarrassed and humbled by it. Yubi who has stood quietly by removes my weapon and web gear from the jeep and gives it to me. "I take. I take." he says, pointing to the jeep. He is like a teenager who wants the keys to the car. It was only last week that I taught him and the other Yards to drive.

"Yubi wants to drive the jeep, Burkai."

"Sure Gai."

I nod to Yubi approvingly. His face lights up. He gives out a call and suddenly a myriad of children come running our way. Yubi places them in the jeep until it is full of naked kids. He sits in the driver's seat, starts the engine, smiles over at me, then proceeds to carefully and slowly motor the jeep into the village. All the kids stiffen with excitement. Their mouths and eyes hold wide open. Life. Around and round the huts a proud Yubi gives the children a ride of joy. I sling my weapon and hang my web gear on my shoulder. Gai, in the custom of his people takes me by my hand. Together we walk to what is the largest of all the hootches, the 'long house', the chief's residence. The chief is Gai's father.

The chief's cottage is built on large round stilts. The floor of the lengthy rectangular structure sits about five feet above the ground. A long, inclined log, cut with notches along its length serves as a stairway up into the hut's entrance. At the base of the log step-way squat several older men dressed in loin cloths and green T-shirts. Gai speaks to them. They smile and humbly bow their heads.

"Friends of my father," says Gai. "They would like you to have a drink with them."

The men squat around a brown earthen jar filled with rice wine. They motion for me to join them. I squat down alongside them. One of the men hands me a bamboo straw.

"Here Burkai, let me show you how to drink." Gai picks up a thin stick of bamboo that lays across the round mouth of the jar. He explains, "...see how there is a small stick along the length of the bamboo." He points with his finger. At the center of the length of the bamboo stick is a small splinter, about an inch long, that is bent at a right angle to the longer piece. Gai places the stick across the mouth of the jug so that the short splinter is pointing down into the rice wine.

"When you drink, you must drink until the wine falls below the little splinter. You understand?"

"I've got it Gai." I shuffle my feet along until I am squatting next to the jug of rice wine. Grains of rice float in the milky looking liquid. A pungent odor rises into my nostrils. I put one end of the bamboo straw into the liquid and take a long draft until the wine level falls below the downward pointing sliver. I hold the wine in my mouth until it is nearly full. I then swallow the drink in a big gulp. The men all laugh in approval. The wine leaves a viscous bitterness in my mouth and throat.

"Good Burkai! Good!" Gai compliments me.

I see Yubi walking towards us. He has discarded his clothes and now wears a loin cloth. His long black hair hangs straight down to his shoulders. Gai makes a comment about 'young people'. "Pretty boy Yubi," he says and grunts a short laugh. Yubi comes up smiling. I hand him the bamboo straw. He squats alongside me. One of the older men pours water into the mouth of the rice wine jar bringing its level back to the top. He then lightly stirs up the fermented juice. Yubi sticks in the bamboo straw and sucks the wine quickly down to the appropriate level. The old men nod in approval.

Gai excuses himself and walks up the log stairway to disappear into the long house. Yubi and I continue drinking with the men. I quickly discover that it is a custom to have a drink with each new individual you meet. Before long I feel the nervous edge of hyper-vigilance being replaced with the ease of slight intoxication. After drinking in acknowledgment to each man, I stand to stretch my legs. Yubi and I talk in what little I know of his language. His English is far better than my Montagnard.

"Burkai, look." Yubi points to his bare foot. "I push." He makes a motion of purposely pushing against the ground. "Earth moves!" He nods affirmatively and his eyes convey the reality of his relationship with his environment. "I push. Earth moves. Yes." His voice holds a seriousness.

For the moment I agree out of politeness, but I would learn many years later, while in a college physics class, that the earth did indeed move when you pushed your foot against it. The movement was small but none the less it did move. Yubi had no knowledge of physics, but he had the sensitive experience of feeling the earth moving beneath his feet…with every step. I had no idea.

The sky above us is turning gray. Huge purple clouds brush over the sun. The air turns cool. The old men squatted around the rice wine jug throw blankets around themselves and grow quiet.

"Rain," says Yubi.

"Oh Burkai!" Gai calls from the entrance of the long house. "Come inside, please."

Yubi and I walk up the notched log stairway into the hootch. Inside, a sprawling rectangular room opens before me. Its entire floor is covered with a light-brown mat, woven from long thin leaves. The walls are woven from green palm fronds. Above my head, latched to bamboo pole rafters, a tightly thatched roof, woven of banyan root, flows in random geometrical patterns. In the middle of the floor is a large round black metal basin that serves as a fireplace and cooking fire. Small yellow flames dance in a pile of hardwood twigs and bathe the entire room in a soft golden glow. Sweetened smoke drifts lazily up and out a smudged opening in the woven ceiling. Several women sitting around the fire make the diminutive noises associated with the preparation of a meal. A succulent fragrance fills my nostrils and tantalizes the back of my throat.

"Burkai, come. Meet my father and family."

Standing in a line, ready to meet me the American, are his immediate family. First is his grandfather. Old, withered like leather and blind, the patriarch stands before me. He extends his hands outward. Gai tells me to take his grandfather's hands in mine and put them to my face. I bend down to his height. His fingers search from the top of my head to my hands. Sounds of approval between soft grunts to chuckles extend from his throat. His head bobs and nods. He occasionally makes a comment to the others. A toothless smile spreads in his brown face.

"Now my father," says Gai. His father's name is La. Despite his old age his energy and eyes reveal a fierceness, but his smile shows his heart. He takes my hand in the two of his and speaks for several minutes. Gai interprets a long welcome and joy at my coming to visit. For now I am not directly introduced to the remaining members of his family. We all sit down on the floor. Yubi brings forth a short squat red earthen jar. More rice wine. Gai speaks.

"It is our custom for you to have a drink with each of my family." Being already familiar with the ritual, I nod in agreement. Then I see a procession of tribal people coming in a line through the entrance to the hut. Starting with friends, then aunts and uncles, then cousins, then siblings, for each one I suck up the rice wine so it falls below the prescribed bamboo sliver. Again and again. Drink, drink, drinkkk.

I begin to feel woozy. Very woozy. Finally, it is time to drink with the chief. The chief sits before me, the jug of rice wine between us. My head is starting to spin. My stomach threatens to lurch. I buckle down and strain to keep focused on the custom presented me.

"And now Burkai, have a drink with my father," enjoins Gai.

I am doing my best to stay coherent. I motion to Gai that I wish to speak with him. He comes close and I whisper in his ear, "Gai, if I take one more drink I am going to throw up. I swear."

Suddenly Gai turns aggressive and loudly exclaims, "YOU MUST DRINK!"

I squint through the haze of my inebriated eyeballs. The chief is glaring at me. Everyone else in the long house is giving me the stink eye. I'm not going to get out of here alive I think…so drink I must, lest I insult my hosts.

"Okay Gai, but I warn you I'm gonna' puke.

"DRINK!" Gai demands.

I shrug my shoulders and take the bamboo straw into my mouth and suck up the wine until the level in the jug falls below the mark. My mouth bulges with the pungent rice wine. I gather all my will and swallow.

The eyes of his village are upon me. I strain to contain the drink but like a whale clearing its blowhole a shower of wine erupts from my mouth. *I'm a dead man.* A stream of regurgitation spews like a river from my gut, through my throat, out my mouth, across the floor…BAWRAAAAH!…

Riotous laughter and unrestrained cheers burst forth from all the people in the hut. The chief rolls on the floor slapping his sides. Tears stream down the blind grandfather's cheeks. Gai tries unsuccessfully to contain his merriment.

"You are a good man Burkai!" says Gai slapping me on the back. The room spins. I manage a feeble smile and feel like the ugly American. "Not to worry, Burkai. Not to worry…Just right…Just right."

No Shame

After being out of the service for ten years I now faced the painful decision of re-enlisting. The last circumstance I wanted in my life was to be a weapon carrying soldier preparing for some possible future battle. But the state of affairs of being jobless, without transportation and shelter, was pressing me towards soldiering.

At the time, joining the military was the only job opportunity on the Big Island of Hawaii. The major newspaper was published only three days a week and the want ads numbered fewer than half a dozen. The construction work I had been doing ended when the project was completed. My only island connection, a friend I was staying with, had to suddenly relocate to the mainland. I was unexpectedly homeless, without work, knew no one else and at the moment was losing the little bit of relationship I had with myself.

If you have to be homeless, Hawaii is a good place for it. Papaya, mangoes, avocado, banana, guava and coconuts were abundant and freely available. The sands of the beaches made for a soft bed. The weather was usually near perfect and most beaches had public showers and restrooms.

But my diet of excess fruit was giving me diarrhea and the little black gnats occasionally feeding on me while I lived under the bushes at the beaches' edges was becoming somewhat unbearable. My only possessions, carried in my backpack, consisted of a few pair of pants, shorts and T-shirts along with some personal hygiene gear and a pancho liner. Other than that and the sneakers on my feet, I was alone with my troubled thoughts and each day they were becoming more distraught. I desperately needed a job.

I wrote down a list of all my skills that I thought would give me a chance at employment: construction worker, carpenter, surveyor, salesman, gunsmith, math and physics tutor, lab technician, janitor, laborer, soldier.

On many different occasions I went to every little shop and place of business in Kona town asking for work. All I got were stares and rebukes. I hadn't looked in the mirror for a month. My mind was weak from lack of proper nutrition. I wasn't aware that I appeared and sounded like a desperate man. I would have been content to work the most menial of labor but no one would have me. It seemed the sole chance I had at surviving was using the skill I wanted least to carry out: pushing troops, training soldiers.

I had been a teacher and leader of soldiers. I didn't want to have to do it again. I needed money but being purely mercenary went against the grain of my once-upon-a-time gun carrying soul.

I didn't want to be in the business of war but no other employment was available. For several more weeks I sat on golden sand beaches and walked the rolling green hills of the Big Island, wrestling the anguish within myself to find just cause and reason to re-enlist in the military and again carry a weapon. Just being homeless wasn't enough of an excuse for me.

****

One particular pensive night the weather was perfect. Perfectly stormy. Howling wind and driving rain blew through the conflict of my world. Waves pounded the shore. Blowing sand in the sea salt air stung my skin and made wild my hair. Palm trees whipped by the wind hurled coconuts like projectiles launched from catapults. I hollered and yelled as loud as the surf crashed. *The anger at my predicament at having no other choice.* My cries grabbed at reasons for war while my heart reached for root in any other reality. Like waves washing over the shore, an insane joyous laughter swept over me. Inundated in the momentum of chaos, I found myself frightfully alive with the belief that *I was all things*, and heard the universe say it was *okay*. The storm continued throughout the night and it was good.

The pre-dawn light arrived in shades of soft gray. The morning air flowed smooth and clean through my lungs and nose. The ocean seemed asleep, breathing deeply as its dark swells rolled in dream. I felt wide awake in the decision I had reached. *I would go back into the military.* My job would be to educate the men I would lead. I would teach young soldiers how to keep close watch on their leaders and perhaps more importantly, how to survive war should they ever have to participate. While teaching men how to kill, I could save lives.

****

Killing. A harsh word but that's the work of the infantry soldier. Engage the enemy and destroy them. *I would again become a weapon.*

****

A weapon has a life within, a character of its own. It solicits use. It exudes fear. It aspires to create death.

The use of weapons is lamentable but there is a time for every purpose. Even the sagacious will use a weapon when given no choice, but they never revel in its skill nor exult war.

When what you hold to be most holy is attended by pain, destruction and death the spiritual expenditure is devastating. But one's own suffering is minimal compared to beholding the suffering of others. The sorrow of experiencing human beings at their worst and regret of not being able to help the victims is forever carried.

In war you sacrifice ideals for personal existence and the rage of killing. The experience will be permanent. The hazard is not risking one's life, but one's very humanity.

I became a sergeant in the Hawaii Army Reserve, "B" Company, 299th Infantry.

****

Like it was in Vietnam, I again found myself working with the natives. I was the only white man in a company of one-hundred and twenty five brown and yellow skinned men. They were mostly of mixed races and very proud of it. If you asked one of them what blood ran in his veins, he would nobly state: “Ah bruddah! I one part Hawaiian, one part Chinese, one part Tongan, one part Filipino…” The more mix of blood the deeper the honest pride flowed.

To the local islanders, I was referred to as a “haoule”. A foreigner. Basically a term reserved for someone who deserved little or no respect. But to the local soldiers I was also a curiosity. These men genetically descended from a warrior society. They recognized the insignias I wore on my uniform, emblems that represented my being a veteran of battles and war. Also, wearing the stripes of a Staff Sergeant said I was a leader. My rank and experience posited the right to be involved with them and the privilege to be somewhat distant.

But in the beginning I was thrown right in the middle of them. Even though I had rank and combat experience, my first assignment, usually reserved for a Private, was the position of a lowly rifleman.

I was assigned to a squad and placed with a “buddy.” In the infantry everyone has a buddy. He’s the guy you’re in the trenches with. The guy you sludge through the mud with. Sleep in the fox hole with. Share your meals with and sometimes sacrifice your life for. My buddy was Specialist Patrick Tinao, a physically thick young man of Samoan and Hawaiian ancestry, whose hobby was “hating, hunting and physically pounding haoules.” It was trial by fire. If I could survive Patrick I would probably gain acceptance by the others.

****

One day we were on maneuvers in the severe terrain of the Pohakoloa training area. Across this vast stretch of arid land, legions of ancient brown and black lava-rock rivers, statically criss-cross each other for miles. The hardened lava's currents once flowed molten from the innumerable mounds of cinder cones that dotted themselves across an expansive khaki desert plain of scrub oak, dry brush and thorn. The infantry of Bravo company, strung out like a line of ants, slowly struggles across it.

****

There are two distinct types of hardened lava. One type, ranging from a few feet to dozens of feet in depth, creates erratically wide and long dark rivers, composed of millions of baseball to football sized rocks. Each individual rock has the property of never being stable under the weight of your step. Their surfaces are richly peppered with knife-tip sharp edges that will literally "eat" a leather boot off a foot in less then a month. Its name is the sound you would make if you stepped onto it with bare feet: *"Ah-Ah!"* If a soldier falls down into it, there is certain injury. Flesh rips. Blood flows. Given time, this unmerciful lava will wear the tracks off a tank.

The other type of lava flow, it too sometimes miles wide, long and tens of feet deep, splays its smooth brown surface in alluvial fans, like a thick river of mud, now solid in time and place after having burned and snaked across everything in its path eons ago. Its name is smooth-sounding like its surface feels: *"Lapahoehoe"*.

Spreading wide as the eye can see and located on rising slopes above the harsh lava desert, is a thick, rich canopied jungle, nourished by rain clouds that collect in its tree tops daily. And above and beyond this mist covered, moist greenbelt, is a constant climbing slope of rough, dark cinder and sundry sized chunks of igneous rock, that eventually reaches to fourteen-thousand feet in elevation and the snow-covered, caldera peaks of Mauna Kea. Six thousand feet below these rarefied peaks, on the lava desert plain, the soldiers of Bravo company make camp and begin digging-in for the coming night.

****

The foxhole is the soldiers' friend. It is a shallow pit dug in the earth that gives him scant shelter and cover from enemy fire. It is the place where non-believers are known to convert.

****

It's time to make camp.

Keeping a proper interval of space between each man, one hundred and twenty-five of us walk in a long irregular line. On orders, we move ourselves into a defensive circular perimeter and prepare to dig our foxholes. In the bivouac area scant tree and bush grow in the sharp *"ah-ah"* rock and hard dry dirt. Using a combination shovel and pick called an entrenching tool, we start our task of "digging in."

It is late afternoon. The sky is clear blue and the motionless air seriously hot. A thick rise of heat waves distort the atmosphere around us.

Most of the men have removed their fatigue shirts. Soldiers' bodies glisten with sweat. Their voices groan with the labor required. I am one of them but my buddy, Specialist Patrick Tinao, sits on his large Samoan ass, in the shade under a scrub tree. He is laid back with his hands behind his head, his thick body snug against the tree's gnarly trunk. His broad Polynesian face looks like it is cut in stone. Bug-eyed sunglasses cover his unseen eyes. A pencil thin brown mustache reaches out to the ends of his terse thick lips.

"Hey! Aren't you going to help me dig this hole?" I ask. He is unmoving except for his lips, tongue and vocal cords.

"Fouck You Hoaule! Deeg it yourself! 'less you like *beef?"*

This was it. The moment of reckoning. Patrick wasn't referring to 'beef' as in meat. In local speech, he was telling me I would have to fight to get him to help dig the foxhole.

I remain quiet and keep digging to move the hard rocks and khaki colored dirt out of the reluctantly growing hole. I can feel him psychically positioning for the encounter he wants with me. I promise myself I'll make no move, until he does and when he does, I'll smack his broad forehead with the entrenching tool I'm using to dig the foxhole.

With curiosity and the slightest aggression, I ask him, "I guess you feel really big because you're here with all your *"bruddahs?"*

"I no need my bruddahs to be beeg, hoaule," he threatens.

"Then all these guys here are your *"bruddahs?"* In gesture I wave my arm in wide arc to present the men behind me. All the soldiers are sweating in the heat, busy digging, but keeping an eye on the growing conflict between Specialist Tinao and myself.

"Shoot hoaule, *these are all my bruddahs*!" he yells. Specialist Tinao stands up and fills himself into his massive torso and limbs. He removes his sunglasses, locks his eyes on me and takes a menacing step in my direction.

I meet his eyes for a moment and say, "It looks like all your *brothers are working hard* to get our job done. But you, you sit on your ass while all *your brothers* struggle and sweat. What kind of *brother* does that make you?" I say it with the authority of the Staff Sergeant I am. I keep digging myself into the foxhole without another glance in his direction.

The only sound is that of dozens of metal entrenching tools picking at dirt and scrapping over rock. I keep digging and internally wait at the ready for Specialist Tinao to make his next move. He steps into the foxhole. Both his hands grip his entrenching tool like a bludgeon. He takes a mighty swing with it and buries the tool's pick end deep into the earth.

"You know, for one fouckin' Haoule, you speak some sense." In personal silence, in sweltering heat, *we* dig *our* foxhole.

****

The next week passed without incident or serious challenge. But there were a few occasions when I was either eating or cleaning my weapon when one of the *"bruddahs"* would perch themselves a few feet from me and look me up, down and over for several minutes, then get up and walk away without saying a word. I took it in stride.

Our last night in the field was one of rest and relaxation. Because everyone had performed well, the officers of the company allowed the troops to be at ease. A trip was made to the Post Exchange to buy beer and food. One of the boys shot a wild pig. It was cut up and prepared for grilling. Cooking fires were built. Everyone was in a good mood from having worked hard and having done a job well. Small groups of men gathered together, they drank, ate and *"talked story."*

I stayed on the periphery and didn't join in. I was observing and listening to my internal dialogue while everyone else socialized. On one hand I was congratulating myself at having made it this far. I never would have guessed I would ever be back in the military. On the other hand I was somewhat disturbed by the *joy* I found in being a soldier.

When we were shooting the M-60 machine-gun, running fire and maneuver drills, tossing hand grenades and setting off claymore mines, an alien personality possessed me. Resistance was futile. A demon released by the joy of war, pleased with its rage, lived itself through *me*. It was sentient destructive energy, immaculate in its love of self.

I am frightened that evil lives within me.

"Yea though I walk through the valley of death, I shall fear no evil, for I am the evilest in the valley..."

I am evil.

****

"Hey Sarge!" Specialist Patrick Tinao yells at me.

I look out from within myself and see Patrick walking my way with other soldiers. Patrick has a plate of food in his hands. Another soldier, Kinny, carries several six-packs of beer. In all, about two dozen *"Hawaiian Bruddahs"* begin sitting near me. Beers are passed around. Specialist Tinao hands me a cold can of beer and presents up his can of beer in toast.

"Here's to the Sarge!"

Every soldier offers up his drink in recognition. We imbibe.

I too make a toast. *"To the Warriors of Bravo Company!"*

"Hear, hear! Guarens, guarens! Shoot, shoot Brah!" The response is unanimous.

"Eh, Brah, some *grinds* for you." Patrick hands me a plate of beans, pig meat and hot dogs in buns.

I look at him. His face is broad with smile. The white of his offering eyes stands out from the dark tanned skin of his face.

"Shoot Brah. Go. Grind!" Patrick smiles. His eyes enjoin me to go ahead and eat.

I take the paper plate loaded with food from his large hands and thank him. He nods approval, takes a long drink from his can of beer then looks out across the vast expanse of lava desert and sighs assuredly.

I begin eating. As I eat, the men make small talk, the sun makes a slow descent behind a line of ancient cinder cones. The talking is subdued. The air around us quiet. My earlier feeling of being evil sneaks back into my psyche.

"Sarge?" Specialist Tinao has a question for me.

"Yes?" I sense the other men going suddenly quiet. Patrick continues.

"Sarge. What was it like?"

"What do you mean?" I ask. *I know what he means.*

"The war. What was it like? What did you do there?"

I look around me into the faces of the young soldiers yearning for an answer. I see the human features of Hawaiian, Polynesian, Japanese, Chinese and some that would pass for North Vietnamese. They want the vicarious experience. They want to know what their life may someday be like. I feel an immense swelling of my psyche and an opposing feeling of shutting down. I hear myself answer:

"It was no big thing. Nothing worth telling."

Immediately, Specialist Patrick Tinao responds. He points his finger at me.

"Eh, Brah. No shame. *No shame!"* It is almost a pleading. I feel his eyes reach deep within me.

"If you have shame your soul 'come bound. Cannot grow," says Patrick.

His perception shocks me. He is so correct. For nearly a decade I have not spoken of my experiences in the war. I have endeavored to bury them within myself but the grave refuses to stay covered over. I feel great shame at having reveled in destruction and having failed to save others. For having made mistakes. Patrick is right. I feel shame. But in this moment, being here in the field with the camaraderie of young warriors, whose lives may someday be thrown into life and death combat, I feel accepted and understood.

I feel a lump in my heart suddenly dissolve into my breath and depart the pores of my being. For the men who sit around me and wait, I take a story from my grave and give it life.

Three Questions

Question Number One

Surviving a war is a blessing, living to understand it is a curse. For there is no easy answer to relieve the pains of guilt, loss and especially the frustration of not even having a clear idea of what in the heart of myself needs answering.

The mind sometimes seems as foggy as a battlefield covered in the haze of cordite, numbed into a purely empty void by the shock of what has incomprehensibly taken place. I couldn't imagine that it would take many, many years before any clear concept of the experience struck a clarity within me. Every time I asked myself, "what the hell was THAT all about?" my ability to focus on the question was like trying to grasp a ghost. And for the time being, my answer to everything was, "it don't mean nothing."

We all live life with many questions going unanswered. After all, being home from the war, being alive, allowed me to return to the life I had left. At the time, there was no question that I had to go on living.

Thanks to the good laws of our land, I was welcomed back to my pre-service vocation with open arms. I had had this job since I was fifteen and worked it for four years before going into the military. My job had even given me some preparation for the military. I worked in a gun shop. Guns of every caliber and size. Sporting and military pieces stood in floor and wall racks like shined soldiers at attention, ready for a command to lock and load.

The "GUN SHOP" was the name of the business establishment. I had first worked here as a kid. I loved hunting and fishing and shooting trap and skeet. I competed in pistol and rifle matches locally and in several surrounding states.

People who enjoyed hunting and guns and the great outdoors came from Maryland, Pennsylvania, New Jersey and Delaware. The business had scores of customers who were frequent visitors. During Fall and Winter there was always a group of hunters hanging out around the free coffee, keeping warm and swapping hunting tales of dogs and game. In the Spring and Summer it was pretty much the same group and the season was filled with shooting clay birds, paper targets and varmints. It was a friendly group, extremely diverse of class and career. A family of men who shared the same interests of the use of guns.

I practically grew up with these men. Because I worked at the gun shop six and seven days a week, although always having time off to hunt or shoot when the season or occasion arose, I spent a great deal of time in the presence of these individuals.

First there was my boss, Joe Moors, ten years my senior, a perfectionist, gun smith and migraine sufferer, who treated me like a younger brother. Because of his headaches, I was taught to oversee the day to day business so he could leave work when his frequent migraines attacked him.

We had several customers who frequented the shop almost daily. George Ward was a vice-president of Hercules Powder company. He was an older fart (as everyone called him) with a Harvard education, who had served in World War I as an artillery officer. He was a non-combatant though, who had only trained men to shoot cannons in the war. He carried a distinguished air of wealth and silver spoon upbringing, speaking with an over-acted Harvard accent.

Jerry Truman was a car dealer in Jersey with links to characters of questionable repute. He seemed to have a lot of free time and pockets of cash and tried hard to be the best trap shooter in the region. He was forever buying a different trap gun blaming the old one to be the fault of his missing targets.

Earl Stewart, a traveling salesman, sold hunting accessories. Such as clothing, boots, gloves, scabbards, game calls, etc. He made rounds of every sporting goods shop in the state and surrounding areas. He was a happy type who would stop in for a cup of coffee every chance he got. Always on the run, he loved being an outdoorsman but had the reputation of having the strangest luck when it came to competitive shoots or hunting of any type. He was the guy who always bought the hunting dog who no one else wanted. He was usually the brunt of everyone else's practical jokes.

There was an array of others who made the gun shop their second home. After work or after a hunt, they would come and hang out at the shop, sharing their stories or professing their skills against the game they hunted. Everyone treated me with kindness and some sort of pleasant attention. They all had watched me as a boy become a skilled hunter and excellent shooter. Many times they took me along on their individual or group huntings. I grew up in their kind company. I was nineteen when I said good-by to them. I went to train and prepare for the war in Southeast Asia. I would be gone for four years…

So here I had returned from the experience of the military and the war. Back to the smell of Hoppes #9 (a civilian gun cleaning solvent), canvas hunting clothes and creosote cork decoys.

I had only been home for a few days when I started back to work. It was the middle of hunting season and the shop was abuzz with activity. Over the next couple of weeks, one by one, the old familiar customers would take time to greet me and welcome me back. They didn't make any big deal out of my return. They were polite but seemed to be looking me over as if they weren't sure of who they were talking to. Obviously, I had changed. I was no longer the teenage boy they had known for years prior and at the time I wasn't aware of all the media stories that were being perpetuated about returning veterans. There were questions in their eyes they didn't yet ask. I went about my job selling guns and hunting goods, cleaning and repairing guns. I had been asked to join several hunts, but I politely declined giving reasons that were untrue.

Then the questions began.

The first question was one I was asked by nearly every one of the hundreds of customers who knew me. It didn't trouble me and I didn't think twice about it until I had been asked it just one too many times. I didn't realize how I really felt until the day Earl Stewart, the happy smiling salesman, asked it.

We were alone in the shop. Earl had just poured coffee into a styrofoam cup. He was stirring in the powdered cream and sugar with a plastic swizzle stick and leaned his elbows on the counter I was standing behind. I leaned back against the shelves behind me quietly observing him. He looked at his coffee cup then looked at me with a smile that told a tale of something else behind it. He stared quietly for a couple of moments and asked, "Well, Lee, have you adjusted to civilian life yet?"

One thing I certainly hadn't adjusted to was being able to sleep like a civilian. Having spent a year in combat my sleep was more like lying in wait. The eyes would close and the brain would still, but the instinct of survival was actively prowling the perimeter. Sleep maybe. Rest never.

"Have I adjusted to civilian life?", I repeated emotionlessly, moving closer to Earl's smiling face. "Have I adjusted to civilian life?" I barked like rifle fire. "Have I adjusted to civilian life?" I screamed like an incoming barrage while I grabbed Earl by the lapels of his suitcoat and nearly yanked him over the glass counter of the pistol display.

"I'll tell you what I've adjusted to! I get up in the fucking morning. I take a shit. I go to work. I pay taxes. I live the same daily fucking mundane life that you do! Tell me for God's sake, what the fuck is there that I have to adjust to!!!...TELL ME! FUCKING TELL

ME…!" I am physically shaking Earl so violently his feet are off the floor and his cup of coffee has exploded in our faces. Bugging out of his reddened face his eyes are screaming for help. I am trapped in a distant silence while the earth around me is being torn asunder.

"Lee! Lee! Stop! Stop please!"

His pleading suddenly brings me back to the reality of the situation. He pulls himself away from the loosened grip of my fists. I have a thousand yard stare on my face. Earl is in shock. He grabs his sales case from the floor and heads for the door and says, "I gotta go" and with coat tails flapping exits the store.

The store is empty and as quiet as if all the sounds of life have ceased to exit. There is coffee splattered across the glass counter top. Like an emotionless robot, I proceed to find a rag and begin to put the mess in order. In the solitary beating of my heart there is activity I can't comprehend.

****

Question Number Two

The cold hammer of winter has slammed its harshness against the end of hunting season. Marshes are frozen and the last of the wild fowl has flown South. Men and their gunning dogs have endured every hunt available to them. Now is the time to give the dogs and their torn feet and severely scratched noses rest. A time to let Old Blue put some meat back on his bones. Hunters are bringing their shotguns and rifles into the shop, dirtied from the woods and fields and weather they've been exposed to. They are muddied and slightly game bloodied, and in need of oil and cleaning care. That's my job. I can strip down any hand held or shoulder-fired weapon faster than anyone. I'll remove the mud and grim and oil and assemble the firearm making it ready for the next seasons' hunts.

****

When I originally enlisted in the Army, I was promised the choice of jobs. I chose to be an arms bearer, which is basically a military gunsmith of sorts. I had it all figured out. There were only two schools in the Army where armorers were trained. One was in Aberdeen, Maryland, only an hour from my hometown. This was a way to prevent being separated from my girlfriend. The other school was in California, a place I thought I would enjoy seeing. Hell yes! I'll give Uncle Sam four years of my time to be in either place. But the government, being true to its bureaucratic nature, assigned me to the infantry. I actually went and complained to my drill Sergeant about the assignment I had been contractually promised and denied.

****

Drill Sergeant Walker was a good leader and teacher of new recruits. Unlike most other drill instructors, he wasn't psychotically mean. He had a way of bringing out the hidden strengths in young men and challenging them to higher goals.

Unblinking, with that stare into the distance he wore, Drill Sergeant Walker addressed my grievance head on. "Troop, combat arms is the only way to go. You'll learn to lead men, have more adventure, and wear the hard stripes of a Sergeant instead of being a fuckin' puke Specialist. Airborne! Understood?"

John F. Kennedy couldn't have said it better. Combat arms was the way I was going.

I snapped to attention and replied like the trooper I felt I was, "AIRBORNE SERGEANT!" I was off to the Infantry…

****

I am just finishing putting together a customer's Browning 12 gauge shotgun and am giving it a final wipedown and inspection when my boss Joe comes into the shop.

"Hi Joe. How are you doing?" I put the shotgun into its fleece lined case and write "complete" on the job ticket.

"I'm having a rough morning. Damn migraine won't quit". He squints his eyes and rubs his temples.

He's never made any mention about the incident I had with Earl a couple of months ago. I know he cares about me, but it's a relationship I find no feelings for.

"Well, I hope your headache goes away".

He goes to the cash register and counts the money, totals the daily take and removes most of the cash.

"I see you've put all your guns up for sale." He states it, but it sounds like a question.

As a kid growing up hunting and shooting competitively, I had collected dozens of guns.

"Yea, after sleeping with a weapon for years, I seem to have lost my interests in shooting. I really don't feel like killing animals anymore or even busting targets."

"Well, maybe you'll feel differently come next hunting season."

"Maybe", I replied indifferently.

It is nearing dinner time. Joe comes into the repair room and hands me a few bucks.

"Go get us a couple of cheese-steak sandwiches. On me". We hadn't eaten dinner together since I returned from the war. When I was a kid, we used to often have meals together at the shop. I head off to the local sub shop and soon return with our meals.

It's a quiet night for business. The evening grows colder and snow is beginning to blow around the outside of the lighted gunshop, framing the store like a cottage in one of those shake-and-it-snows glass balls. The blowing snow outside the window gives me a comfortable feeling of being wrapped in seclusion. Joe and I eat our philly cheese steaks in silence. The silence feels peaceful. Then Joe asks the question nearly every customer known to me has already asked.

"Would you do it all over again? The war, I mean. Would you go knowing what you know now?"

The hundred or more times I'd already answered this question, I did so by just answering,..."what's done is done. There is nothing I can change about what happened, so why even ask?"...and the tone I used to answer said "subject closed, end of conversation".

But to my surprise, I heard words coming from within me and off the end of my tongue that I had never even thought of nor ever heard before.

"Well, I'll tell you how it is. If there was a war, and I was called by my country to fight, I would take a close look at the situation. If I decided the cause was a just one, I would go to war. But if upon seeing the situation as unworthy or unjustifiable, I would refuse to go. And you know what would happen then?"

Joe holds his sandwich in two hands in front of himself as if to take a bite but has stopped eating. "No. What would happen?"

I am experiencing my self and Joe from the perspective of a third person. From some space and time outside the both of us, I watch the answer unfold on its own.

"Well, I'll tell you what would happen. If I refused to fight for my government, they would send someone after me. I would be forced to march off to the war they support or I would be forced into prison. Forced. And you know what would happen then?"

Still holding the sandwich in suspension of eating, Joe answers, "No. What would happen?"

"Then there would be a war on my front step, because there is no difference in me traveling half way around the world to kill someone for what my government believes in, then me killing someone on my front step for what I believe in!"

Joe says nothing but I can see his brain trying to compute who I have become.

From the vantage point of being outside of my body watching and hearing all this take place, I see Joe is still holding his sandwich before himself as if he is frozen in space and time. The snow outside the shop is a full blown winter storm, complete with howling winds and strangely enough, lightning. The shop lights go out and I am glad the world has disappeared. In the dark Joe says, "Let's call it a night."

****

Question Number Three

Next evening several of the shop's regulars are sitting on stools gathered around the coffee pot. George Ward is talking about his newly purchased bird dog, an English setter costing George five thousand dollars. Roughly the same amount the government paid in insurance for the death of a soldier in Vietnam...*"what'll it be Mamma? Do you want the cash for the death of your son or would you like this fine bird dog?"*

George is complaining how the dog is having trouble learning a new lesson he is trying to teach it. It seems every time the dog is let loose in the house, the first thing it does is to go straight to the garbage and spread it over the floor.

Jerry, who is sighting down the ventilated rib of a new Winchester trap gun sarcastically comments, "You'd think a dog that costs five grand would know better."

Earl the salesman, trying to contain himself, starts laughing and has a choking fit from the coffee that goes down the wrong hole of his throat. The rest of the group have a good loud laugh on George who holds his head a little higher and acts as if he is above the fun had at his expense.

The laughter even gets Wayne Barter to snicker. Wayne's short, wiry frame is always dressed in worn hunting clothing. He has the bright blond hair of a teenager although his age is sixty-something and considers himself the hunter's hunter. He has made a living from hunting by selling game meat, illegally. His main objective is body count when it comes to the hunt. He senses the timing of the group and in the lull of the laughter starts in on a tale of the best hunting dog there ever was.

Attached to the entrance door to the shop is a small bell that rings when a customer enters. I hear its signal and leave the story circle to wait on the customer who has entered.

Immediately I smell liquor. A squat, broad-shouldered, red-faced man slams the door shut and stands where he has entered. He is staring directly into the long row of racked guns. A particular piece has caught his blood shot eyes. I ask him if I may assist him with something but he doesn't hear me. His inebriated body slightly weaves, he stands transfixed, talking in a private whisper to himself. I watch him carefully.

The group of regulars are deep in storytelling and chuckle among themselves. The newly arrived customer is in his own world. The look on his face and in his eyes is that of someone who has just discovered a long lost acquaintance standing in front of them. He walks in slow steps of disbelief at his discovery. His arms outstretch as he approaches the rack of rifles. Halfway down the row he reaches into the rack and gingerly lifts out a thirty-caliber M-1 military carbine. He holds the weapon at a "present arms" position and looks at me for the first time since he has entered the shop. His face spontaneously displays both disbelief and hope. He speaks in low tones and closely examines the carbine he dearly holds in his hands. I realize he is talking to the weapon.

"I can't believe you're here. Two-two-one-eight-six." He looks at me with a start.

"This is mine. Me and this baby were in Korea together. It's my old partner. Right here on the breech. The serial number 22186. I carried this baby. I slept with this baby. From Pusan to Inchan to…" His speech mumbles off to foreign distances and visions known only to him. He holds the carbine close to his breast. Out of the distance of his stare a few tears run down his red cheeks.

"Tired…cold…my baby…my bad girl…another ridge…tired… cold…cold." His voice sobs gently. He lies down on the gunshop floor and wraps himself around the weapon. "My baby…my girl…" He holds the carbine tightly against his body and gyrates and rubs his crotch against the wooden stock and metal receiver. "Oh baby, oh my poor baby…"

The group of regulars, George, Jerry, Earl and Wayne have come over and gather around the customer who now humps the carbine and whispers sweet nothings in its muzzle. He is lost in a time forgotten but to himself. He loves and lusts on the one thing that gave him memory of an experience known only to combatants. He lies there on the floor moaning in pain and pleasure steadily giving alternative meaning to a soldier humping.

"Somebody throw some water on him," snickers Wayne.

"Get a two by four and I'll break them apart." laughs Earl uneasily.

"Leave him alone damn it! Break it up. Get away from him!" I yell, throwing shock into them all. Without word they disperse and return to the coffee pot area.

I gently shake the sad soldier's shoulder. He responds with a start and realizes the compromising situation he has put himself in. His face reddens even more.

"Come on, let's get ourselves up," I encourage him to his feet. He hands me the carbine but can't take his eyes off it. "It's mine you know?"

I lead him to the shop door and open it for him to leave. He takes one long last look toward the weapon and says, "She saved my life." He sighs crestfallen and with heavy feet walks out the door and gets into an old Chevy pick-up. He starts the engine and drives off without a glance backward.

I close the door and listen to the small bell ring until its vibration stops. I look over at the regulars. Each holds a cup of cold coffee in his hand. Every silent eye sticks itself on me. I pay the regulars no mind and go to my position behind the sales counter.

The group awkwardly shifts around and settles back into their previous seats. There is a moment of quiet then wiry Wayne asks, "How about you Lee? Did you see any action in the war? Were you in combat?"

"Yea, I did. I was." I say no more and go to the front window of the shop and reverse the 'open' sign to 'closed'. The group watches me as I empty the cash register to tally the day's take.

Wayne gets off his stool and walks over to the counter I stand behind. He grins like he is about to do something he considers smart. The others watch us.

"Lee?"

"Yea? What is it Wayne?"

"Would you answer a question for me?" He leans closer to me as if to share a secret. He looks to his left then his head turns to look at the group of regulars to his right. There is an unspoken eager acknowledgment from the group. He then motions for me to come closer to him. I lean across the counter impatient with his antics. He searches my face then asks, "Did you kill anybody in the war?" He straightens up and stands in a posture of waiting. I look to the men around the coffee pot and see them also lying in wait for my answer.

"Wayne, I'll answer your question, but first, would you mind answering a question for me?" I speak candidly and loud enough for everyone to hear. I know he won't mind. No one ever has before.

"Yea, okay. Ask away!" He feels relieved that he has asked *"THE BIG QUESTION"* and somewhat smug in having done so.

"Okay," I say. I motion him closer as if to share an intimate moment, then in the most forceful combat clear voice I reply, "TELL ME WHAT THE FUCK IT IS WITHIN YOU THAT WANTS TO KNOW! TELL ME!" I am holding my fist in his face and burning a hole through him with my intention. "TELL ME, GOD DAMN IT!"

He gives me an incredulous look and backs away. The regulars start to fidget. Earl the salesman is the first to move.

"Time for me to get home. See you fellows later." He grabs his coat and goes quickly out the door.

The others, George, Jerry and Wayne all uneasily give an excuse to say their good-byes and go out the door shutting it quickly behind them. I stand alone and listen to the door's bell as it vibrates its ring through the empty air…

Have you ever wanted to know what it is like to kill somebody?
Why? for the love of god…Why?

Prayers

Lock and load. Take three balloons (approx. nine doses) of Asian white, carefully tear each open and pour white powdery contents into a tablespoon. Add eight cc's of water and gently stir with tip of clean pen knife blade until mixture becomes clear. Hold spoon over the flame of three matches until mixture momentarily boils then remove from flame. Repeat being careful not to spill contents. Take a very small piece of cotton and roll between finger tips until you have a cotton ball half the size of a BB. Place cotton ball into the solution in spoon. Set the spoon on firm surface then place the point of a ten cc syringe gently into the small cotton ball in the solution in the spoon. Slowly draw back the plunger of the syringe to suck all the contents of spoon into it. Add two or three drops of water into the spoon and using the needle's tip, run the cotton ball around the spoon's surface to collect remaining fluids. Remove cotton from needle. Hold the syringe with the needle tip facing toward the sky. Draw the plunger to the ten cc mark. Tap the syringe with your fingers to make sure any air bubbles in the solution float upward toward the needle's tip. Then carefully push the plunger inward so as to remove all the air from the syringe allowing a very, very small amount of solution to escape from the needle tip. If you have followed these instructions carefully you now have enough prepared heroin to kill a horse…

****

Have you ever played with Death? Have you ever taken any action that rushed you to Death's door? Have you ever had IT run at you then stand laughing in your face only to turn and walk away from you? Ever had Death violently snatch away everyone around you? Did you shake in your shoes? Piss yourself? Shit your pants? Feel positively excited?

****

IT is a star struck, dark moonless night on the chilly slopes of Mauna Kea. I and my platoon of soldiers of Bravo Company sit circled within the warm amber glow of a keawe fire. We are quiet. Burning hardwood snaps and cracks sending swirls of sparks whirling into the ethers of the universe as the earth, Aina, spins through the Milky Way. After several months I have been tested and accepted by these Hawaiian men, my "bruddahs." They take soldiering as a way of life. Ancestral warrior blood runs in their veins. Each day we train for battle to prepare ourselves for the ultimate. I sit on the dirt meditating as the firelight dances in my eyes.

The men are conversing in low melodic tones. It's a frequency that resonates with the most subtle vibration of life.

"What's it going to be like, Sarge?" A question from one for the many.

"Huh?" I stir from my ephemeral nothingness.

"What's it going to be like to be in the middle of combat?"

I look around me into the Polynesian faces alight with the fire's glow. Behind all the eyes I see the eager egos glorious for the enlightenment of mortal combat. I hold the moment's pause then answer straight out.

"You're going to be scared shitless."

"No Brah! No!" Doubt uproots them. Knocked into a psychic imbalance, they don't want to believe it. The thought of being afraid makes them afraid. They can't imagine it. Without having been there, no one could. I continue.

"Oh you *will* be afraid, but if you're a good soldier, it won't matter. You'll be scared beyond anything you've ever known and fear will become your companion. Fear will be by your side. Together you will throw yourselves into the foray. It's either that or you will wilt into a puddle of your urine and cry for your mama. Guaranteed!"

The men are still shaking their heads in disbelief. Some of them turn their backs to the fire and walk away fighting revulsion at the periphery of their personal darkness.

Personally, I relish confronting the fear of death for it was this fear in battle that shot me out of myself into previously unexperienced dimensions and into a realm of perfect peace. A reality where every worry or fear I ever had seemed wonderfully, clearly, perfectly ludicrous.

My life has been so changed by this experience that for years afterwards I put myself in the most fear producing situations again and again hoping to be propelled out of my everyday numbed existence into freedom's bliss. Fear is the vehicle.

****

So I sit on the bathroom floor, insensate about my lack of feelings other than the occasion of rage, depression and numbness. Nothing excites me anymore. Nothing moves me. The thrill of flying by helicopter into a battle could never be matched. The excitement of standing straight on as the enemy shot at you and you fired back now only relived in errant dreams.

To lose my numbness I have become an Epicurean of fear. Eventually I feared my numbness. Not an exhilarating fear but a leaded fear that said as a normal human being I was fucked.

My realization of my predicament came when my son was born. I had left the hospital waiting room to go to the lavatory. While I was taking a piss into a urinal, the doctor came in and brightly exclaimed, "You have a son!"

Nothing within me stirred. Absolutely nothing. The doctor's smiling face turned to a puzzled look.

"Oh," was my only reply. What was supposed to be a blessed event only revealed the nihilistic depth of my being and I suddenly dreaded my existence.

That was a year and a half ago. Now my common law wife Diane has taken my son Nicky and left me. *We never have anything, she says.* Alone. *It takes time to make a stake in life, I say.* So what. *I'm tired of sitting around the house while you're gone all day, she says.* Be patient. *I work all day. We have food. You have a car, I say.* It don't mean nothing. *I want to go back East. I hate the mountains, she says.* And I was tired of feeling nothing. *Look. You go to work and earn us a living. I'll stay at home and raise our son, I say.* A life of numbness has no value. *Oh, you'd like that wouldn't you, she says.* I longed for that long ago feeling of peace and well being that I knew Death held for me. *I'm doing what I can, I say.* Struggle.

So I sit on the bathroom floor holding the syringe in my right hand. I squeeze my left hand open and shut several times and pump my forearm back and forth. The veins in my left forearm bulge, my blood thick and full of a life not worth living. I think of the line from the Beatles's song, *"Happiness is a Warm Gun. Bang. Bang. Shoot. Shoot..."* I stick the needle into the plump blue vein and slightly draw back the plunger. Rich red blood rolls to the inside of the syringe mixing with the pale solution of heroin. *"When I hold you in my arm I know no one can do me no harm. Bang. Bang. Shoot. Shoot."* I play with the plunger and push it in slightly. Immediately an ashen taste of bitterness coats the back of my throat. I push the plunger in a little further. *I'm scared I'm going to die.* Honey-coated hot waves of euphoria saturate every atom of my being. *Now is the time.* I shove the plunger to its base...*I'm sorry Hein, I'm sorry Sam, I'm sorry Gai, Hyak, Yubi...*

****

Several hours later I partly regain consciousness but the heroin has squeezed my pupils so tightly I am blind. The darkness is warm. The tile floor I sit on is cool. I feel my back against the wall I lean on. I feel the syringe still hanging in the cradle of my forearm. A gentle breeze floats through my every pore. I fly in formation with a dozen other people across a brilliant blue sky above a turquoise sea. I hunger to be in the water. Like a school of fish the souls I fly with spontaneously respond and we dive, soaring downward and plunge into the sea. Immersed in the aqueous, we glide effortlessly in our continuing flight. Easily, comfortably, I deeply breathe in the water and I am nourished, soaring through the undersea, smoothly like a breeze across silk. I am alive! I am alive!

****

"Shiiit!" I moan as I struggle to my feet. My eyes look through the grayest of haze. I recognize the porcelain sink, turn on the faucet and cup my hands beneath the water's flow. Again and again I splash the water into my face. Slowly my vision, although blurred, returns. A salty residue coats my throat. My guts cry nausea. I kneel before the toilet bowl and wrench, pondering what to do now that it's come to this. In my mind there is rummaging.

"How did I get here?" I ask myself. *Because of what you know!* This voice! I must be turning psychotic. I am here because of what I know? I sigh. Without reservation I have to agree it is true. If what I know has brought me to this moment then it is obvious I need to learn something more, something new, for I have arrived at my present predicament operating under the knowledge I possess. It is starkly apparent to me that I need to expand the information my head holds. *You need a teacher!* How? Where? When?

When was the last time you felt your life was over? The voice again.

It's three A.M. Sunday morning. I've got nowhere to be and nothing to do. I guess I'll sit on the bathroom floor and somehow figure this out. Okay, so was there a time before when I felt like my world had come to an end?

The heroin captures me dream-like. I feel as though every atom of my being scatters throughout the universe. Ethereal. *The War!* A feeling of endless falling suddenly coalesces my atomized being back into solidity. Yea, the war. It's been four years since I've given any conscious thought to it. Outside of the nightmares I kept the experience buried.

But now I recall times in battle when men were dying around me and the enemy was trying to overrun me and I was screaming aloud, "This is it! This is it!"...Yes, it was a time when I thought my life was over. Yet here I am. I didn't die. I survived it. What was it, how did I get myself through it?

As my mind slowly sucks out the memories even the heroin can't subdue the climbing adrenaline levels the forming recollections bring.

God! What a rush! A few feet over my head fifty-one caliber fire is tearing through and exploding tree trunks into splinters. AK-47 fire from dozens of NVA soldiers in the jungle vegetation to our front, who are attempting to flank us, kicks up dirt around me. I fire back. Across the tree tops F-4 jets and Cobra helicopters rumble, firing cannon rounds at enemy in the open. I am screaming into the radio, to the pilots, the enemy's positions. Cluster bomb canisters falling from A1E Skyraiders rip open and spread metal finned, yellow baseballs of deafening deadly detonations. The noise is surreal. An enemy B-40 rocket round hits a big tree next to the bomb crater the four of us take our last stand in. I sporadically drop the radio's handset in the dirt to fire at NVA soldiers to my right. *Shit! They're getting into flanking position.* I crouch on my knees in the dirt of the crater's berm trying to make myself small enough so my backpack will cover me from small arms fire. I pick up the handset. I'm taking fire on three sides. I'm shooting my CAR-15 and yelling into the handset, "They're closing in. Bring your fire onto us. Bring your fire onto us. You have my permission to bring the goddamn fire onto us!...

THIS IS IT! Heaven rips open. *THIS IS IT!!* Fire and jagged hot metal roar and whine from its gates. *THIS IS IT!!!* Gai, Hyak, Kinnear and I huddle face together in the dirt of the crater's center. Explosive concussions pummel us. The ongoing noise is beyond comprehension. Explosions assault the Earth. She screams, tears at Her face and hair and like us cannot escape. Chaos, fucking Chaos. I shriek a prayer. It plunges into my personal abyss and out through the erupting universe around me. *Help me! Please help me. Somebody, something, somewhere. PLEASE FUCKING HELP MEEEE!!!!!*

I prayed. I remember in my worst moment. I prayed.

I certainly wasn't a religious person nor did I feel anything spiritual to life. I didn't know to whom or what I prayed. But I prayed and here I am. Alive by all definitions. Fucked up but alive. It worked then maybe it will work now…

I recall the depths in that moment of Death kicking in the door. I recall the deepness within myself and the overwhelming Infinite engulfing me. And my prayer penetrating it all. Being answered.

First light scratches on the bathroom window. I look up from where I sit on the floor and quietly, so quietly, into the depths of myself and out into the spaciousness of life around me, I begin praying again, over and over and forever over. *Please teach me. Please teach me. Please please teach me how to be a good man…*

A Father and No Son

"Look at me Dad! Look at me!" *The pain comes telling me it needs healing. I look.*

I hear my son's cry and look up from the task of washing the family car. He cries out in glee. "Look at me Dad!"

I look and am hit with sudden terror. I watch my bright and courageous three and a half year old son, seated on a tricycle, careen past me on a steep downhill lane dead-ending in a cul-du-sac. He has his feet lifted in the air off the riotously spinning pedals, his small soft hands grip the handle bars securely and his head bends round with a face full of joy and laughter, '…Look at Meee, Dad!!'

I run like a man on fire three feet behind the accelerating tricycle and my laughing son. He doesn't see that in less than a few seconds the tricycle he rides will crash into a concrete abutment at the lane's end. His face is bright with laughter, mine must be filled with horror and desperation as I strain with all my being to get my extended arm and hand to him. *Life and Death.* Nick laughs harder. *I disappear.*

At a pace as fast as I can run, the tricycle crashes into the concrete abutment…In the lawn of the yard beyond the road's concrete end, I lie on my back. My son sits on my belly and is laughing uncontrollably. *I realize we are safe.* I am angry and upset. I am dead serious explaining to him the danger he was in but he is in a blissful joy of consummate giggles and laughter.

I clearly see the perfect state of his present existence. Innocent of fear and painless. I lose my anger and momentary need to educate him. I look at his joy and let it infect me. We laugh. Father and Son…

****

"For the longest time Brooks, I wouldn't even use the word 'my' son. I was the father of a child. I wouldn't, couldn't say, I 'have' a son. 'My' son.

And I guess I did it because I knew I couldn't 'possess him' or 'own him.' The war taught me that you can't possess or own anything. Life as you know and experience it is here one moment then gone the next. If you hold onto it, part of you suffers."

I can feel Brooks taking my words in. I sense his connectivity with me and my stupid fucking anguishes. Somehow I feel he was born for me and the other combat veterans that talk to him. He wonders if I realize that the man who knows he owns nothing cannot be owned?

"What does this non-ownership do for you?" asks Brooks who sits in his big body and chair. I feel his heart outdoes the size of them both.

I pause…for twenty-some years…because before now I didn't believe I could admit that I didn't want the responsibility. I guess selfishness is made no less the crime through a guilt that sometimes disables me…

"Brooks, there is something in me, some part of myself that is like the fire-tender of a steam locomotive. The fire he tends keeps a vigilant effort at continued self-wounding. Guilt. But the tender is more like a brakeman to feelings of well-being." I chuckle in the midst of my embattled anguish.

I have crossed the battlefields of guilt caused by making decisions that resulted in friends being killed. The guilt of killing. The guilt of living. And now I find myself journeying further, following the familiar marked path that leads to the recorded pains of life. I excavate.

"Brooks. Do you remember me telling you about what I felt when my son was born? *Congratulations! You have a son! I feel nothingness. Oh!? Empty without response.* God, how frightening that was! But later there was a change."

We were living in Colorado. Nicky was six months old. Every morning at five I would rise for work. After I dressed I would go to his nite-light lit room. Most times he would be asleep and I would wake him by gently rubbing his back. Other times I would softly lullaby his name luring him to wake. Sometimes he would already be awake standing at the rail of his crib and waiting with a beaming face. I would raise him with my hands out of his crib and hold him in my arms. I'd talk softly as if he understood every word. He giggled and smiled and pumped his pajama-covered little body and limbs in movements of joy. For a few minutes, father and son. I would place him back in his crib (he preferred on his belly) and gently rub his back until he fell asleep. For many months, in the wee hours of every working morning, we began our day this way.

But one morning was radically different. *I awoke feeling radiant, deeply in love.* And I remember an accompanying happiness. I was a father in love with his son…What a wonderful morning that was…

****

There was a period of time during my weekly visits with Brooks that I would bring a large beach towel with me. In my sessions with him I discovered there were 'events' from the war for which I had need to grieve. I knew I had to cry and found it nearly impossible to do.

"Today we're going to get at it, Brooks!" I would announce on many a different day and show him my towel like it was proof. A mission. To cry. To wail from the battle within.

I pursued my pain as much as I could, but all I ever mustered in his office were one or two tears, then the emotional spigot would choke off. Numb. Slightly frightened. *Why does a warrior fear crying?* It seemed so silly and stupid to fret over events that occurred more than a dozen years ago. And now delving into the loss of 'my' son another wound that needs healing. For how long does the human condition for suffering extend?

I remember experiencing enormous relief and an immense feeling of freed-up space in my heart and chest when I was finally able to grieve and cry over some of the losses I experienced in Vietnam. I need to cry again.

Perhaps I am owning the pains of losing my son rather than face the deeper hurt of having let him go. But I felt I had to. The only other choice was to be engaged by his mother's creation of disharmony she perpetuated and overtly blamed me for. *"It's not good for you to be around him!"* So I left. I couldn't fight the false calls to the police, the stealing of him from my sight and touch when I came near. It was too painful. And I couldn't live with the separation, so I had to realize I couldn't own 'a son'. If I couldn't own him then I could never lose him.

****

I think I would rather relive the experience of war than suffer the heart's loss of love. I cannot possess anything. I can only experience it. And experience it I must.

Leave No Man Behind

We will tell you exactly what we have decided. We will not be persuaded by our country nor by anyone else because it seems one receives no good by fighting in unjust causes. You can stay at home or you can fight all day. Equal pay you will earn. You can be a coward or you can be brave. Equal honor you will share. Death is coming if you shirk. Death is coming if you work. We found no spiritual profit in the unbearable suffering of risking our lives in neurotic politicians' godless wars. We are the starving children who gave a hungry mother country every morsel of bread they could find and came away with less ourselves. (a paraphrase of Homer's Odysseus during the siege of Troy)

****

The last several months of group therapy have not come easy. Everyone in the room has gotten a chance to tell his story. But they tell it like it happened to someone else. Now we have to feel the story. I feel like I've been on this emotional patrol awhile, deep now into those areas of truth and I've been where these guys are at the moment. Emotions threatening to release. You are doing everything possible to keep them at bay. Not just the emotions of anger and rage, but the pain, guilt and grief that fuel them.

There is an unspoken grief the group as a whole is currently avoiding. Two of our members have met untimely deaths. The first to die was Sam Kakina, a pure blooded Hawaiian. Sam had been an infantry soldier when in the war. He was a father and husband who worked hard in the service industry and worked harder to understand his feelings that made day to day living an added burden. It is common for those men of Asian or Polynesian decent to feel guilt at killing people who looked like them. "Like killing a part of myself, my people" he would say. Sam died after complications during hemorrhoid surgery at the VA. The other death was Jimbo's, another infantryman, who like some others in the group held great shame at their unit's systematic burning of villages and consequent civilian casualties. Jimbo was from the hills of Tennessee. A poor white boy who one night chose the biggest mango tree on South Kona Road to crash his little Nissan into.

So the group, unable to admit pain, focuses on incoherent rowdiness and one-upmanship over who did the most outlandish stunt while in the war. Everyone is talking at once. I think no one is listening but me. In the cacophony I hear a quiet single voice…

"I feel like crying, but I'm afraid if I do I'll never be able to stop," says someone in the chaos of all the avoiding of the real issue that flies around the room. Repressed emotions bounce off the walls, careen around us but can find no portal of exit. In each man, even those medicated to some level of non-involved comfort, feelings strain to be expressed.

****

Most soldiers serving in Vietnam were just out of adolescence or in its final stages of development. In the circles of psychological theory, it is held that the influence of social context, during and after this developmental period, heavily weighs its imprint on the individual's psychology.

Imagine this: you are conscripted by an authoritarian power into a society that imposes the rigor of preparing for direct participation in warfare. This is a time when most adolescents are individually stepping into the waters of the world at large. During this time identities are solidified and tested in the given social context. Normally this is a period of learning to be responsible in supporting yourself with employment, learning how to interact with the immediate social environment and searching for the peer group within which you will function.

The first step taken into the society of the military imposes a de-identification of any previously learned self. Your head is shaved. No face hair is allowed. You will wear a uniform identical with everyone else. You will not speak unless spoken to. You will do what you are told or suffer physical, emotional and mental consequences for your taking initiative to be an individual.

Then your daily life will be subjected to purposely arranged twists and turns in expectations. Training to expect the unexpected. You will be pushed to limits you will learn to go beyond, because life is about your survival. Your need to survive is what the training all points to. Combat. Kill or be killed.

You will learn that use of force is a power that brings results. You will learn to use labels that de-humanize. You will learn that there is a time to kill. A time to kill. A time to kill. With your rifle, with your grenades, with your bayonet, with your bare hands…

And as an adolescent you will go forth into the world of war. Travel to distant exotic places, meet strange people and kill them. For whatever reason authoritative powers dictate.

You learn the world is a dangerous place. You learn that you are a pawn of others. You learn that you are expendable so others might impose their rule. And of course you may agree with it all, but then again you might not. Then what? Then what?

A Call to Arms

Fools bugled by the laughter of hell,
a herald to death in the unforeseen.

Righteous hearts, troubled minds,
Souls adrift beyond heaven's reach.

Pain's companion, wandering, warring youth,
led by patriotic lies.

Hallowed ground beneath each footstep taken
in search of the past path of being...

Carefree and young, peace of mind, rift of care.

Who would dare?
Who would dare?

****

A fist fight has broken out in the rap group. Miles, a foot soldier and Japanese-American from Hawaii and Dale, a helicopter door gunner and white boy from the East Coast, roll and wrestle on the floor. A fight from an argument over who got the most combat awards but really a fight to somehow, some-fucking-how get at the pain rooted deeply within themselves. Within seconds the other members of the rap group have separated them.

****

In 1967 military officers in the Surgeon General's office published a report on Combat Psychiatry. They presented statistics of medical evacuations during World War II, Korea and Vietnam. During Korea and the conflict in Vietnam, approximately five percent of all evacuations were for psychiatric or neurological reasons. In 1943, during W.W.II, psychiatric evacuations were at twenty three percent. In the early years of 1943 more soldiers were being discharged medically than were being inducted.

The military psychiatrist is in expedient position to easily conserve or diffuse manpower. During World War II, because command considered the psychiatric evacuations as weakening to the number of overall forces, they enforced a policy with a decree that… 'no discharges from service will be given for psychiatric reasons other than psychosis.' Although arbitrary and unpsychiatric, its affect did halt manpower loss. *[Amer. J. of Psychiat. 123: 7, Jan. '67]*

It is probable that this reasoning coming from upper command continued during the Korean and Vietnam eras. This may be the explanation for the much lower incidence of reported combat trauma during those wars.

****

This war comes packaged with a warning label: *Caution: Studies have shown there is greater than a 20% chance of becoming mentally disturbed by participating in this conflict.*

****

Our rap session is ended for the evening. Miles and Dale have shaken hands and come to realize that it isn't each other they are mad at. They understand that there is a common enemy that lies at the depth of their anger. It's called the government. They feel used by men who sought power and personal profit from the war. They've experienced chastisement by their country. We've researched about warriors of past wars and it is obvious the powers-that-be historically discredit and intentionally ignore any notion of war causing harm to the soul and psyche of men. War is business the powerful profit from and the conscripted suffer from…

Several years later Miles would lie down in bed and forever go to sleep with the help of a drug overdose.

Gray Dog Afternoon

The Yards and I are having a lazy day at Dak To. Thick gray clouds are at a ceiling of just a few hundred feet above our heads. It was raining heavily earlier this morning and the areas of unit operations in Southern Laos and Northern Cambodia are experiencing severe thunderstorms and rain, making airborne operations impossible. The recon teams in those areas are at the mercy of the 'socked in' weather. If there is any trouble for them, they will have to go it alone. Not a pleasant thought.

But for us, we endure the boredom of war, although an occasional 122mm rocket comes flying into our area. Such is life. It is early afternoon and the day bathes us in uniform gray light. The Yards sit atop one of the bunkers and play a game of cards with cigarettes as high stakes. The Vietnamese artillery compound behind us is quiet. In its watch tower I see two guards sleeping confidently. I am antsy.

"Hey Gai! How about some dog for dinner?" I interrupt the card game.

"Ho!" Gai answers and the other Yards turn their faces to me also. All their eyes open a little wider and a slight smile raises their cheeks. Dog is a delicacy for the Montagnards. "Where is dog?" asks Yubi. I entice them on. "Oh, I know, I know."

****

A few months ago when we were here at Dak To, two new Americans were assigned to fueling duty. A few hundred meters from our little compound are several large aviation fuel bladders that are surrounded by dirt berms. Two American soldiers are usually stationed at the Vietnamese artillery compound next to us. The Americans' job is to refuel the helicopters and aircraft that fly in and out of here. At night these guys sleep in the artillery compound, but in the daytime they have their own bunker near the end of the air strip to call home. Being neighborly, I went over to introduce myself to the newcomers. When I approached their bunker a little white dog came charging out and sunk its teeth into my calf. The bite bled. I yelled and the two soldiers hustled out of their lair. They scooped up their pet and made profuse apologies.

"We're sorry. He usually only goes after the indigenous. We're really sorry."

To say the least, I was a little pissed. The bite needed a bandage. I grin and bear it.

"I'm Sergeant Burkins. I'm over there in the special operations compound." I point across the runway. "I just wanted to introduce myself."

"Hi. I'm Slim and this is Rob." Mutt and Jeff I muse. "We're from Texas."

"Where you from?" I again point across the airstrip to my tiny compound.

"Over there." They appear confused. I have no intention of making new friends.

"We're really sorry about the dog."

"Don't sweat it. If you have any need for me and my men you know where to find us. Sometimes it rains rockets so identify as many holes in the area as you can." I'm not sure if they understand my meaning. I walk back across the runway to my area and plan to do some first aid to the dog bite…

****

The very next morning, before the sun comes up, I am in the watch tower of our perimeter. It's that time of morning when shapes materialize out of the darkness and what do my eyes behold but a little white dog sniffing around in the concertina wire. I switch off the safety of my carbine, take aim and POW! One clean shot echoes in the stillness. Before the dog stops twitching Yubi is in the wire and scooping up the critter. The rest of the Yards are awakened by the shot. They come up out of the bunkers. Yubi brings the dead dog into the compound. He and the Yards immediately start butchering the animal and preparing a fire. A large pot of water starts to boil. Pieces of dog and assorted dried vegetables are thrown in. The morning is chilly. Mists form along the ground. We huddle around the cooking fire's warmth. The Yards giggle and fuss with each other in delight. Dog soup for breakfast.

****

Later that afternoon one of the refuelers, Slim, comes over to our compound. The Yards are a mean looking bunch and Slim stops short of the gate uncertain of what is going on here. "It's okay guys, he's one of us," I say. "What's up Slim?"

In a long Southern drawl he asks, "Have you seen my dawg?" Gai looks at the other Yards and interprets for them. Immediately they all make like they are busy with something else.

"No Slim, can't say that I have."

"Well, if you happen to see him would you let us know?"

"Sure Slim. Will do." I can hear the Yards trying to stifle their laughter.

Slim looks and sounds really sad. He turns to leave. I feel bad (just a little), and deem I have to make some kind of amends to the twinge of guilt.

"Hey Slim, while your here, do you want some soup?"

****

The Yards are biting to my gambit. "Dogs. I know where there is a dog. You like some dog soup?"

Gai responds. "You know we like dog. Where is the dog?"

I point to the far east end of the runway where there is a large plain of scrub brush and grass.

"Out there. Come on. Tell the men to grab their weapons and a bandoleer of magazines. We're going hunting."

Gai gives the orders. Deng and Boon stay behind to guard the compound. I have Gai, Hyak, Yubi and Diu load up in the back of the 3/4 ton pick up truck. This vehicle is equipped with straight pipes, no mufflers. It has a rag top and runs like a bat out of hell. We use it to move rockets and other armaments around the airfield when we have to reload the gunships. Today we are going to use it to drive the wild dogs out of the brush. I fire up the engine. "Lock and load", I yell to the Yards. "And hang on!"

I pull on to the runway and race down it towards the field. The engine's pipes roar like a stock car. We hit the end of the runway and dash into the grass and scrub field. The Yards are whooping it up like cowboys. I smash the truck into the short scrub brush. The vegetation folds and crumples underneath the running boards. I drive a pathway of lazy "S's" through the bush. After a while of careening around the field, a short-hair brown and black dog darts out to our left. I gun the engine and race after it. The Yards open fire with their CAR-15's. Bullets kick up dirt around the fleeing dog. It zigs. I turn the truck to follow. The vehicle bucks and we bounce around in it. We hoop and holler. The Yards keep shooting. A bullet finds its mark. The dog flips paws over head. I quickly brake the truck. The Yards leap out of the back before the vehicle slides to a complete stop. They run to where the canine lies. Hyak reaches it first. He holds the kill up for all to see. Hyak beams a large white smile across his dark brown face. The other

Yards do a spontaneous little victory dance. The gray day shares our good fortune.

Hitting the Wall

"Are you going to go visit the traveling 'Wall' in Hilo?" Brooks asks.

"No. It's not the real thing." I answer uneasily.

The Wall. The black granite memorial that's a tribute to the dead soldiers of the Vietnam war. It sits in a hole in the ground in Washington, D.C. exposed like a desecrated grave. The traveling 'Wall' is a scale replica of the original. The traveling 'Wall' has come to Hilo, Hawaii and I am adamant about not visiting it. No way.

****

I walk across the sprawling green grass field of Hilo Park. Behind me the sun shines in a blue sky and thc sea rolls gently in the bay. Inside me feelings of uncertainty weigh heavily. I slow my walk as I approach the 'Wall'. I stop. I can't bring myself any closer than this. A hundred meters from where I stand a long, low, shiny black triangle stretches across the green grass of the park. A plethora of palm trees and birds-of-paradise plants serve as a backdrop to the black granite memorial. Etched in the Wall's face along its entire length are the names of the 58,000 people who were killed in the war. A few veterans, wearing jungle fatigues, walk slowly, almost reverently, along the black walls with their friends or families, searching for a name they know. Their fingers touch the black stone and trace the engraved letters as if they were touching the owner of the hallowed name. A few individuals stand unmoving and stare deep into the Wall's reflection.

I decided to come here when I realized it was my fear that kept me away and it is fear and uncertainty that now keep me at a distance of several hundred feet from the Wall. I take a labored breath and move a little closer still. I feel the ocean's soft breeze at my back.

A tall familiar figure standing near the Wall's apex looks in my direction and begins walking towards me. It's Michael Cowan, one of the vets from the rap group. He reaches his hand out to me. I take it firmly. "Hi, I'm Michael." He doesn't recognize me. He came into the group just before I left it. As a matter of fact he was partly the reason I left the group. He quickly commandeered all attention in the sessions. For the first time ever, he had a chance to talk openly about the war with other vets. An outpouring of need. To hear him talk, one would think he won the war single-handedly. "Hi Michael. I'm Lee."

"I see you were a member of Special Forces." He points to the green beret that sticks out of the pocket of the jungle trousers I wear. "You guys did some of the most dangerous work in the war." He says it with authority and sincerity. I just nod. "Have you been up to the wall yet?" I tell him I'm slowly building up the courage. "I understand brother." He lays his arm across my shoulder and says, "If you need me I'll be over there." He points to an information booth that several vets gather around. "I talk to you later." He turns and walks away.

Michael ambles toward the information booth. He takes a seat and begins the task of helping vets locate a name on the memorial. I take a deep strained breath and move another step closer to the 'Wall'. *Right foot.* Then another. *Left foot*. And another. *Right foot*. I am moving forward but the walk is like a dream. No matter how many steps I take, the Wall remains out of my reach. My thoughts float in a dilation of time. I think how much Michael has changed. He was a latecomer to the group sessions. I immediately recognized him as a bearded street person I had seen dumpster diving around Kona town. He was an Oklahoma farm boy who had been raised by loving folks and instilled with the idea of someday becoming governor of the state. Military service was a planned step in his political career.

Michael came into the group like he had just gotten off a helicopter fresh from the chaos of battle. His eyes were wide open with fire. His long arms waved in the air accentuating his story. Michael was recently released from a mental hospital where he was sent by a judge after shooting a Hell's Angel biker. His court case was nationally famous. After shooting a man a Vietnam veteran had been judged insane by reason of war.

****

Only several days after leaving Vietnam and the military, Michael and a good friend of his went to a bar in California for a drink. They had a few beers then decided to go elsewhere. Michael went to the bathroom while his friend walked out to their car in the parking lot. Outside his friend was confronted by a group of bikers who quickly proceeded to beat him unconscious. Michael came out and saw his friend on the ground being kicked and beaten. He ran into the midst of about twenty bikers and tried to help his friend whom he feared dead already. A biker pulled a .44 pistol and stuck it in Michael's face. Without a thought Michael snatched the weapon from the biker's hand. Point blank he shot the biker in the head. The rest of the bikers started running in all directions. Michael started screaming in Vietnamese and continued firing at the fleeing bikers.

The pistol empty, Michael picked up his unconscious friend, put him in the car and drove straight to the local hospital. Sitting in the emergency room Michael realized what he had done and called the police to turn himself in. He was arrested and charged with murder.

At his trial Michael was found innocent by reason of insanity. He was sentenced to serve an undetermined amount of time at the State Mental Hospital. It was instructed that the doctors 'make this man remember' everything that happened to him in Vietnam. After two years of time the docs had him talk about everything he could remember of war. Then they put him back on the street…He ended up in Hawaii living out of a dumpster and found his way into our rap group. In time Michael and I would become the closest of friends.

I watch this big bear of a man Michael gently talk to a vet who is looking for a name on the wall. Michael consults the book of the deceased, runs his finger down the page and says,.. "Here he his. Date of death: January, 14th 1968. Panel number 27." The names on the Wall are in the order in which they died. Michael scribbles the panel number on a piece of paper and hands it to the veteran. I walk up to the table and stand in front of Michael. "You've really changed," I say to him. He looks at me puzzled. "I was in the rap group, but I left it shortly after you arrived."

"Well I hope I didn't do anything to run you off," he smirks.

"No, I just needed to focus on the private session time I spent with Dr. Brooks," I say.

"Who are you looking for?" he asks. I give him the names of the friends who lost their lives. Michael looks them up and writes down the panel numbers. I suddenly get an undefined urge and take a sheet of paper and watch my hand write something down. Michael hands me the panel numbers and asks, "..are you okay?" I can't answer. I've fallen into a vacuum. Michael is right in front of me but he looks and feels a million miles away. I turn toward the Wall and like a magnet to iron an invisible force pulls me along in undulating silence.

All along the Wall there are placements of flowers, pictures and notes. I find the panel I am looking for. I look for the names fearing to see my own. There they are: Hein, Pool, Wilson,...I take the paper on which I have written and tape it to the holy panel inscribed with my friends' names.

"...I am so sorry Chuck. I am sorry Sam. I am so sorry Gai, Hyak, Yubi, Diu, Boon, Deng, Bhun, Pei, Than...I am so sorry. I stand alone and quietly, covertly fight back my tears.

Suddenly there is the distinct feeling of chopper blades beating in my chest. My eyes start to the blue sky. If any sound reminds me of Vietnam it is the voodoo cadence of helicopter blades beating the air. *Fuck. What are they doing here?..* I am almost angry at their presence, the disturbing noise they bring. Here they come. Two of them, flying directly toward the memorial. They slow and hover above me and the long black grave. Then…thousands of flowers begin floating and falling from the belly of the choppers. Soft and fragrant Plumeria petals gently rain to the earth on me, the memorial and everyone else. Restrained tears work their way down my cheeks. In my ears the beating blades transcend to become the drums of ancient Hawaiian warriors. The flowers fall softly. My soul for the first time in years feels a little lighter. Only in Hawaii. Only in Hawaii.

The air ships have emptied of flowers. My mind and heart return to where I am. The receding beat of helicopter blades reminds me once more of being left in the jungle. I shake my head. The ground is covered in white, pink and red silky flower petals. Michael is standing at my side.

"Hey. Do you want to go have a drink? I'm living at the Hilo Hotel. There's a great bar there. It's right out of old Saigon. You'll love the place…"

I look at Michael. Between our eyes I look through the evident overlay of thousands of memories…"Sure. I could use a thirst-quenching iced-paregoric about now. How about you?" I chuckle. Michael isn't sure he heard me right. We turn and walk away leaving the flowered grave to the long war dead.

Torture

A faceless enemy unknown by his name, given Dink, Gook or something more inhumane…

****

I control the North Vietnamese soldier by the rope leash attached to his hands handcuffed behind the small of his back. A black cloth blindfold wraps across his eyes and ties behind his head causing his evenly cropped hair to bunch up like a broom head crown. He is a few inches shorter than me and slightly pudgy for an Asian. He wears a dark green cotton shirt and pant uniform. His tree bark brown feet remain bare. I keep my carbine pointed at the man's back. He lifts his chin and moves his head side to side as if trying to discern an unseen scent. His brow furrows and in his mind he worries for his future.

Several hours ago this well fed, healthy and free man was an enemy soldier driving his truck along the Ho Chi Minh Trail, transporting troops and materials of war in the obscurity of night. His misfortune was to be ambushed by one of our recon teams. His fellow soldiers were killed. He was captured. Towed along in bonds he cried and wept all the while the ambush team made their escape through the jungle night. Only after being pistol-whipped did he finally keep quiet.

I am the prisoner's armed escort. Along with me, Sergeant Plaster, the leader of the ambush team, Colonel Bushy Brows, the camp commander and a Vietnamese interpreter wait on the edge of Kontum airfield. A C-123 Hercules flight will land then fly us to Saigon and MACV-SOG headquarters where the prisoner will be interrogated.

As we wait I keep my eyes on the enemy soldier and notice he is fidgeting in place and making muffled whining sounds. Plaster adjusts the prisoner's blindfold and makes believe to arrange the POW's hair and uniform to make him 'presentable'. Colonel Brows' face belies a confused curiosity as he watches Plaster play fuss over the NVA.

Colonel Brows' uniform is crisp. His five o'clock shadow shades his large jowls. His jungle boots shine uncomfortably. The fluctuating wrinkles in his forehead perplex over the fact that only a few weeks ago he was assigned to a desk job in D.C. Because of some military/political failing on his part he now finds himself in command of a group of proud unconventional operatives. Men who wear no rank, insignia nor have concern for protocol. Having never been on the receiving end of a weapon or gotten dirt under his fingernails the Colonel is out of his league of command.

"Sergeant Plaster, what are you doing?"

"Just making the prisoner respectable sir," replies Plaster as he adjusts the NVA's collar. Plaster steps back and smiles admirably. The prisoner groans and squirms as he stands bound and blindfolded.

I know the prisoner is obviously discomforted at his situation but he increases his squirming and worming. I tell the interpreter to ask the enemy soldier what's up with the increasing body contortions.

"He says he has to go to the bathroom."

Plaster and I look at each other. The Colonel pretends to take an interested stare at something on the other end of the runway. The interpreter shrugs.

"I'm sure as hell not untying the motherfucker," I say. The prisoner wiggles and squirms more desperately.

"Tell the bastard to be still," Plaster commands the interpreter.

"Dong lai! Du mame! Dong lai!" The interpreter yells.

"Keep the fucker covered, Burkins."

The prisoner tries to resist but cannot do anything but squirm against submitting. Plaster grabs the POW by the pant waistline and begins unbuttoning the man's pants. The NVA wiggles and tries to move away from Plaster's manipulations. I grab the prisoner by the back of his shirt collar and hold him still. Plaster finishes unbuttoning the man's fly then reaches into the barn door and pulls out the North Vietnamese's dick. The blindfolded man turns several shades of red embarrassment.

"Tell him to go ahead and piss," Plaster orders the interpreter.

The interpreter speaks to the captive in his native tongue. The POW shakes his head back and forth in personal torment. After a long, low agonizing groan the prisoner lets flow a yellow steaming stream of piss. The blood red embarrassment on his face fades as he empties himself of nature's call. The Colonel stands to the side but watches out of the corner of his eyes.

When the prisoner finally finishes, Plaster gently takes him by the pecker and gives it a few healthy shakes. The NVA's face turns bright purple and soft whines leak from his throat. Plaster gives the man's dick a final quick shake and puts it back into his pants, buttoning them up. The NVA looks as if he is going to shit himself…Plaster tells the interpreter, "Tell the bastard I'm not going to wipe his ass…"

The Colonel stands his mouth and eyes agape. Plaster smiles and tucks the prisoner's shirt in and sets the gig line straight. At the end of the runway our flight drops onto the tarmac and roars to a stop in front of us. Its engines continue running as the back end of the aircraft lowers to allow our entry on. Plaster, the interpreter and I get on board with the prisoner. The Colonel stands off the runway shaking his head in disbelief.

The Hercules aircraft sucks its rear cargo door closed then pivots to align itself with the runway. It locks its brakes and revs its engines until the entire ship vibrates madly. Suddenly the aircraft lurches forward then accelerates even more as the pilot ignites the jet assist engines. The plane races down the short air strip and leaps nearly vertical up into the blue sky. Our air transport levels and speeds itself across the carnivorous green jungle below.

The prisoner sits at my side. He hangs his head. A few silent tears escape from under the blindfold. I look at him and feel a moment's compassion knowing that in Saigon his future will be a lot worse than having his dick shaken by an American soldier.

The War Room

Several of us vets from Doctor Brooks' rap group sit around the kitchen table in Michael Cowan's apartment. Michael, a forward observer in Vietnam, has taken the lead in organizing the combat veterans living on the island of Hawaii. Hanging on the wall in the kitchen is a sign that says it all:

"IF YOU KNOW YOU ARE RIGHT, THEN FIGHT!"

****

Truth is there has never been a war fought that has not been to increase the value of a country's dollar. It doesn't matter what intentions follow the original blow. The seminal intention in war is to gain economic influence and power at the expense of others. The greatest expense lies in human suffering.

****

Every war has produced its share of "hidden casualties," those who came home so debilitated mentally and emotionally crippled that their health would remain precarious for the rest of their lives.

After the Civil War, "irritable heart" syndrome, symptomized by palpitations, quick fatigue, shortness of breath, headache, dizziness, diarrhea, chest pains and disturbed sleep was often diagnosed as insanity. A label attributed to psychological casualties was the term, "nervous disease". Psychiatric problems accounted for six percent of Union Army medical discharges.

So great was the public outcry that Military Hospitals for the Insane were established in 1863. But after the Civil War's end the government closed the hospitals and no more effort was made to treat those soldiers afflicted with 'the stresses of combat'.

After the Vietnam War, soldier's who sought help for combat stress related disorders were told by the government that such claims had no merit. Consequently many of these men suffered alone.

But in 1983, due to continuing public pressure, Congress passed laws requiring the Veterans Administration to recognize, treat and adjudicate monetary relief for the veterans' claims related to combat stress.

****

Statistically, in Vietnam, approximately twelve percent of all military personnel participated in direct combat.

****

We vets are gathered at the 'War Room' in Michael's apartment to discuss the Veterans Administration's treatment of veterans. By federal law the VA is supposed to be an advocate for a veteran seeking relief. However, in Hawaii, the VA is doing every thing it can to thwart, stall and deny veteran's applications for entitlements. We are meeting to explore what choices we have in changing this situation.

"How in the hell are we going to get medical care for veterans if the goddamned VA's offices and medical center are located on the island of Oahu?" Chuck, a Marine, asks the question.

Currently VA policy requires a veteran seeking medical care to travel to Oahu. All the other islands have no VA services. Having to go to Oahu for help is expensive and time consuming considering several trips are required. Most veterans don't have the resources.

"Nobody listens to our arguments. The fuckin' bureaucrats laugh at us because we don't have any power," states Brian.

"We need to go over to Oahu and blow up a fucking building!", angrily quips Nash, one of our group. "That will get their fucking attention."

"No, we can't do that," I say. "That would make us just like the men who sent us to war. We've got to do it this way..." I hold up two thick paper back books. They are the Federal Code of Regulations, Title 38. "And this!" I hold up a copy of United States Code, Section 38, Veteran's Benefits and Entitlements. "We are going to learn the law. Then we are going to shove the law down their throats and pull it out their ass!"

"Precisely," says Michael. "Most of the bureaucrats at the VA are non-combatants. They were a bunch of desk jockeys during the war, they are desk jockeys now, and they treat us combat vets with disdain because they missed the opportunity to fight for freedom."

"That's right" adds Chuck, "they're a bunch of REMFS (rear echelon motherfuckers).

"The first step will be to get us some *bona fides.* We need to get us a position of power to function from. We're going to establish a Congressional Chapter of the Veterans of Foreign Wars. This will make us authentic. When we speak, we'll be heard. We'll use the letter head to get attention to our cause. This will establish us as legitimate." Michael makes his point.

There is some underlying uneasiness in the group. Joining what is known as an "institution" goes against our distrust of such groups.

"We will be the group. Our members will all be combat veterans seeking to right injustices against all veterans."

Michael is right. We need some bona fides.

****

Some two million men served in combat during World War I. "Shell shock" a state of depression, thought to be caused by brain concussion, disrupts a man's physiology. Because of shell shock, over 69,000 U.S. soldier's were permanently evacuated from the fighting. Nearly 36,000 men were hospitalized for lengthy periods of time because of this disorder. Eventually almost 160,000 soldiers were deemed psychiatrically unfit. "Shell shock" centers were created to treat psychiatric casualties. World War I shell shock cases accounted for over fifty percent of VA patients by 1942.

****

We began our mission of forming a chapter of the Veterans of Foreign Wars (VFW) in Kona, Hawaii. Almost immediately the Veterans Administration (VA) in Honolulu attempted to undermine our actions. They did their best to rally several military retirees (lifers: those having a one-track military mind) in Kona who believed, like the VA, that any psychological complaints due to combat were crap. These 'infiltrators' came to our organizational meetings and accused us of being cry babies. On more than one occasion the meetings came close to becoming a brawl. Our point was made one night when one of the vets screamed at the 'lifers' that any tears they saw in our eyes were "...tears of goddamned rage." Rage at the lies perpetuated by politicians to justify war and rage at the loss of our brothers' lives for someone to make a dollar.

We eventually formed our VFW chapter and got our Congressional charter, but it took more than a year of putting up with these 'disbelievers' who themselves would ultimately fall apart emotionally from the years they spent in denial of the horrors and pain they experienced in war.

We decided our war against the government and VA would be conducted like the Viet Cong waged war against the United States. Ours would be a war of attrition. We would wear the motherfuckers down. We would not give up. We would hit them with everything we could. We studied the law. We helped each other file our claims.

When we gained an inch we took a foot. When we lost a battle we let the powers that be in the VA in Honolulu know we were waiting for them to fuck up and that we were watching them.

****

Michael, Chuck and I sit under the shade of several large palm trees on the grass of the lawn that surrounds the Veterans Administration Regional Office. Inside the government building the 'adjudicators', the VA employees that hold power over a veteran's claim, gather to go to lunch in downtown Honolulu. They exit the doors of the monolithic VA building. Michael, Chuck and I sit in the shade and observe their movements. Then we follow them.

Within minutes we have quietly walked up behind the group of unsuspecting VA workers. When we are within a foot of their backs, the three of us scream as loud as we can, "HEY!" With the force of our voices we startle the group of a half-dozen individuals. They nearly jump out of their shoes and before they can regain their composure we grab their hands for a stern, friendly shake and launch our presence directly into their psyche, "HI, I'M MICHAEL,…I'M CHUCK…I'M LEE…WE'RE THE VETS FROM THE BIG ISLAND WHO ARE GOING TO MAKE YOU GUYS OBEY THE LAW. WE JUST WANTED TO SAY HI! SEE YOU LATER…" We turn and quickly disappear into the throngs of people on the busy city street…

****

Filing a claim for medical entitlements with the VA is a lengthy, time-consuming process. Once the initial forms are filed the veteran has to wait about four or five months for a response (veterans have been known to die while waiting for health care). Several of us from the rap group filed our claims. Six months have passed without word from the VA. In the meantime, we have been busy notifying Congressional leaders of the VA's non-compliance with federal regulations. In addition, we have made known the fact that of all the states, Hawaii has the largest number of veterans per capita and that Hawaii is the state with the least amount of accessible health care. We gain the ear of Congress. To our delight there is going to be a Congressional Inquiry into the VA health care system in Hawaii. Incoming!

****

The VA is out to fuck with us. Six months after filing our claims the VA notifies us that we vets who filed have missed our 'scheduled appointment' for evaluation. We were never notified of our appointment. The VA claims it sent notices to us. Bullshit! We are told we will have to re-apply which will take an additional six months of waiting for justice. We expected this from the VA. A delaying tactic to forestall our aim. If it's war they want, it's war they'll get.

****

Meeting directly with an adjudicator is an impossible task. They are the ones directly responsible for the process of a vets claim. If they fuck you over ('oh, sorry we lost your papers…') you can't get at them. Or so they think. Today we will penetrate their defenses…

****

We have managed to secure an insider within the VA bureaucracy. Our mole has provided us with the direct dial-in phone numbers of the adjudicators.

It is zero-seven-forty-five hours. In fifteen minutes our assault will begin. Michael, Chuck and I prepare.

We sit in comfortable lounge chairs outside Chuck's beach-side cottage. The morning air is fresh with ocean breeze. The sand beneath us shines golden. The bay's water is deep blue, calm and voiceless. Before our assault we check our equipment. List of secret phone numbers: *check.* An operable phone with dial tone: *check.* Colt .38, locked and loaded: *check.* Determination: *check.*

It is zero-eight-hundred-hours. Michael, Chuck and I look into each others' eyes with affirmation. The time has come. I pick up the phone's receiver. I dial the phone number of the head administrator at the VA. It rings. It is answered.

"Hello. Tiano here."

"Mr. Tiano, this is Lee Burkins, a veteran on the Big Island and charter member of the VFW in Kona." I also give him the phone number I am calling from.

"How did you get my number?"

"Several of our members got a letter from your office stating we missed scheduled appointments. The truth is the VA never notified the veterans of the appointment. We request to be quickly re-scheduled."

"Screw you guys. You got your congressional investigation. Now we got you. All you guys are going to have to re-file your claims and wait until we get around to processing them. Fuck you."

"Mr. Tinao, if you don't re-schedule these appointments,...***WE ARE GOING TO COME OVER THERE AND START KILLING PEOPLE!..*"** I scream into the phone then quickly hold the receiver out at arms length. Michael puts the .38 Colt alongside of the phone receiver and fires a round. ***BOOM!*** I slam the receiver down onto the phone's base. Chuck screams at the phone.

"Take that you motherfuckers!"

For a moment we three rest in the silence of a deserted beach and the fading echo of our gun shot. Then we break into hysterical laughter. When we have cleared the tears of joyous retribution from our eyes, I pick up the phone and dial another number. We repeat the tactic for the benefit of four other adjudicators. Once our calls have been made, we sit and quietly wait for the phone to ring.

Within twenty minutes of our 'request' we receive several phone calls from several different VA offices. All our appointments have been rescheduled.

****

Attention to WWI veterans' problems, particularly payment of pensions and medical care, reached a threshold in 1932 when an estimated 15,000 veterans marched into Washington D.C. to petition for justice. This first-ever mass demonstration in our nation's capital was dispelled after the unarmed veterans were attacked by the government's militia and several veterans were killed. Congress immediately passed legislation meeting veterans' demands for justice.

****

The inquiry of the Veterans Administration in Hawaii by the Congressional panel of Senators from Washington, D.C. was a huge success. Congress quickly provided funds to build new medical facilities on all the outer islands in the state of Hawaii. Also established were employment positions for over fifty new medical personel to man the treatment centers.

****

In World War II, the proportion of support troops to combatants was ten to one.

****

The stress on the heart, mind and soul of the soldiers of W.W.II was profound. Battle fatigue, sometimes called combat neurosis, troubled over one million men. According to Richard Gabriel in *No*

More Heroes: Madness & Psychiatry in War, more than thirty-seven percent of all W.W.II Army combat troops were discharged for psychiatric reasons. The minds and nerves fractured in battle possibly represented the greatest challenge to healing.

****

Today is my day of truth. I stand alone in a room used for "evaluation hearings" at the VA. I have arrived early for my scheduled appointment with three medical doctors, an adjudicator and an unknown party whose purpose is to oversee the actions of the hearing personnel. In truth, a yes-man of the higher powers in the VA.

The meeting room is ornately finished in heavy, dark woods. It resembles a court room. There is an American flag hanging silently on its short staff. I stand before it and journey deep into the feelings within me. Today I will demonstrate to these government bureaucrats the war that lives within me. As I stand before the flag of my country, my back is turned to the room and I ruminate. Behind me I hear the entrance of my judges come into the room. One by one they enter and take their seats at a large rectangular ostentatious desk. I keep my back to them and wait until I hear that everyone is in the room. I then stand silent looking at the flag for a good five minutes more. No one says a word. I make them wait. Before I turn to face them I open up my psyche and suck every goddamned bit of energy out of the room and men into me. I turn around.

Seated on one side of the long desk sit the doctors, the adjudicator and the yes-man. On the other side of the desk sits my representative from the Disabled American Veterans who will help me present my case to the VA. I take my seat beside him. One of the doctors immediately asks me a question.

"Mr. Burkins, how many guns do you own?"

Without hesitation I quickly come out of my seat, lean across the table into the doctor's face and yell, "What do you want to know for?"

My actions shock everyone. *Bam! Take that!* A psychic grenade detonates.

The doctor responds nervously, "Well…the number of guns a veteran owns…is in…direct relation…to how severe the PTSD is."

My DAV representative lays his hand on my forearm and gently restrains me.

"Take it easy, Lee."

Without withdrawing my intent from the bureaucrats I slowly sit back into my seat. I sit silent for a few moments.

"One." I answer. "I own one gun." *Never let the enemy know what your true firepower capability is…*

For nearly four hours they drill me about my tour of duty in Vietnam and my life after the war.

Warrior's Cry

It's been a month since I've seen or spoken to anyone. Doctor Brooks was my last contact with society and I've missed our last three scheduled sessions. I remain hidden in my sanctuary, locked behind numerous gates and at the end of a nearly impassable four mile long rocky driveway. My flower farm is my sanctum.

Sometimes it is so quiet here that the quietness can be heard. And beyond the quietness the stillness makes itself felt. I think I have been sitting on the floor of my cabin for days. My body has ceased to be capable of moving and my mind has stumbled into nothingness. Nothingness. I experience an overwhelming alone-ness in this nothing-ness.

Sun rises. Sun sets. Dew forms on petal. Rocks grow ever harder. I observe words recalling the past trying to realize the present…I am a bystander.

****

Once upon a time, I was a soldier. A military man who was highly trained in the art of battle. A member of an elite unit that endured many casualties in a war. I was trained and battlefield educated to overcome the greatest of odds. My personal power of mind and determination carried me through. When the war ended, I believed there was nothing in the world that could shake me or break me. Now that is being proved wrong…

My being a warrior defines certain aspects of life as an internal struggle with the daily use of power. Power being the ability to take action to get things done. The everyday, common social undertaking of the necessity of earning a living can sometimes be an uphill battle. The familiar ways in which we propel ourselves forward toward our goals may themselves become casualties. What then is the power that endures?

Making a living as a warrior is not quite the same as being a provider of services or a maker of goods. The providers and makers earn a monetary living by their trades' identities. Being a warrior is more of an attitude, philosophy and idea of ones' self-identity which in today's world is not readily financed. Soldiering is a paid military skill. But soldiers follow orders. Warriors know their duty. I like to think I know my duty, especially after having survived a real war.

The likes of myself and others of my kind can be found in any social vocation or position, under any identity, immersed in the battle of earning this life as every moment dictates. To earn is to acquire the power of money. Fiscal responsibility of normal social living requires us to provide for our sustenance and shelter. So it is with me, my warrior self.

I worked, earning my living six days a week, eleven hours a day as a construction project engineer, getting soaked in rain forests, caked with dust on warm wind blown plains and chilled to the bone on snow covered peaks, daily, while commanding crews of complaining laborers. The work environment got me so grimy and dirty I sometimes went unrecognized by people who knew me.

My life felt an urgency for change. My "toughing it out" tired. Sanity and well-being were packed and ready to leave. Surrender was not a word in my vocabulary, but my body, psyche and soul were on the verge of leaping from the precipices of stress my vocation had pushed me to. When the project was completed I quit and set my sights on another vocation. I saved enough money to lease a small flower farm that had previously failed to be successful. The Protea flower farm I now called mine was more of a rock and weed strewn graveyard for dying flora than a blooming business.

Several years before I acquired the farm land of predominantly lava rock, thirteen acres of potentially flowering trees and shrubs had been planted with high aspiration and hope by previous occupants. Drought dried up the water system. Human mismanagement of the plants' needs proliferated. Five years after seeding, all seminal hope and planted endeavors withered. The farm was abandoned to Nature and a natural course: death. Weeds strangled root and branch. Trees twisted with thirst. Disease grew in a field where dreams once played. Alone and isolated on a remote mountain in Hawaii, a flower farm slowly gave up its life.

I had quit my job to flee to a dying flower farm situated on the slope of a mountain, four thousand feet in the clouds, four miles of serious four-wheel-driving off a secondary road exit. No electric. No phone. No running water. No orders to follow or to give. Just the quiet and stillness of isolation. Me and the trees and a view of the surrounding sea. Perhaps I could find a new life in saving the life of a flower.

My previous vocational slavery provided me enough money (power) to endure several months' expenses. In that time, I planned to save the farm by caring for the plants that had a chance to survive. I had no picture of my future. I worked day by day. For months I cut wild weeds and dug viperous vines from roots. I cleared the lava rock field of dead trees and shrubs. I pruned. I drove my truck, laden with tank, on a nine mile round-trip of four-wheel-drive, down and up the mountain to bring water to the thirsting field. From the truck I carried a water bucket in each hand while carefully navigating my steps over boot-eating loose lava rock terrain to relieve the thirst of each protea plant fighting for reproductive survival. I looked to the gift of living in Nature's solitude for my own clinging to life.

Many months of watering, weeding, pruning and nourishing passed. A field of thirteen original acres was now down to less than three acres of barely living plants peppered across a hostile rock field of broken black lava.

I too was feeling black and spread out. The solitude I first looked for was now being invaded by fear in my thoughts and worry in my heart. During my intensive to save the flowers, I had neglected to keep watch on my power, my capital savings. Cash flow dried up. It hadn't rained for months. It had been three months since I last made a payment to the bank on my farm truck. Lease money was past due. I was hungry and getting weaker.

The striving-to-live flower trees produced an average of two dozen marketable blooms a week. About fifty dollars. That alone could barely feed me and fuel my truck.

I received threatening letters from the bank. Repossession was the order. Failure to pay the farm's land payment meant good-bye roof over my head. At least as a grumbling construction worker I expected a paycheck. Alone in a struggling play of nature, I was needing a reality check.

I had become a warrior in battle with the enemies of confusion and loss of hope. No job, no money, no future but debt. No well to draw from. I felt powerless.

Standing in the quiet of the farm's cabin, gazing through the windows across the mosaic field of varied Protea plants and trees, I saw the few faces of flowers ready for harvest. Representation of six months of effort and hard work produced only fifty or so dollars a week.

I was losing hope. I was at a loss to carry on. No matter how many orders the old sarge in my head barked, my feet couldn't follow the commands. I was losing what little internal strength I had. A hungry warrior, drained of energy, exhausted of emotion, too weak in spirit to carry one more bucket of water or fight one more battle. Powerless. You can't buy rain.

While worry ran amok through any comfort my mind knew, my emotions and body's buttocks sunk to the floor of the farm's shack. I sat and looked through eyes without intention. I saw flower plants waving their branches in the dry wind. In a way I understood, I heard a cry of thirst.

Within the shack's structure I saw emptiness. I lived with neither table, nor chairs, nor bed. I slept on the bare plywood floor in a sleeping bag. I bathed in a five gallon bucket. My propane powered fridge was empty. There was barely enough gas in the truck to drive the twenty-five miles to town to sell the few flowers that needed to be cut.

Without thought to the future, I spent the last half year of my life in the field of the island's mountain giving my all to the flowers. Day by day, moment to moment, I cared for them, talked to them and caressed their boughs and leaves. Kissed their blooms. I knew every plant by heart. I knew exactly where each bud grew, where each flower waited. I knew that a dozen flowers waiting would not make a living for this failing farm, nor empower this weary warrior.

Worry wracked my heart. The fatigue in my body and weight upon my soul wrestled weary for resolve. Non-plussed, I reflected. Days ago I sat down on the floor and fell into this nothing-ness. My alone-ness echoed empty and my mind could only observe itself struggle.

During other hard times in my life, I had always managed to pick myself up and carry on. Break on through…There had always been this driving drill sergeant voice inside me that would bark mental commands: "Let's Go Troop! Move It! Move It! Pick up that left foot and plant it ahead of your right! Pick up that right foot and plant it in front of your left. Eyes to the horizon! Let's Go! Left, Right, Left. Move Out!!"

Now…I couldn't be motivated. No matter how much my mental drill sergeant persisted I couldn't respond. Part of me gave up. Then all of me gave up. Nothing-ness.

****

It's a clear morning, I sit in my shack on a bare wooden floor, alone with voices in my head and a few flowers in the field. Alone on a secluded mountain island in the middle of a great sea. Alone, I cry in waves.

A voice in my head says, "Get up! Get up on your feet!" I answer, "I can't."

"Why?" it asks of me.

"Because I am without strength. I haven't the power to move."

Then the voice of sarcastic consciousness asks, "What is the greatest power?"

Absentmindedly I speak aloud to a cabin empty but for me and the space made by the enclosure of walls..."What is the greatest power??!" Clear as a bell that's what the voice asked. Again and again.

"What is it troop? What is the greatest power?"

At this point I am set to lose all I believe I own, so I figure losing my mind as surely as I feel I am, is only natural. I think about nothing but this: What is the greatest power, oh penniless, powerless warrior?

In the realm of trying to 'think' I hear a whisper. Clear and resonate. A whisper. *Love. Love is the greatest power.* Written in literature. Spoken in the words of the saints. Love is the greatest of powers. *Love conquers all.*

For a moment the weight on my shoulders and soul seems to shift. My damaged ego adjusts.

"Oh yea?" Ego quickly retorts. "And where am I going to get some *love?*" I growl. I'm alone, in the wilderness, on a mountain side, on an island in the middle of the ocean. Where in the hell am I going to get some love?" I yell at the walls and windows and world around me. I feel my voice swallowed by the expanse of Nature surrounding me.

I start babbling to myself. "Love? Maybe I can call out for some love." I hold an imaginary phone receiver to my ear and dial. "HELLO! Love Delivers!? Yea, its me. I'd like an order to go. Two quarts of bountiful warm love. Yea, make it quick and keep it warm and radiant. Thanks. Good-bye, good-bye, good-bye…" Tears fill my eyes. My face succumbs to sadness. I lose control. I begin whimpering, slide into crying and fall into sobbing. The snot out of the nose sobbing.

While the drill sergeant of my mind kicks, berates and yells at me, I hear one word spoken clearly and softly between and around the dog barking orders I can't follow.

"FRIENDS."

Again through the noise of my suffering self the word passes as an arrow in flight. "FRIENDS!"

My eyes are squeezed shut trying to stop the tears. Now they open and through my lips the word "friend" whispers to me. I hear it. I feel it.

The few friends I believe I have are thousands of physical miles distant, but the thoughts, feelings and spiritual bonds I experience with them are here and now.

Immediately the thought and image and feeling of my spiritual (same soul in two different bodies) brother, Mitchell, comes to me.

I close my eyes. I give my thoughts over only to him. Mitch and I met years ago at the university. After graduation we went separate ways. We wrote to each other from all parts of the world. We viewed the full moon as a time to think deeply of each other. We were brothers by spirit. He was ten thousand miles around the world from me. Images of us being together appear in my mind. Feelings of being close to him follow in my heart. I love Mitch. I don't know why but I do. I always have. The brothers we never had, in each other we loved.

As I sit on the cabin floor, in the middle of nature with my eyes shut, I pour every memory of our being together into my present reality. In my mind I hold him fast. We embrace. We hold each other. I love you Mitch, I think. I love you Mitch, I feel. I love you Mitch, I say.

My words echo to no one, but in my mind I see the love I have for him fan the cold coal in my heart to ember. I mentally stoke my feelings of love for my friend until my heart becomes flame. Warmth begins to burgeon into my chilled soul. Even though Mitch is thousands of miles away, in my mind and heart I hold fast to what is between us, to what made us what we are to each other. Brotherly love.

For nearly an hour I revive and relive all the experiences we once shared. All the love I had ever felt for him. Over and over. Again and again.

Suddenly the image of my mother appears in my mind. Without diminishing or letting go the love I feel for my friend, I think of my Mother and how much I love her. I hold her and Mitch inside my brain and bosom for an hour more. Loving them, pretending as if they were actually present. My mind's eye holds fast to the beautiful images of embrace. My heart entwines itself in the images as well. My feelings respond to the reality my memories and reflections create.

Other friends came into my awareness, into my mind and heart and I make them real. Everyone, everything I have ever loved is with me and I love them as though they are here at the farm, in the cabin, being close to me.

I first heard the word 'friend' in mid-morning. It is late afternoon when I finally open my eyes. All the love I began to feel at first and then built upon, friend by friend, is still with me. From my heart, feelings of love as great as I have ever known flow. My blood and being warms radiant. Love fills my breast and overflows.

Through the tears in my now open eyes I recognize the empty cabin but I feel a fullness of being and warmth. A smile surprises me on my face. I am physically alone in a wilderness, poor to the demanding world, yet inside and beyond me I feel rich. I have *love* alive inside me. I feel it radiate outward from me like light from the bulb. I sit unmoving on the floor and feel timeless by the liquid life-giving feelings of love. After immeasurable moments, the love imbibing me gently begins subsiding like a good-bye kiss left on one's cheek.

As the sun makes way for long shadows reaching across the protea field, my thoughts return to the reality of my situation: I am broke and afraid of losing what I have worked so hard for. The wolves of turmoil still at my door gnaw at the hinges of my mentality.

For the moment I am feeling better than when the day began but a small heaviness presses me more into the present earthly moment. After a long sigh, I stand on stiff and shaky legs and tell myself to get on with the task at hand. "Let's go feet!."

I will go and cut the lonely few buds turned to flower I know exist. I will sell the few and go on from there. I can't bear another thought beyond that. The further into the future I look the dimmer the vision.

My feet get me to my truck. My mind says cut the flowers. I drive through the field's gate, up the small rise to the back of the farm's boundaries and stop. I know every plant intimately and where each bud and flower grows.

In a few minutes it will be over. I get out of the cab and sigh heavily. The love left in my heart is losing resonance. I move to gather the few beautiful flowers that await me.

Walking on loose rock and dead weeds I head toward the proteas. The first tree presents a prize flower. The "pink mink" is a large shuttlecock shaped bloom made of what seems to be long, narrow pink bird feathers tipped in black mink. Inside at its center is a yellow dome, soft as teddy bear fur. I gaze upon it, stroke it, thank the tree and cut the flower. A small smile crosses my face. A moment of rest lays in my heart.

I move to another tree and cut. Another tree another flower. I cut another and another and…I suddenly realize there are flowers everywhere! In every direction from every tree and shrub, hundreds of flowers cry out in bloom! I cut and cut until the truck bed is entirely filled. Entirely. Flowers everywhere. Flowers everywhere. I am breathless with amazement.

This is a miracle. I knew where each bud was. I am with the plants everyday. I knew there only to be a dozen or so flowers to cut. I know my trees. Hundreds of flowers don't bud, mature and bloom in an afternoon!

But the field is fully flowered. It shouts with flowers.

In this moment a feeling inside me, from my again-glowing heart speaks:

"If you are not seeking the greatest power you seek less. Seek love and let it wield you."

I hear it. I see it. I feel it.

****

It is the warrior in the silences of his personal despair that will bring about the change society so desperately needs.

Author with AK-47 and CAR-15

HYAK THAN YUBI (in rear) GAI DIU DENG BOON

Hyak. Team leader of the Yards

Hein, the day before his death.

Yubi and Author at Dak To

Yubi, Than, Kinnear, and Author

Author and Bhun at Dak To

Author, just before leaving Vietnam

Author(kneeling center) with other SOG members

Collateral Damage

Language is the power by which we construct our world. The spoken word binds us as a people, secures us in harmony and strengthens us in war.

It is said 'truth is the first casualty of war', but veracity is wounded long before the battlefields are born. The first shot is fired when language is twisted and sometimes invented for the benefit of authorities to justify their actions, usurp laws meant to keep peace and convince others to fight.

The politicians and the particular individuals whose need for war endures seldom choose to view the battle from a tour of duty on the front lines of fighting. So, to exhort others to take up arms for their cause, they create a vernacular that is soft and inoffensive for convincing those whose backing is necessary. It's a makeover of the hard cold facts of fighting. Who in their right mind is going to run headlong into battle if the certain realities of maiming, death and war psychosis are used for incentive. If war doesn't sound so bad, what the hell, let's get in there and get some.

A "skirmish" is an innocent sounding term meaning a minor battle. I've personally never known a soldier who thought a fire fight was minor. It may be if you're not the one getting shot at.

Then there's the phrase "coming under friendly fire". Friendly Fire isn't and never will be friendly. It's as deadly as enemy fire.

The Israelis really came up with some of the best terminology ever. "Preemptive Strike" is a classic. "No, no, we did not attack. We conducted a pre-emptive strike!"

The war in Korea brought us the terminology 'police action'. The word 'police' connotates a relationship with justice and the word 'action' is an ambiguity that draws little or no attention. War is war.

A more recently coined term is 'collateral damage.' We exhibit need to remove ourselves from the personal acts that are revolting to our deeper self. These words could never confine the painful guilt nor justify the act of killing innocent men, women and children…

And "ethnic cleansing" is far too polite a definition for mass murder.

A weapon is a tool. A war is an action. Torture is an examination. Killing is re-inventing. The incarceration of a different philosophy is justice. A mass facade of words to make hypocrisy invisible.

But I believe the most hypocritical of words ever used are those of prayer for victory. The utterances of patriotic orators and pious leaders that fill the hearts of the masses with exalted excitement in the glory of war…

****

Hear us O Lord! as we send our Fathers and Sons and Mothers and daughters forward into battle…

****

The slow coming daylight divulges the carnage of last night's attack. The tactical operations center and several other buildings that housed many of the Montagnard soldiers are a flattened rubble of crumbled cement blocks and twisted tin roofing. Small scattered fires burn as men busy themselves looking for survivors. The company commander whose sleeping quarters was below ground level of the now destroyed operations center has been found shaken and only lightly wounded with scratches. The Montagnards have been less fortunate. Already several dead bodies have been pulled from the dregs and lie waiting for the appointed body bag.

****

Give thy blessings Lord to these noble patriots. Help them to crush our foes and dress our heroic actions in the glory of flag and country...

****

A dozen other men and I have readied ourselves to make a pursuit of the enemy responsible for the attack on our compound. The morning's light is dim as we depart in single file through the now opened barricaded gate of the company area. We walk cautiously along the outer perimeter as we search for possible signs of a trail left by the attackers. We find where the sappers cut their way through the defensive wires. Here they entered straight between two bunkers that were left unoccupied in the night. Creating a chaotic melee in the dark early morning hours, several sappers infiltrated the company area and detonated a half dozen satchel charges. The attackers were so skilled they got in, did their destruction and got out within minutes.

Because of a scheduling error the team assigned to the bunkers was also assigned to night ambush. The team went on ambush not knowing they were also assigned to occupy the bunkers. The enemy probably waited indefinitely and patiently for such a fuck up. Farmers and shop keepers by day. Viet Cong by night.

In the dirt of the small road that runs along the perimeter of the compound we find several distinct sandal imprints. The pattern of the sandal's soles is unlike the familiar tire treads. We also find droppings of fresh blood. By the looks of the sandal prints and the continuing splattering of blood it appears one of the sappers is being helped along by two others. There are maybe five or six sappers from the looks of the trail they left. We pursue.

****

O Lord, Let thy rod be our might and justice that we may endure, overcome and rejoice in our cause...be ever merciful and watch over our soldiers so they may return to comfort of family and hearth...

****

We follow the trail of blood and sandal prints along the narrow dirt road that shortly ends and turns into a footpath with the surrounding jungle closing in. The path splits with one branch extending towards a large open field surrounded by an ominous tree-line. The other branch leads towards a small cluster of huts sheltered under shade in a grassy glade about a hundred meters from us.

****

*And in our supplicants O Lord hear what we dare not say...**bless our shells that they tear our foes bodies to bloody shreds...***

****

The Montagnard on point suddenly yells out. We spy two men running from the large open area to disappear into the black shade of an opening in the far treeline. I catch glimpses of the men moving behind the treeline. I quickly take the grenade launcher from the Yard and fire a round to what I believe will be an intersection of the grenade and the two running men. We watch the 40 mm grenade loft across the open field. The grenade explodes behind the treeline and there is a larger secondary explosion. It is quite possible the grenade hit its target and set off ordnance carried by the escaping men. Or perhaps there are Viet Cong waiting in the treeline for us to cross the open field.

The Master Sergeant in charge of our group decides to call in air support to blast the treeline. Within minutes a fastmover is on site and dropping two-hundred and fifty pound bombs on the treeline. While this is in progress half of our group head back to investigate the cluster of huts at the end of the other trail. We maneuver through the standing trees until we are close to the hootches. There are about ten of them. We see no visible movement of people. We wait and watch until the other part of our group returns from searching the bombed treeline. We split into teams and move in to search the bamboo and thatched huts. Our sudden entrance causes commotion. People, mostly older men and women and a few children, are forced to leave their homes.

****

Help us O Lord to cover their fields with their patriotic dead. Help us to lay waste to their homes. To turn them out and break their spirit…

****

I enter one of the hootches and search the room for trap doors and other possible hiding places. There is a raised slat bed in the corner of the room. It lay covered by many blankets. I remove the bedding. Under the bed is a large hole that is carelessly covered with a straw mat. I pull away the mat. Hiding in the hole is a young man, probably my age. He cowers in a fetal position. He wears what looks like a large diaper. He is dirty, sweaty and has cuts and scratches on his body and legs that slightly bleed. His hair is cut like that of the North Vietnamese soldiers. On his feet he wears sandals that have the same pattern soles that we followed from our compound.

"Chu hoi! Chu hoi!" (give up! give up!) I yell pointing my weapon at him. I call to the team Sergeant.

"I've found someone!" The young Vietnamese man turns his head and looks at me. His eyes convey hatred and contempt. "La day!" (come!) I yell and keep my weapon pointed at him. I motion for him to come out. He slowly crawls out of the hole and from under the bed. He puts his hands in the air. I get behind him and march him out of the hootch.

Outside the hootch the villagers have been gathered together by our group of men. A man and woman in the group begin yelling hysterically. It is their son I have taken prisoner. They and others of the villagers are protesting loudly and angrily. The parents of the prisoner break from the group and run towards their son as we bind and blindfold him. Two of our group physically grab the couple and push them to the ground. Weapons are turned on them and the other villagers. Our patrol's yelling and threatening with weapons make the villagers realize there is no hope in stopping us.

****

For our cause we cherish thee Lord...curse our enemy's longings...

****

We have returned with the prisoner to our compound and handed him over to the Vietnamese Special Forces for interrogation. My team and I have to crew the mortar pit for the coming evening.

****

...blight their lives...protract their suffering...burden their reason dear Lord,

****

I spend the night firing illumination rounds from the mortar tube up into a dark heaven to wash our compound in an eerie dance of shadow and phosphoric light.

Even though the mortar pit the Yards and I serve is far to the other side of the compound from the Vietnamese Special Forces building, we do at times hear the clear scream of the methods of inquisition.

****

and make difficult their escape...drowning them in their tears.

****

At dawn's first light members of the Vietnamese Special Forces drag across the hard dusty earth a limp body by its legs. They tow the near lifeless, diapered body to the tiger cages near the mortar pit. I watch them slide the beaten man, face up under and into the barbed wire rectangle box that is built on the ground and less than a foot in height. The Vietnamese soldiers tie up the cage's end. The man inside lies on his back. The barbed wires of the cage lay so close to his body that he can neither turn over nor move his limbs. All he can do is lie facing the sky.

I climb out of the mortar pit and stand next to and over the tiger cage. In it is the young man I forced from his home and family. He lies looking like one large bruise. The eyes that yesterday stabbed me with hate and contempt are now swollen shut. But I swear I see tears run from them.

****

Dear Lord we ask this in the spirit of love and seek your aid with humble and repentant hearts. Amen.

****

The throes of war do not allow for convenient musings as to cause or effect. Lost is seminal reason in the patriotic words of right versus wrong and good versus evil. Perhaps evil is born pure and lives only out of that purity, but I believe more so that men, or a single man, out of the experience of abuse and fear, becomes addicted to a need for power and dominance over others. When these men seek to rule the world they stop only at their death, and it is true that men not dominated by fear will be called to kill them and suffer alone in that victory.

Let the speech of our thoughts and feelings be such that it includes the sharing of well-being and peace with all, despite the travails of the human condition or the burden of present conditions. Because words are imperfect every generation of humanity rewrites itself. Truth is the facts presented as they are for the benefit of all.

When Lives Fall Out of the Sky

Dear God,

I read the peaceful battle back in the world is gaining momentum. Here it suffocates in humid jungle. Remember that refreshing autumn day on campus before the moratorium march? You and I organizing the dissidents, galvanizing their glands. Hell no we won't go!. Hell no we won't…shit! I'll never forget the blue-eyed gaze a young woman threw me when I told her I couldn't make the march on D.C. because I was going to the war I was leading them against. That's why I'm here. Fighting a psychic wrath in a perfect background of turmoil and dried tears. On a stinking hot yesterday, I sat in a soft, green park, Victory by name, Tudo Street, Saigon. Visions of immolated monks surrounded me. "Why?" I cried.

"There is only purpose, no reason in killing," one spoke.

As their flaming bodies burned, their lucid eyes rolled to the heavens. Their guiltless smiles fell silently to ash. At that perspiring moment a fleeting of love pierced my heart. The smell of burning flesh raked my nostrils. Vomit spewed down the front of my fatigues.

God I'm so fucking tired. I cannot wait for love to find me. War is darkness and I fear going blind…

****

Inside the olive drab walls of our canvas tent, a single candle's light barely infiltrates the darkness that has steeped the Dak To launch site. Tonight, because of an absence of enemy rocket fire, we prefer to sleep above ground rather than in the damp depths of the bunkers. In the tent, a new guy Wilson, the six Yards and myself settle onto our army cots for the evening. It is quiet except for the incessant shrill of insects. Each of us, in silence, religiously examine our gear and weapons for completeness and function then set them within a hands reach should there be sudden need.

Wilson and Yubi walk outside to take the first watch on the bunkers. Gai, Hyak, Diu, Deng, Boon and I stretch our clothed selves into our cots for the light sleep of soldiers. The candle's light waves and flickers dancing with our distorted shadows upon the tent's walls. Some of the Yards speak in low, soft conversation. I drift.

"Burkai." Gai's voice gently pulls me from the floating space between wakefulness and sleep. My eyes which I didn't think I had closed fill with Gai standing beside my cot. I blink.

"What is it Gai?"

"Boon wants to tell you something."

Boon is the oldest member of my team. He has lived through numerous invasions of foreigners. He speaks no English. I sit upright on my cot and cross my legs. Boon's cot is next to mine. Gai speaks to him. They talk for a minute. Understanding very little of the tribal languages I can only feel for the meaning of their words. Gai turns to me and speaks:

"Boon wishes to tell you of his ancestors."

"Tell him I will listen," I say to Gai as I look into Boon's dark eyes and face illumined by the candle light.

Boon looks at me as he always has. Quietly and questioningly. His unblinking eyes hold me firmly while his lips release a soft melodious incantation. His words which I do not understand lull me back in time. I release my mind and feel. As his continuous singsong story reveals his ancient connections he meticulously uses his hands, arms, face and eyes to accentuate his tale. His voice sometimes climbs, then falls, sometimes stays even, then trembles. His eyes smile and on occasion tear. His heart remembers anger. His song laments of loss. On and on he sings his family's story. I sit fast but my blood threads with the invisible emotions of his family's lives. The candle's flame burns bright as does Boon's soul. Four hundred years of family history pours from his spirit. He lulls late into the night. I become his dream.

****

Morning brings activity.

"Gai, tell the men to grab their gear. Leave the rucksacks. Bring only weapons and ammo. Covey's been shot down. We're going in hot."

Gai's face reflects the seriousness of the situation. 'Going in hot' means there is enemy on the ground near the crash site. There are two men in that downed plane, an Air Force pilot and one of our men from the Special Forces camp.

The helicopter's turbines begin their windup. The whine of the turbo-jet climbs higher in pitch mirroring the ascending intent of the chopper crew and my team. We are geared up. Gai, Yubi, Diu and I load into the lead chopper. Hyak, Boon, Deng and the new team member Wilson climb aboard the second bird. The rotor blades of the ships thunder, beating the air harder and harder. I look over to the four Cobra gunships that have already aligned themselves on the runway at Dak To. In tandem, they lift their tails and point their noses downward as they start their inclined take-off from the pot-holed airstrip.

Our helicopters vibrate, rumble and lift a few feet off the ground to jockey into position over the runway. Slowly we lumber up into the air and follow the sleek gunships westward towards the Laotian border. I go through the routine of making a radio commo check with the pilot of the helicopter. Once that is done I attach the handset to hang at my breast on my web gear. I move to sit in the chopper's open doorway and check my weapon making sure a round is in the chamber. I rest my thumb on the safety and slide my index finger onto the weapon's steel trigger.

The warbird flies at tree-top level and careens at one-hundred and thirty miles an hour along the winding To river. Time is of the essence. Last report had enemy elements moving toward the downed aircraft. In my mind, gut and bones I feel the solidifying concrete of determination.

****

We've reached the crash site. Our chopper circles the downed aircraft. The gray twin-engine plane has cut a swath down the jungle slope of a small valley. I strain my eyes to locate an area in the jungle below where we can disembark the helicopter. The green jungle foliage beneath us is a patchwork of canopy cover, scattered tall trees and modcratc cover of bamboo, brush and tall grasses. About a hundred meters from the crashed aircraft is a small opening in the tree tops just big enough for the chopper to hover down into. The ground is covered in tall, thick elephant grass. I tap the pilot on the shoulder and yell, "THERE!" I point to the area. He nods affirmatively.

The helicopter begins a descent into the hole in the tree-tops I've pointed to. Off to my left I see the Cobra gunships diving and firing rockets into a gully area on the opposite side of the little valley we are preparing to enter into. As the helicopter lowers itself into the opening, I use the radio to check in with the Cobra gunships. They have engaged an enemy element that is making its way toward the downed aircraft. The enemy is less than a few hundred meters from the crash site.

Our chopper has maneuvered into the trees' opening and hovers over a section of thick grass. It looks about four feet to the ground. I signal to the Yards. We move out of the ship to stand on the helicopter's struts. I'm the first to jump off. The Yards follow my lead. The four foot drop turns into a surprise ten foot fall through very tall elephant grass. My feet hit solid ground and I roll into the grass. Gai, Yubi and Diu do likewise. Quickly the four of us form a defensive perimeter. The second helicopter hovers over us. The other four members of my team jump out of the chopper. They too take a long first step to the ground.

I make radio contact with the pilot of the lead ship letting him know we have gathered safely on the ground and are making our way up the slope toward the crash site. On the other side of the ridge above us I can hear the Cobra gunships firing their mini-guns and the explosion of cannon fire. The team moves in single file. Because the brush around us is sparse we make quick time getting to the downed aircraft. The humid air is thick with the smell of aviation fuel.

I place the members of the team in a defensive perimeter around the downed airplane. Gai and I survey the mangled wreck.

The aircraft we call 'Covey' is a push-pull twin engine plane. One engine in the front. One engine in the rear. The plane is a two-seater with all other available space filled with communications equipment. It appears the plane was flying at tree top level. It had passed over the ridge above us and did a sudden nose dive down into the trees on the slope of the valley we are in. A wing is ripped from the aircraft. Aviation fuel soaks the entire area. The cockpit windshield is shattered. The rear engine and the heavy wall of radio equipment in the back of the aircraft have pushed their way toward the front of the aircraft crushing the right seat rider into the front engine. The pilot was thrown forward through the cockpit windshield. He hangs over the cowling of the front engine with his foot pinned between the crush of radio equipment and engines. Both men are dead. In the air, the sound of the Cobra gunship's firing gets closer to us.

What a mess I think and try to figure out what to do next. I lift the head of the man crushed between the engines and recognize him. It's Winchester. I know him only slightly. I remember him as quiet and attentive. He chose to fly above the jungles lending his clear voice to give hope and support to the team members down on the ground. I remember his voice. He has a bullet hole perfectly placed between his eyes. The skin on his face feels soft and lifeless. There is no way I can remove his body from the collision of radio equipment and engines.

The pilot's body lays splayed across the front engine's cowling. He wears the standard gray jump suit of the Air Force. Around his waist is a belt, holster with a Colt .38 revolver and a very large knife in a sheath. Stenciled in the leather sheath is the name 'TEX'. Tex is a big fellow. Probably six-six and two hundred and fifty pounds. I look at his ankle and foot pinned between the engines. I look at the large Buck knife on his belt. I remove the knife and use it to cut deeply into the exposed calf of his trapped foot. I cut down to the bones of the lower leg. A small amount of blood coats the blade…Suddenly there is the sound of small arms fire coming from the ridge above us. Some of the Yards in the defensive perimeter return fire. A Cobra gunship rakes the ridge with mini-gun salvos. I hear ricochets buzz through the air. I immediately think of all the fuel around us and the possibility of it igniting. I yell.

"Wilson! Hyak! Are you okay?."

Wilson yells back, "Yea! We're good. We spotted a single gook. I think I hit him!"

"Hold your position!" I command.

I get on the radio and talk with a pilot of one of the slicks. He tells me that about two dozen enemy soldiers are making their way up to the ridge above us. The staccato of the firing of the gunships works into a steady frenzy.

"Hurry it up!" yells the pilot's voice out of the radio handset. I look at Gai. His wide eyes have taken on that big round voice that says,…'oh shit, what's next?'

I grip the big black handle of the Buck knife and begin whacking at the bones of the dead pilot's lower leg. CHOP! CHOP!

CHOP!..CRACK! The fibula breaks. I cut through more of the muscle and start chopping at the larger tibia bone. I chop and chop and chop…As I work away sweat grows on my face and body while in my mind I hear Boon's ancestral song singing. As I chop the knife into the pilot's leg, I can't help but ponder if his family is suddenly aware of this very moment. I wonder if the lineage of his soul is singing lament into the tapestry of his family's history. Somewhere a mother faints. Somewhere a father begins dying of grief.

The bone reluctantly gives up its matrix a little piece at a time. Finally I hack through the bone and finish cutting the flesh and sinew holding it to the ankle and foot. The body falls off the cowling into the mangled vegetation. The lead chopper pilot calls me on the radio.

"Burko, you better be getting your ass out of there. The gunships are almost out of ammo." The sound of mini-guns, cannon and rocket fire continues on the ridge line above us.

"There is a ridge I can get the helicopter near enough to pick you guys up. It's just about seventy-five meters up to your left." I look up at the helicopter that hovers about fifty feet above us. The crew chief is leaning out of the chopper and pointing in the direction he wants us to go…I yell into the mike. "Okay! Okay! We'll be there as soon as we can. We'll pull out of here in a few minutes! Roger copy, over?"…

"Got your copy, Burko. Out."

I look at the wrecked aircraft and Winchester's trapped body. There is no way I can get him out. Standard operating procedure is for me to destroy the radio equipment and remove any weapons once the bodies are recovered. I cannot recover Winchester. I call the helicopter pilot again and explain the situation. He relays it to a higher command. The order comes back. Leave Winchester and destroy the ship entirely. I remove two thermite grenades and insert timed fuses into them. I call in the rest of the team to gather at my position. We make ready to move out.

I place the thermite grenades among the wreckage and squeeze the timers to activate them. I then turn to Tex. Using the fireman's carry, I drape the body of the pilot over my shoulders and across my back. I sling my carbine over my neck. It hangs freely at my waist.

"Let's go! Move out!" I point in the direction I want to take. Yubi leads. The firing of the gunships has now focused on our side of the ridge. I can hear AK fire. We move as fast as we can in the direction the helicopter pilot has directed us. The body I carry is large and heavy. Tex's hands drag at my feet. His one foot drags on the ground behind me. I hold the body across my shoulders and keep it secure with one hand. With the other hand I grip onto bamboo stalk and pull myself step by step up the slope.

We are approaching a narrow protruding ledge on the ridgeline above us. The extraction chopper hovers about four feet off the ground and to the side of this precarious open area. One of the crew is frantically waving us on. The door gunner is systematically firing at the ridge across the gully and above the wreck site we just came up from. I reach the hovering chopper's struts. A member of the crew reaches down and helps me to lift up Tex's body. I make a final push upward. Tex is pulled into the metal belly of the warbird.

The members of my team are firing across the gully at the red and yellow flashes dancing in the shadowed tree line. A lone gunship screams a few feet above the trees and covers the hostile firing with its own fusillade.

Hyak, Boon, Deng and Wilson climb up and into the helicopter. It lifts off and rolls to the left of the ridgeline. Another chopper quickly hovers into position near me. Gai, Yubi, Diu and I scramble on board. As our ship pulls into the air I see two F-4 Phantoms make strafing runs over the ridge of enemy soldiers. Below in the gully the thermite grenades ignite the aviation fuel at the crash site. A large billow of black smoke shoots into the air and gets smaller and smaller as our helicopter ascends to safety and turns homeward. Below us the funeral pyre of war machinery and the flesh of Winchester burn to ash. The whirling wind rushes around my head and into my ears. I swear I can hear Boon singing.

****

Back at home base in Kontum I have just finished my debriefing and after action report. The company will make plans to take a larger element of men back to the crash site to retrieve the remains of Winchester. His bones wait alone.

I walk out of the headquarters building and am met by one of the Recon members of FOB 2.

"Burko, you better come quick. One of your Yards is flipping out!" He points over to the Yard housing area. I see a flurry of people dashing about. I hear yelling and what sounds like out-loud crying…I run over to the area.

It's Boon. He is wailing, crying and staggering around like a man ravaged by sorrow. He holds a grenade from which he has pulled the pin. As if in a gesture of prayer, both his hands tightly hold the grenade's handle from releasing. He is sobbing and moaning lamentations.

Because of the danger Boon presents to those around him, everyone else in the area is huddled behind one of the many sandbag obstructions near the buildings. I duck behind one of the sandbag walls where Gai, Hyak and several other Yards crouch. Boon continues wailing and sobbing, staggering like a drunk this way then that way. When he moves toward those around him they quickly scatter to a safer area. Many of the Yards gathered around the area yell to Boon. He is indifferent to their callings.

"Gai, what the hell is going on? What is wrong with Boon?" For a reason I've never understood Gai seems to be stifling a laugh.

"Ah Burkai, Boon's only surviving relative, his cousin Prek was killed yesterday. Boon is all alone now. He has no one." Gai turns his attention back to Boon and yells, "Yahoo! Yahoo!" (friend! friend!) But Boon is mentally absent. I can discern a few words he keeps repeating over and over, ones that I heard him sing just last evening.

"He is calling to his family. His ancestors, Burkai." Gai looks at me and nods his head in resigned affirmation.

Boon lets loose a painful wail then falls silent. He looks at the grenade he holds to his chest. He loosens his hands. The handle flies off. Boon's face wears the agony of…why? Gai and I and the others around us duck behind our cover of sandbags and cringe. BAWOOOM! The grenade detonates. Boon's soul is released to the song his ancestors sing. I too can hear it.

Last Shot

We have spent the sunny day walking patrol along the vegetated rock and sand shores of Ahn Tre Island. The island floats at the mouth of Nha Trang Bay where the South China Sea begins. Here ends my tour of duty, but unbeknowst to me at the moment, the war would continue to be with me. I halt the patrol for a break.

The patrol consists of a mix of nationalities of seven men. There are two Thais, two Koreans, two Australians and me, an American Special Forces buck sergeant. I am their leader and their teacher. For the past two weeks these men have studied how to become recon team leaders. They've learned advance methods of map reading, directing air fire support, rappelling, extraction from operations by unconventional means, small team leadership and immediate action drills for contact with the enemy. These last few days they spend patrolling this tiny island with me as instructor and evaluator. It's their graduation patrol.

For the most part, the island is a safe place to patrol. It is no bastion of enemy forces and is surrounded by sea. Shear craggy rock walls jump up from thin sand beaches scattered around its perimeter. The Air Force has a large radio and radar operation on one of the island's peaks. They have a capable contingent of security plus the fact that the Special Forces routinely conducts "training operations" around the base of the island. This patrol is one of those operations.

Tomorrow morning is the scheduled date of extraction for the team. The patrol has been uneventful. The weather has been tropical balm. We are setting up our night's perimeter just inside a small stretch of black sand beach inhabited by palm trees, large fern and a tangle of thick vine. Behind us climbs the dark rock face wall of the island, to our front gentle swells of the South China Sea lap the beach. Twilight now seeps into the approaching darkness. In the barely discernible distance lay the city of Nha Trang, alight by candle and firelight, floating eerily as a mirage over smooth obsidian water.

There is no talk save for a few whispers. To be recon is to be silent and invisible. The team, via hand and eye signals, situates itself in a small semi-circle. Our backs to the rock wall, claymore mines deployed to the right, left and front. Half the team will be on guard, the other half will sleep. Guard will rotate every two hours after dark. I will not sleep. As quiet as the patrol has been, there is no sleep for the truly restless. Veteran combat soldiers do not rest they only lie in waiting.

The sun has been swallowed by the jungle's distant mountains. As the white points of stars pierce the purple turning to black sky, I squint my eyes laying my vision on the sandy beach to my front view. You never know what to expect in war. It's best to expect nothing but to be ready for anything. I never expected to see my tour of duty end. I just took every moment as it presented itself. I never counted down the days. Every day was just another day. There were no weekends, no holidays, no Mon-Tue-Weds-Thurs-Fri-Sat-Sun days of the normal week. I called the day Po-day. Every day was Poday. Past and future had no meaning. Living in the present was what kept you alive. I realize that in a few days I'll be leaving this life of war. Not once in the forever-ness of being here have I given in to the thought of going home.

The night has covered everything in sheets of blackness. I sit my butt on the sand. Cool dampness seeps into the ass of my fatigues. I lean my back into my rucksack as if it were a lawn chair while my legs stretch away from me into the darkness. Sea sounds lap the beach. My carbine cradled in my arms lay across my chest with my thumb on the safety and my finger lightly on the trigger. Soothing sea air fills my lungs. I have never seen so many stars. The night begins slipping smoothly through the quiet awareness of my mind.

****

The lapping sound of small waves has been ceaseless all night. Dawn stirs the darkness moments before it wakes. This is my favorite time in the jungle when reality begins to take shape out of the nothing of blackness. A sudden thread-thin white line of sea foam is the first manifestation my eyes experience as substantiality. Blackness covertly makes its unmarkable transformation to grayness. From the invisible sea come unnatural sounds. It may be a change in tide playing a new sound along the shore but I'm not certain. Then I hear it clearly as the first hint of gray reveals a blob of shape bobbing in the water to our front. The blob turns into a small round boat, woven like a large basket. In it are several men. They are quiet except for the sound their paddles make scooping the water. I signal the soldier next to me with a touch of my hand. I nod my head toward the approaching craft. The team is ready and quietly waits for my signal. We will hold our fire and wait to capture the unsuspecting men by surprise.

Through the cover of dim light I count six enemy. They paddle directly onto the beach and jump out of the boat thinking how fortunate they are for arriving before dawn. Then I scream, "Chu hoi!" (give up!) In their brief moment of ease at having reached their destination they have been lax in securing their weapons from the boat. My team and myself have stood up and point our weapons at them. The intruders know they are caught and put their hands in the air.

Like any farmer from the area these Viet Cong are dressed in the standard black pajamas and rubber sandals. Three of them wear green bandoleers slung over their shoulders and across their chests carrying what looks like explosives. Their eyes hold the look of sudden illness and fear. They are desperate for life to be different from this moment.

I order three members of my team to carefully remove the bandoleers from our prisoners. The captives stand on the beach with their hands in the air over their heads. After each prisoner is searched they are forced to lie on the beach face down in the sand. Four of my men begin the job of blindfolding and binding the arms of our captives. Suddenly in a valiant effort, the Viet Cong closest to me jumps up, takes one giant step and leaps towards the water. His body lengthens gathering every inch it can in a dive for freedom. Straight as a board, his torso hits the water with a belly-flop. The staccato blast from my automatic carbine and two other men's fire sprays several bullets into his body making it go limp. It rolls lifeless in the water. The sea's smooth current quickly takes the man under and out to sea. One of the prisoners begins quietly crying. The rest remain silent their faces in the sand. I feel an incessant drumming in my heart. The sun's first rays streak across the water and into the distant mountains. The helicopters approaching our site sound like thunder.

****

After the mission I had a day of stand-down time and planned to sleep in but life has its changes. The morning clerk is shaking me awake and putting papers in my face.

"Get up Sergeant Burkins. You've got orders for stateside! The Army is discharging you a few weeks earlier than scheduled. You're flying the freedom bird today at 1500 hours from Bien Hoa!"

In a second's movement comes a lifetime of change. One moment you're living a permanent life of presence and suddenly it ain't so. I've not thought of a life different than this. It's been nothing but one step at a time. Leaving now is just another step.

****

I arrive at Bien Hoa's departure area on time, but monsoon rains and several typhoons in the South China Sea delay my leaving for several days. Even though the flights are canceled, troops due to be discharged from service keep arriving for their departure making the staging area look like an overcrowded refugee camp. All the billet areas are filled including any available floor space. A few hundred men are left without a bunk and have to sleep scattered throughout the sandy grounds area around the billets. No one is allowed to leave the area. Nothing to do but wear your poncho, sit in the rain, wait out the storm, eat cold c-rations and smoke pot. A lot of pot. Hundreds of men ready for departure, sit gathered in many small groups, each enjoying the passing of a pipe or joint. Many murmurous low voices whisper of the possibilities of tomorrow. Tomorrow, for the first time for many of us, seems a reality within reach.

Along with the gray skies and rain exists a general anxiety as to whether or not we are really going to make it home alive. The odds are that the closer a man is to leaving Vietnam the greater his chances of getting killed. There could be a rocket attack or perhaps some careless act of someone discharging a weapon accidentally. Until that freedom bird lifts off and flies away from the war, the 'real world' is still an uncertain distant dream. On the third day of waiting the skies finally clear and the freedom birds begin their departures.

The government has chartered civilian aircraft for our ride to stateside and my group has filled the seats of our United Airlines jet. As the plane taxies onto the runway the pilot announces that the take-off will be an accelerated steep ascent. The surrounding jungled hills are still alive with the possibility of producing enemy fire. The quicker the aircraft can ascend the greater our chances of being out of range of danger. The pilot aligns the Boeing jet on the runway. The turbine engines begin a whining climb of rpm. The brakes of the aircraft hold fast until the engines are at full scream. The jet vibrates violently in place then suddenly leaps forward. Acceleration presses me deep into my seat. The aircraft's nose lifts upward. We leave the ground like a rocket let loose toward space. Long cheers of exhilaration explode from every man onboard. As our aircraft makes a turn out to sea, I take my last look down on what has been my life. I see an F-4 Phantom jet swooping over exploding red napalm on the lush green slope of the mountain that gets smaller and smaller and smaller as I am lifted away. Deep in my chest I feel an ache.

The Need for Healing

Dear Lee,

I am Charles' sister. I want to thank you for the photos of my brother and providing me with some glimpses into the life my brother had in the service. It is like having a little bit of him returned.

I don't think any of the family ever recovered from what happened to him.—My Dad grieved himself to death.—Charlie's high school buddies still cry when they see me. I cannot help but wonder what life would be like had he lived.

Thank you again.

Denell

****

The following is a discourse on the art of non-dualistic weaponry. The art of these weapons is in their power to overcome internal conflict, to create change in the external world and to heal the individual who practices their usage.

There comes a time in a warrior's martial study when he must realize that the greatest challenge and most formidable opponent is not an enemy outside of himself. It is within the warrior's emotions, mind and psyche that the greatest of confrontations occur. How does one confront an attack of ill feeling or adverse thought? Of what good is a conditioned body, techniques of physical engagement and the wielding of conventional weapons against the sometimes hostile energies of our heart and mind?

Using a blank mind, a hardened heart or psychic numbing as defensive or offensive weapons will not secure victory nor protect us from harm. Their use only ignores the complete reality of a situation and eventually they are the cause of ill health.

Without strong health a warrior cannot expect to endure against any enemy, be they physically to our front or mentally and emotionally within our being. A hand cannot hit, a sword cannot cut and a bullet cannot pierce the anger, confusion, doubt, worry and fear that can assault our inner well-being. What are the weapons and the techniques that calm and heal the battles within the self?

In the martial world, use of a stick, sword or other hand held weapon is a relationship of duality. I pick up the sword. "I" wield "the sword". It is a condition of two distinct entities: "Me" and "the sword". An "I" and an "it". Duality. In the highest levels of weapons training the warrior seeks to become "one with the weapon". However, even though the sword becomes an extension of the self there is still the existence of one's intention. It is my will that powers the wielding of the weapon. Me "doing" something "with" something or "to" something. Duality. Action through doing. It is our excessive "doing" that can limit our ability when engaged in war within the self.

The weapons that are used in the battle within the self are **non-dualistic**. They are not something an "I" picks up and "wields". The only action of the "I" is to manifest the weapon into existence and then set it free. Once the weapon is accessed and set free, the weapon does what **its nature dictates** without an "I" wielding it, without any personal intention directing it. A weapon with its own mind. The weapons I speak of are *energetic feelings*. Feelings are a powerful energetic force. Rage, for instance, can have such power as to be uncontrollable. More powerful are the feelings of Thankfulness, Forgiveness, Love and Surrender. Like a sword, they can cut through the unwanted feelings, inimical thinking and unbalanced psychic energies that bind our spirit and disrupt our relationships with the world and others.

Unlike a sword that is picked up by the hand and wielded, the weapons of Thankfulness, Forgiveness, Love and Surrender must be manifested within the self. Feelings are an experiential energy we are all familiar with. Anger, joy, sadness, laughter, confusion, clarity…to name a few. Like different musical notes in a symphony, each feeling has a *distinctive frequency* or *vibration* giving it a quality unique unto itself.

Feelings are extremely powerful. Grief can knot a stomach. Fear can weaken the knees and loosen the bowels. What then is the vibratory nature of the weapons I speak of? What does Thankfulness *"feel"* like and how can a warrior access this *frequency of feeling*? And what does the warrior do once the feeling is located and identified? What is its affect?

To begin, settle yourself in a quite environment where no outward distractions are likely to occur. Quieten your mind, calm your heart and then ask yourself, "what does Thankfulness *feel* like?" Look, listen and be sensitive for the experience of this feeling. Search your memory of mind and feeling. Perhaps there is a time you can recall when someone did something for you that gave you an opportunity to feel thankful for. Recall this feeling. Once you feel it, <u>gently increase your awareness of the feeling</u>, so the feeling becomes more prominent. Feel this 'Thankfulness' as much as possible. Continually increase your awareness of the feeling to such a degree that there can be no doubt it is truly the distinct feeling of Thankfulness you are experiencing. Focus and enhance your awareness on the feeling's vibration. Resonate with this feeling <u>until your sense of self and doing disappears!</u> **This is the most important part of the practice**. Your awareness of the feeling (within yourself) must be of such a great degree that your consciousness of self ceases to exist. All that exists in this moment is the energy of Thankfulness you have discovered within yourself. It is an experience similar to darkness generating light within itself. When the light radiates where does the darkness go?

The moment of disappearance of self is a moment of **non-duality**. You are no longer taking any action with respect to the feeling you have found within your being. Your intention does not exist. All that exists is the vibratory energy of the feeling of Thankfulness. By your disappearance of self consciousness, this "energetic thankful feeling" **is set free**, like a wave piercing space, taking its own course and spreading its affect. The action of the nature of Thankfulness is let loose into the world through your inaction. We have not taken a moment of thankfulness and expressed it in words to "something or someone" (duality). We have not directed it by our hand. We have set the immense nature of a unique feeling free to do its own biding (non-duality) without our assistance. A metaphor would be that of turning on a light. When we turn the light on, we don't spread the light around the room ourselves. We flip the switch and the light does its thing. The same holds true for turning on the Thankfulness switch. There is no personal aim or desire for it to "do" anything or "go" anywhere. Light fills the room of its own accord. Like the light, the energy of Thankfulness, its vibratory frequency, permeates every direction, crosses every distance and touches all.

The technique is to have the complete experience of finding the feeling of Thankfulness and with our awareness "amplifying" the feeling until the "I" **disappears in it**. In the moment we "return" to our consciousness, to the realization that we have in fact "disappeared for a moment", we need not concern ourselves with wondering whether or not something has happened. Let it be. Do the practice again or just get on with whatever you have to do for the moment. Don't contemplate or inquire as to what was accomplished.

So what does this self generated "energetic feeling" accomplish? **It assists healing within the self and the world.** Thankfulness is a resonant condition to the heart and soul. The energy of its vibration is nourishing. It will set previously blocked energies in motion, create space and free energy for other uses. This is the nature of Thankfulness. All that we have to do is find it within ourselves and set it free. Like a pebble dropped into the pond, the manifested wave journeys to every shore. Like a victorious army on the move, the wave-like energy of Thankfulness will steadfastly transform the enemies of conflict and resistance within you and beyond you. Like water wearing through a rock, the force of thankfulness will eventually come to obvious fruition.

The weapon of Forgiveness. For many people it is difficult to forgive the injustices they feel they suffer. Some people would rather die than forgive. Even those who reluctantly make a conscious decision to be forgiving sometimes do so only because they mentally believe it is the right thing to do. Intellectually, "they" forgive "them". "I" forgive "you". This is a dualistic relationship. Even though there is a beneficial nature to being forgiving, doing it with a sense of duality is not as powerful or effective as the non-dualistic reality. We need to remove ourselves from judgment and personal intent. We need an action to take place through our inaction. Forgiveness must be set free because being unforgiving will deny you room to move.

We must discover within ourselves the energetic *feeling* of Forgiveness. Like Thankfulness, Forgiveness has a frequency, a vibrational quality that is distinctly its own. We must look for that feeling within ourselves. What does Forgiveness *feel* like? Search your memory of past experiences and recall a time you felt Forgiveness for someone. Maybe a good friend couldn't keep a promise they had made. They are feeling bad but for you it is not a problem. Perhaps you've been the one forgiven by another for some transgression. Recall this event. Search deep within your feelings for the "vibration" that is forgiveness. Once you find it evident, use your awareness to increase the intensity of the feeling like an ember fanned into flame. Be calmly persistent until the feeling of Forgiveness gets so incredibly large that you disappear within it. In the moment you lose your sense of self, **Forgiveness will be set free to impose its nature**. Its "tune" will play upon your being and like light it will extend its reach toward the ends of the universe. You do not have to think or have the intent of forgiving anyone or anything. Forgiveness is set free by your resonance with its vibration. Resonate and you disappear into it. Any judgment you have held against anyone (including yourself) will begin to dissolve and transform the energetic stasis of having been unforgiving. Life will open up and you will begin to find more potential in which to roam.

Be aware that the use of the "Forgiveness weapon" may require much practice. Don't be on the constant lookout for miracles or other effects. Healing the hardness from being unforgiving may take time. But guaranteed healing will begin. By setting free the energy of Forgiveness you will experience opportunities opening up for you in ways you never thought possible. It is said, "forgiveness is not so much for the forgiven as it is for the forgiver…" When we are unforgiving, we burden ourselves, we place limits on life. When Forgiveness is set free **it will do what is needed** to create balance within our lives and the lives of those with whom we are entwined.

Throughout the history of written literature Love has been quoted as the greatest of all powers. Power is the ability to bring about change. Love existing without the construct of duality opens the realm of infinite potential for change.

With your awareness recall the feeling of Love. Feel energetic Love and help the feeling grow until it overwhelms your egotistical sense of self and you disappear into its radiant nature. Let its energy permeate you and spread like light through darkness. Have no intention for where it goes. Care not how it goes. Do not wield it. Do not guide it. Allow yourself to be transformed into the energetic feeling of Love free to live its own nature. Have no afterthought of what it has done or how it does it. Just find it, amplify it, set it free. Love helps heal all. Wounds that are physical, mental or emotional will begin to heal from exposure to the energetic frequency of Love. Find the space within yourself where the feeling of Love exists. Enlarge that space. Let the feeling resonate within you, throughout you. Set it free by transforming and disappearing in its essence. The weapon of Love is a tangible feeling. Only one more word is necessary. Practice.

The weapon of Surrender is in the realm of finality. Surrender is an energetic feeling. In the practice of *disappearing* and *transforming* into the "energies of" Thankfulness, Forgiveness and Love, the weapon of *Surrender* may be needed. There will be times in practice when it will be difficult to ***give over*** to the idea of letting loose of all control and identity. The energy of Surrender can help us release the final strands that hold us in a dualistic experience where we have a life that is sensed as separate from another life. A life we feel need to control. This perhaps is the most difficult act for the warrior to complete, for whom can we trust to "aim" the arrow other than ourselves when we sit on the cusp? Surrender does not mean "giving up". It means allowing something **other than one's self-identity to exist as our life.**

What does surrender *feel* like? It is a feeling of great release. In this release is great relief. In this relief is immense clarity and calm. In this clarity and calm is a peace where all things are made possible. In this feeling one can finally let go...When your conscious self returns to the realization of an act having taken place within you and beyond, think not of outcomes. Sit quietly, then slowly return to present daily concerns or continue practicing. Surrender eliminates confusion, doubt, worry and fear especially after much practice in the energies of Thankfulness, Forgiveness and Love. Practice will enhance our lives. Practice. Practice. Practice.

****

Even the warrior who kills for his king and believes he does so with the blessings of gods and nation must nevertheless purify himself. Somehow the cleansing must absolve the soul. All killing, no matter the sanction of state and country, is a transgression to the fabric of what makes us human.

What Do We Do Now?

A mother may tell her son he is home from the war and to forget the battles, but she knows in her heart he is not home…

****

Our flight escaping the Vietnam war arrives at Fort Lewis, Washington around midnight. The moment the landing gear screeches against the asphalt runway loud cheers erupt from everyone on board but myself. I didn't cheer when we lifted off from Vietnam either. Again I only experience a deadpan observation of events around me. I feel like a character viewing himself in a silent film.

Within a few moments our plane rolls to a stop. The whine of the turbo engines slowly dies. The jet doors open making a sound like the far away muffle of a mortar round leaving its tube, a sucking *"frump"*. From my seat window I see stairways roll up to the aircraft. I sit in my seat as the rest of the soldiers move to the exits. After the last man moves into the doorway, I get up and start my walk toward the free world. I exit the aircraft's doorway and take a deep breath of the air of America. An air free from the fear of harm. An atmosphere free from the psychic vibration war generates. As soldiers below me step off the plane's stairway onto the ground, several of them pause to kneel, bow their heads to the earth and kiss her.

We are met by cadre who assemble us into formation and march us directly to an area of the army base where we begin our out-processing. Some soldiers will be continuing on with service but for the majority of us this will be our last day in the military.

Our first stop is a large building where we are issued a new dress uniform. After being issued our new set of military greens we file into another large building where the new pants and jacket will be tailored, the proper insignias sewn on and the awarded medals pinned on. A small army of tailors work without pause. We are told our 'wardrobe' will be ready for pick-up shortly after daybreak. We stand in long lines waiting our individual turn to be 'fit' into our new uniform. It is now zero-three-hundred-hours. An announcement is made. Chow will be served immediately, just outside the building we are in. Cold baloney sandwiches and black coffee are on the menu. One big groan rises out of the throats of the hundreds of soldiers hungry to be civilians. Tailoring measurements are quickly taken. The hum and drum of sewing machines vibrate the building as a mass of men mooing like dissatisfied cattle herd themselves in the direction of the exit doorways. Elbow to elbow within the restless drove, I too slowly shuffle out of the building.

Good news comes with the baloney sandwich. The "Steakhouse" mess hall will be open at 0600hours. We are each given a chit to redeem for a t-bone steak breakfast. A small reward for making it back in one piece from Vietnam. We have fifteen minutes to finish our baloney meal before we move to the next stage of our processing, a physical exam. Because of the night's darkness, I feel I could still be in Vietnam. I expect the rising sun's light will bring the proof of the 'world' to quell my doubts.

The medical examinations are conducted in several large brown tents that have been set up alongside the existing medical buildings. This helps handle the larger than usual influx of returning GI's due to the weather delayed departures from Vietnam. Flights were backed up. Now masses of men are backed up. There are only a few doctors to examine us all. In the large tent we are seated at tables set in multitudinous rows. Before us is an official military form and a pen. An officer appears at the front of the tent and begins reciting orders as to how to complete the paper set in front of us.

"Listen up!" His voice mechanically barks each word like it carried equal importance. "I'm gonna say this once. Because there are only a few doctors and so many of you men, if you got anything wrong with you, it's gonna be at least two weeks before you get it checked out and get outta this man's army."

From the back of the tent several voices of dissent cry out simultaneously. "Fuck the Army!"

The tall, thin officer maintains composure. "Just because you returned from Nam doesn't mean you aren't still in the Army. Any more FTA's and you'll all stay here!" In response are a few chortles. The officer ignores them and continues.

"Pick up the pen in front of you and fill out the blanks where it asks for your name and service number. When you've finished that, draw a vertical line with the pen through all the little boxes on the left side of both sides of the paper."

I look closely at the boxes he speaks of. There are a several dozen of them, each one referring to some sort of physical condition or ailment. I begin to draw a line down through the check boxes. I'm feeling I want out of here now. Right now. But my hand stops at the box marked "mental." In my mind I feel a space that is deep and uncomfortable, a feeling of standing at the edge of an abyss and molecule by molecule I am being sucked in. I skip the pen's mark over the 'mental' box leaving it unchecked and continue drawing an ink line through to the end of the boxes. The officer in charge continues.

"When you have finished drawing a line through all the boxes on the form, then write in the space provided on the back side of the form, this sentence: I... AM... IN... GOOD... PHYSICAL... CONDITION. Once you have done this, fill in the date and sign your name in the space provided. When you have completed this task pass your paper to the right. Don't move from your seat until ordered."

The forms are passed and collected. After the officer has all the papers presented to him he barks his final order to us. "Listen Up! When you are dismissed you will move outside where you will fall into formation and be taken to a billet area where you can shower and shave before leaving this man's army. Now, in an orderly fashion...DISMISSED! Get out of my tent!" His searching eyes take one last look at the soldiers exiting the tent and under a breath that belied his emotionless words, you hear him say, "…and good luck."

Our formation is marched to the billets area. Each of us finds a bunk for himself. On each bed is a plastic bag containing showering and shaving amenities plus boot and buckle polishing needs. It is four-thirty in the morning, most of us either sit or lie on our bunk. A cadre comes into the barracks and makes the announcement that breakfast will be served at zero-six-hundred-hours. We are to shit, shower, shave and be in formation at zero-nine-hundred-hours to have our pay records processed.

Some of the men already have their uniforms. The tailors are finishing our monkey suits ahead of schedule. The conversation in the barracks is busy and excited. The closer to getting out of the Army the higher the pitch of conversation and emotion. I lie on my back on my bunk, my hands behind my head. I look up at the ceiling but my eyes are unfocused. I lie so still I can feel the vibration of the ambient atmosphere, its contents of anticipation, its plans for the future, its current of change. The vibrations increase until I feel as though I am strapped to the nose of a jet bomber that streaks faster and faster, plunging through a dark, turbulent storm of thunder, lightning and psychic wrath. Flashing explosions fill my eyes. A scream escapes from my lungs.

Out from my inner world and into the barracks air an unbridled scream suddenly freezes everyone into motionless silence. For a moment all life is voided and I feel lightened by my action. A soldier's single comment manifests itself in the frozen air, "Christallmighty!…"

Another soldier answers, "Yes?" There is some uneasy laughter then the pulse of life unplugs itself and begins moving again. Soldiers continue about their business of showering, shaving, shitting and spit-shining, preparing for release into the real world…

I am running through thick jungle. Vines and boughs impede my motion. I feel the weight of my gear slowing me even more. The *ground turns to deep sand. My legs move like molasses. I suddenly realize my weapon is missing. Behind me I hear the enemy yelling, breaking brush and getting closer. A straightjacket of anxiety slowly constricts me. I struggle against immobility. Struggle, struggle,...struggle...*I bolt upright from lying on my bunk. The panicked thought of *where am I* rings in my head. Cold wet sweat clings to my skin.

"Hey dude. You okay?" A soldier next to my bunk speaks to me. "Man, you were really into it. You okay?"

My brain strains to get my bearings. *Stateside*, I tell myself. Yea. Yea. I'm at Fort Lewis, Washington. I take a difficult deep breath into a tight chest. "Yea, I'm okay."

"It's chow time. Steak and eggs on the menu. You sure you're okay?"

My mind is having trouble focusing. My heart pounds in my chest. I see the concerned face of the GI standing at my bunk's side. He says it again.

"Chow time, brother." He shrugs, turns and leaves.

The barracks is empty. Everyone is probably at chow. Six A.M. I've been asleep for over an hour. I rise from the bunk and go into the latrine and throw some cold water into my face and over my head. I look into a mirror that reveals a face with eyes stuck in a permanent stare. I rub my eyeballs into their sockets, splash more water into them but they remain locked in a perpetual stare. I tell the face, "it's okay, it's okay..."

The sun is rising as I make my way to the mess hall. Across the distance I can hear a freeway with cars, American cars. I see a subdivision with rows of neat houses, American houses. America. It's hard to believe but I've returned. I see I've returned and I've got all my limbs and today, within a few hours after four years and a life time of war, I'll be a civilian again.

As I near the mess hall, I see a few men wearing green berets standing outside the mess's entryway. They turn their attention toward me. One of them calls out.

"Burkins! Burkins, you made it!" It's Gersh and Dorn and Lawton. We were at JFK Special Warfare School at Bragg. We went through Special Forces training together. They had returned from Nam a few days ago. They too were scheduled to get out of the Army today.

After a few back slaps between everyone we talk of our time in-country.

"Can you believe it?" says Gersh. "Here we are!"

"Fuckin' A!" adds Dorn.

"So what's up, Burkins?" asks Lawton. "Where did you spend your time? Me and Dorn were with B-55 Mike Force out of Nha Trang. We did all right except for Dorn gettin' shot through the balls. Missed his jewels but put a hole in his bag." Lawton laughs.

"Scared the shit out of me more than it hurt, you fuckin' stoner." Dorn punches Lawton in the arm.

"And Gersh here," Lawton points a finger at him with a feigned seriousness, "Gersh here ain't right. He spent his time at an A-camp. Fuckin' went native." Gersh doesn't comment but quietly looks at Lawton his expression saying, 'I got your number asshole.'

"So what about you, Burkins?"

"I was at Command and Control Central. Ran a recon team for a year then got lucky because the Army considered me a security risk.

They sent me down to the Recondo school to be an instructor for my last month. Here I am."

Lawton continues rapping. "Hey Burkins, why don't you come with us. My parents' house is only a half hour from the base. When we get our walkin' papers, we can go there and get ready to party fuckin' party. We're going to hang out for a few days then we plan to buy an old school bus and head down to California. Wadda you say?"

"Sounds like a plan," I reply. The smell of sizzling steak floats out of the mess hall. I realize I'm really hungry. "Hey you guys ate yet?"

"Yea, we're gettin' ready to go get our monkey suits", replies Lawton. "Hey we'll catch you at the final formation then we'll all head out together. You with us?" I had nothing scheduled, nothing at all. I had no idea of planning so far ahead yet.

"Yea, count me in."

"Fucking outstanding!"

Lawton, Dorn and Gersh head out to the building where an army of tailors work non-stop. I turn and head into the mess hall. Steak and eggs. Not too bad.

After a quiet and uninterrupted breakfast I head over to get my dress clothes then return to the barracks to shower and shave and get ready to go get paid. If I've figured it correctly, I've got about six-hundred dollars coming to me. With the thousand I've got on me that would do just fine for a trip to California. Why not?

The time to leave the Army is getting closer. I've showered, I've shaved, I just got paid and a call for final formation has been issued. I grab my duffel bag with the few belongings I brought back from Nam. Mostly a collection of different army camouflaged fatigues, my jungle boots and a few pancho liners. As I fall into place in formation I see Lawton, Gersh and Dorn standing in the next platoon. Lawton is still talking. A cadre comes out of the building to our front and calls for attention. I make a quick adjustment to my beret. As soldiers are supposed to do, we all fall silent and stand erect in place.

"Listen up! In just a few minutes you will be dismissed from the Army. A word to the wise. You will be in this Army until you leave the base. Until that time you will conduct yourself in the manner becoming of a military man. You are not out of this Army until you leave that front gate. If you screw up before you get outside that gate your ass belongs to me. Am I clear?"

A resounding response: "CLEAR SIR!"

The officer faces our formation and shifts himself to attention. "All right then. GROUP! A-TENNN-TION!...DISS-MISSED!"

There it is. That's it. Twenty four hours ago I was in the jungle killing people. Now I'm a civilian headed for the streets of America. There it is. Here I am.

Lawton, Gersh and Dorn along with two other Berets, Sanchez and Goldmen, walk over to where I stand. Lawton introduces me. They both served at CCN, another covert organization like CCC where I served.

Together we all start walking for the bases' front gate which is a few hundred feet to our front. As we approach the guard house at the gate's entrance a black '57 chevy roars by us. A GI is hanging out the passenger's side window. In his hands is a duffel bag which he shakes vigorously. Army clothes and shoes spill onto the road until the duffel bag is empty. He screams repetitively, "FUCK THE ARMY, FUCK THE ARMY..." He laughs histerically. The MP's standing at the gate jump out of the way of the speeding '57 Chevy. Two Military Police jeeps with sirens blaring, pursue the Chevy out the gate. Other soldiers in the immediate area clap and cheer at the spectacle.

We watch the Chevy and MP vehicles disappear into the traffic. The noise and moment's excitement have passed. Lawton, Gersh, Dorn, Sanchez, Goldmen and I walk through the gate, then stand encapsulated and unmoving. There is a long period of silence. Dorn speaks first. "Well, what do we do now?"

"Let's go buy some real clothes and get out of these monkey suits," suggests Gersh. We are all in agreement. The five of us pile into one of the yellow cabs fishing at the gate's entrance for soldier's fares.

Lawton directs the cab driver. "Head downtown, my man. To a men's clothing store." Without reply the cabby pulls down the fare lever and off we roll leaving the Army base and Army life behind.

At the clothing store we all buy jeans and an assortment of collar shirts and sweaters. Penny loafers are the shoes in style so we buy them too. Rain begins falling outside the store. We've got our military issue trench coats, so no need for us to buy rain jackets. Lawton has called his brother to come pick us up at the store. By the time we are finished changing into civilian clothes, Lawton's brother has arrived at the store.

Lawton is animated. He gives his brother a big "Hey little brother" and a quick hug. "Hey everyone this is my brother Joe. He's a college kid. No military service for this guy."

Joe sheepishly shakes hands with us all. He turns to Lawton. "You should have told Mom and Dad you were coming home, Bill."

"Hey, I wanted to surprise them. No harm in that is there?" Joe looks uncertain. Lawton appears a little anxious. He doesn't hesitate though. "Hey, let's move out! Home little brother."

We leave the store. Joe's car is parked directly outside. We load ourselves into the vehicle. Joe starts the car and pulls into traffic. The ride to Lawton's house is without conversation. Even he is quiet. The rain pours down. The windshield wipers drum a hypnotic cadence. The ride is a timeless thirty minutes.

We arrive at Lawton's parents' house around one PM. The rain is a steady drizzle falling from dark gray skies. There are towering pine and fir trees growing throughout the neighborhood of scattered houses. Joe shuts off the car's engine and speaks. "It's Saturday. Everyone's home. Let me go in first."

"What the hell for?" Lawton asks.

"Just give me a minute to prepare them. They didn't know you were bringing your buddies."

"So fucking what?" demands Lawton.

Without answering, Joe gets out of the car. He runs to the front door and goes in. The door closes behind him. We wait. Joe opens the front door and waves for us to come in. Our duffel bags in hand, we follow Lawton into the house.

Inside the living room, standing oddly huddled behind the couch is Lawton's family. His brother Joe, his two sisters, his mom and dad. They are obviously scared. I am puzzled. There is a short silence. His dad says, "Hi Bill. How are you?"

"I'm home dad. Aren't you glad to see me? Mom?"

"Of course we're glad to see you son, only we weren't expecting you. You caught us by surprise. We aren't prepared...We didn't expect you to bring guests with you."

"Well hell, these are my friends. We're home from the war. How about a welcome home?" Lawton has lost his animation. He seems to be begging.

The six of us are still standing just inside the front door. Lawton's family stands behind the living room sofa. An immense space of uneasiness fills the gap between us. Finally his mom and dad move from behind the sofa and come to greet Lawton. His father shakes his hand. His mother gives him a quick hug then steps back her eyes searching her son for answers.

The stifled atmosphere in the room slowly lifts and in a few minutes there is a normalcy of function. We are greeted and welcomed. Lawton's mom shows us to a large den area where we can put our bags and sit ourselves down. We leave Lawton to his family and the rest of us hang out in the den.

"Man what was that all about?" asks Sanchez, one of the Berets who came with us.

"I have no idea," answers Goldmen, "but I do know I'm getting hungry and I'm ready to go out and dance the night away tonight! How about you Burkins? What do you want to do?"

"I think I want to fall in love," I reply. "I remember that feeling and to be truthful I can't wait for it to happen again."

"Round-eye women are the meal I want," Dorn says licking his lips loudly.

"Do you think we should wear our uniforms? Women fall for men in uniform don't they?" asks Sanchez.

"Screw you, you fucking lifer," laughs Gersh. "I don't need nothing but my personal charm."

Lawton enters the room with a plate of beef sandwiches and a six-pack of beer. "What personal charm is that Gersh. You gonna use your fucking 'quiet man' charm?"

We all laugh and grab a sandwich and bottle of beer. As we eat and drink, Lawton closes the double wood doors to the den room. "You dudes ready to blow?"

"You got some shit?" asks Goldmen.

"Boo-fuckin-coo papasan. Customs was a joke. I walked through with a kilo of some of Bong Song's finest herb. The smoking lamp is lit, gentlemen!"

"Airborne!" cries out Dorn.

Lawton opens his duffel bag and pulls out a well-wrapped package of Nam weed, sets it on the coffee table and rips it open. The potent perfume of Vietnamese gansa wafts upward. "Help yourselves gentlemen." He throws several packs of rolling papers onto the table. Everyone rolls a dubee for themselves.

"What about your folks?" asks Sanchez.

"No sweat. They went shopping for food. My sisters are gone for the night. Staying at a friend's house, so you horny bastards can't get at them." We laugh as we light up.

Soon the den is filled with pungent smoke. The smoke enters my brain and I can feel the pleasing sensation of nary a care. Life is okay.

We all sit quietly for a while then Dorn makes a statement: "Pussy! The mission is pussy!"

Myself along with the others readily volunteer for that mission. The plan is for Lawton's brother Joe to take us to a college hangout. A bar with a live band and dancing. Airborne! Tonight, our first night of being in the world, is going to be special.

****

The six of us stand closely together at the edge of the dance floor. The intense staccato of strobe lights freeze frame the frenzied dancing of a sea of oblivious youth buzzing to an amphetamine vibration of rock music. We stand huddled within an invisible shell that slowly cracks with the disbelief of the world we've entered. We are of one mind, a small collective consciousness separated from the people gyrating around us. Guilt. We have entered a land where the Vietnam war does not exist. A land where people could care less that other young Americans are dying in a faraway jungle. We think and feel for our comrades we have left behind. We don't belong here. It's not fitting for us to be alive while others have died. We are a million miles from nowhere.

"Let's get the fuck outta here!" yells Goldmen over the noise of the music.

We move as a unit encased in separation. On our way out we grab Lawton's brother Joe and tell him we want to leave. His face wrinkles with confusion, but he comes with us and drives us back to the house. It is late in the evening and no one is at home. We all go into the den and begin heavily smoking reefer. I break the quiet.

"What the fuck is it Lawton? Why did your family act so strangely towards us. They acted like we were aliens."

Lawton's eyes search for escape. "I think I made a big mistake."

"What mistake would that be?" asks Dorn.

"I sent home some things from Nam. You know. Keepsakes."

"Like what?" Everyone of us has our attention on Lawton.

"Pictures of me wearing a necklace of dried ears."

"Man oh man oh man. God have mercy on your soul, Lawton." Sanchez says.

Lawton explodes, "Fuck God. He don't give a shit!"

Silence hangs heavy in the smoke filled room. We continue smoking. Suddenly I am yearning to see my Mom. A great urge to go home fills my being. I begin changing out of my civilian clothes and put on my uniform. I use the phone and call a cab.

"Burkins. What? You're not coming to California with us?" asks Dorn.

"No. I've got to go home. I don't know why but I gotta go. Now." I hear the cab blow its horn outside. "Good luck guys." I pick up my duffel bag and leave the house. I have an ache wondering if home is still there.

I catch a red-eye flight from Seattle to my home on the East coast. I am the only passenger on board the large jet. It feels as empty as I do. I don't sleep and it seems within minutes we land in Washington, D.C. For sentimental reasons I purchase a bus ticket for the final leg of my trip home. During my entire time in the military using the bus was my major mode of transportation when going home on leave. I use the two hour bus ride to float through my mind's memories of what seems my past lifetime. The memories are slippery. I can't seem to focus on any one moment. Scenes of events void of feelings roll through my inner vision like a TV constantly changing channels. I don't have the strength to attach to any one thought. They carry me along. The bus arrives at the depot in my home town. I'm not sure if I've slept, but I feel like I've been dreaming my entire life. The terminal is busy.

I exit the bus and look for my duffel bag among the other passenger's bags. As I reach to pick it up, I feel a sudden compulsion to turn around. Standing immediately behind me are a small group of flower child types. A tall bearded young man wearing a fringe jacket and head bandanna sneers at me.

"Baby killer!" he says with the slightest uncertainty.

I remain quiet. All the eyes of the boys and girls in the hippie group are on me waiting for some reaction. I stay silent. Death silent. I feel every feeling war can generate grow like a storm within me, yet I feel unmoved. Without conscious effort these feelings that range from rage to horror pour from my eyes into the eyes of the young men and women now shaking in their sandals. They want to run but they feel held fast by an unseen force. I realize that it is something from within me that strangles their will. In this moment their lives belong to me. I lean my face into my accuser's. Distinctly and without malice I say.

"You don't understand…"

They are freed from the demon that now returns to the abyss of my experiences. They sheepishly retreat saying no more. I pick up my duffel bag and walk to the taxi stand outside the bus terminal.

I think to call my Mom before I arrive but decide not to. She hasn't heard from me for the last several months because I quit writing letters home from the war. It seemed to be pointless. Home was a place I couldn't think of. Now here I was. Almost home.

I hail a cab. From a crumpled piece of paper I read him an address. My Mom has moved from the residence we used to live. Her place is close by. Within minutes I am standing at her front door. I ring the bell. The door opens. I greet her.

"Mom! It's me. I'm home!"…I wait.

She immediately smiles then a look of motherly concern crosses her face. She holds my shoulders and asks, "What's wrong with your eyes?"

I feel a flash of slight disappointment and hear myself say, "I've seen a lot this last year Mom."

"My son. My son. Welcome home." She hugs me like the Mom I remember.

"Welcome home. Welcome home."

Final Visit

...I want to hate you for making me feel dirty, making me feel guilty, making me feel a criminal while it is you and only you who makes killing lawful...your arrogance knows no shame...your craving addiction to power is inimical to peace...but this hate I will not harbor...in terms you can understand, hate is worthless, my king...you do unto me what you would have me kill others for having done unto you...

****

"How is the war with the VA going?" asks Doctor Brooks.

I sit somberly. Because Congress ordered the VA to improve health care services on the Big Island of Hawaii, we vets can no longer use Doctor Brooks as our primary care provider.

"You guys wanted this. Now you're going to have to use OUR doctors..." spewed the vindictive VA powers.

My visits to Brooks will soon end. By edict of the VA, I and the other veterans are scheduled to meet with *official* VA psychiatrists. Beyond our wildest imagination these men became guardian angels. These were doctors who would do what was necessary to tax the efforts of war and help heal the men once conscripted to it.

"I'm going to miss you Brooks. Going to miss the exploration we've shared for...how many years now?" I question.

"Two and a half years." Brooks responds.

Deep and hidden are my thoughts to myself. Thoughts of events that dare not posit word. How dark can a side of oneself become and still feel a part of humankind? Extracting satisfaction from the dark side of life is how the evil live.

Brooks looks into me. He just nods his head. I think he feels my sadness at this deep loss that hangs on me for the moment. A moment of grief.

"Guess what Brooks?" A sudden gleam comes into my eyes.

"Yes?" He resonates with my mood swing.

"The VA thought they had trouble with Congress, but shortly they are to receive a barrage of incoming that is sure to cause havoc among their ranks. I've spent the past week with a TV news anchor dragging him through the jungles of Hawaii to visit and record how disabled veterans and their families are living due to the VA's neglect. We are going to be on prime time news, ten minutes every night for the next week.

Brooks chuckles and shakes his head side to side.

****

The television airing of disabled veterans living in the jungles of Hawaii brought a full frontal attack and final foray deep into the ranks of the Veterans Administration in Honolulu.

News Week, Time Magazine and the TV show 20-20 all came to visit and make veteran's stories known. Veterans of Korea, World War II and Vietnam had for years been neglected and denied entitlements by the VA. When Time Magazine did their interviews with the head administrators of the VA the final shot found its mark:

The top administrator, when asked for the reasons why disabled veterans and their families were living isolated and homeless in the jungles of Hawaii, replied...*"these veterans are living like this because they want to!"*

****

The statistics of the psychological casualties of war are somewhere between six and seven percent of the *total number* of people who served in the war. But these numbers are misleading. ***Of all the soldiers who participate in war, roughly only ten percent of them are involved in actual combat.*** This means that of the total number of combatants nearly seventy to eighty percent suffer psychological damage. A slight of hand in the accounting makes war seem more acceptable.

****

Is there a Doctor in the house to hear the beat of a combat soldier's heart?

Is there a Healer in the house to feel the pulse of society?

Is there a Consciousness in the house to know what is just?

Doctor, have you ever heard the story of your peers and how they helped tens of thousands of young men evade the selective service system? Perhaps you were one of these conscientious souls who protected innocence from the greed of men and the murder of war.

You know why I am here. I am a disturbed individual in mundane existence for evaluation of such disturbance. I am disturbed for having murdered innocence at the expense of my own. The consequences of war are unpredictable. I am a consequence of war…

All war is based on deception. The deception coming from the hegemony of men addicted to power. Men who do not seek to end war but to become dominant in it.

Doctor, are you familiar with the "Tonkin Resolution"? It was born out of the fabricated 'deception' of the Tonkin Gulf Incident in North Vietnam. The President and the Secretary of Defense said there was an attack on a US ship in international waters by North Vietnam. It is a well known fact that the Tonkin incident was a 'fake'. The power junkies lied and that deception began the Vietnam War for the United States.

Beware the power junkies. They are criminals of the most heinous of all crimes: the forceful conscripting for murder. *You will go forth and kill for me. You will go forth and risk your life for my philosophy. If you do not serve my purposes I will have you jailed as a criminal. If you live through the ordeal you will accept the fact you were used and quietly find your place in the society I control. If you don't, I will crush you...*

And they take men like you doctor, and subtly educate you to believe and certify that war is acceptable and not unhealthy in the least.

"We can't have these poor excuses for patriotism acting damaged and harmed from the effects of war. Why, how could we continue our plan of profit from violence if we let these malingerers malign war."

That's why I'm here. My 'dis-ease', my disturbance finds no escape from the malady of society's acceptance of war. 'Adjusting to civilian life' requires me to acquiesce to the war-minded leaders who would conscript humans to kill. Kill for the profits of power.

The flagrant hypocrisy of men who would shape the world in their image, shape the world through violence, keeps me in a state of hyper-vigilance. Who knows when these petty tyrants with sweet mouths will instigate a war to line their pockets with profit at the expense of all else.

Beware men who instill fear in people and then promise to banish this fear by requiring personal sacrifices of individual freedom and the relinquishing of your hard earned dollars to the war machine.

In my insanity I must endure to help heal these men. I don't know how. I only know I must. And I admit there is fear in me that the darkness that lies at the periphery of my soul seeks release upon these autocrats. But this is my battle, to withstand any assault on my dignity to be lowered into the pit of violence I so much abhor.

Good Doctor, you have the power to help in this need for the growth of peace and the death of war. It is the words you put on paper that will keep the war machine from spending the pennies I receive for this war induced malady on more and more bombs. Your words will help give me the time and space I need to focus on what must be done: I will not rest until the violence in the world is silenced. I am a peacemaker. To be anything else would be evidence to the insanity that is war. I do not accept the insane acceptance of war. Support me in this fight. Help provide me a meager means to be of service to bringing peace into the everyday world. I will live with the flashbacks, the lack of restful sleep. I will wrestle with the darkness of violence and work for the light of peace…Is there a good Doctor in the house?

****

Congress' investigations and the aggressive onslaught of the media's search for truth have forced the VA administrators and adjudicators into surrender. It has been five years since we first began our mission of justice for veterans.

We receive the call: *"What do you guys want?"*

****

Wars have come and gone and come again. A great sad truth to the state of affairs of men is this: No one has ever saved the world. Absolutely NO ONE. Even the greatest of spiritual beings that have graced this earth have never succeeded in bringing peace to the world. Despite the plethora of religions and spiritual intentions of individuals, humanity remains the same as it ever was. Men seek to rule the world and do it through the use of force. Until men begin to understand what pain is and how it motivates humankind, the healing needed to make a lasting change in our penchant to neurotically control life will fail to make a lasting peace. Pain is an illusion of devastating separateness; its epitome lies in the joyous feeling of safety in killing. We kill only ourselves. Our suffering is our common blood. It will not be an intellectual dissemination of knowledge that makes a change in the way humans treat each other. Peace will be born through the alleviation of human suffering.

As individuals we are all wounded. Wounds left untended fester deep into our souls and in our anguish we lash out at others. Because of our wounds, our words harm. Our actions injure. Until we make healing ourselves and others a priority, we will continue to make war. Healing. Healing ignorance. Healing hunger. Healing homelessness. Healing poverty. Healing separation. Healing. Healing. Healing.

****

The Vietnam war has come and gone. The fight with the VA has passed. The battle within the souls of the combat soldier lives on. Of the thirteen men who were in the veterans rap group in Hawaii, only four of us remain alive today.

If any one word could describe the rap group it would be frailty. We were hardened warriors made frail by the epidemic of violence and the fear of relapse. As damaged in soul as we were, each one of us wanted never to do violence again. I think many of the men passed on because of the frustration they experienced at not knowing how to bring an end to the ongoing violence in the world and within themselves. Once violence has been set in motion, non-violence seems impossible.

****

A great myth that needs to be uncovered is the arrogant presumption that governments and the men that run them are god ordained or divinely sanctioned. Never has a greater lie perpetuated itself.

Wars are fought to protect the value of a dollar. Wars are fought to feed the addiction of power. Wars are fought because we accept them. An animal has no choice in the action of preying upon other animals. Man, in order to rise above his animal nature, must make a choice.

Win or lose there is no happy ending to a war. Time alone will eventually erase the combatants' wounds.

Seek not to rule the world. Learn to be sufficient. Exercise love and learn to empower others. Like a warrior the soul must be in constant training.

****

Brooks sits in his chair and pulls a thin, dark-brown cigarette from its hard pack. I get up from the couch and offer him the flame from a lighter I hold in my hand. Surprised but pleased he accepts my gesture. He takes a slow inhale and comfortably exhales. We both know that this moment is good-by. He stands and takes my hand in his.

"What are your plans?" he asks.

I think to myself for a moment. I am now armed with my 'war pension' and the small freedom it gives me from society's conventions. I feel no joy in the victory over the inhuman bureaucratic machinations that view war as necessary. The casualties the rap group suffered remain a reminder of the contagion of war.

"I'm going to continue this healing process Brooks. I need to become a door through which all healing comes. As a warrior my greatest goal is to be able to heal an angry man if he gets within ten feet of me. If I can cover enough ground, perhaps I can make a difference in the way we humans treat each other."

Brooks smiles and gives me a warm embrace. I return it then step back and give him a well earned salute.

"Thanks Brooks." I turn to the door, open it and take a first step in the direction of peace.